The Obama Presidency

Promise and Performance

Edited by William Crotty

LEXINGTON BOOKS
Lanham • Boulder • New York • Toronto • Plymouth, UK

Published by Lexington Books
A wholly owned subsidiary of The Rowman & Littlefield Publishing Group, Inc.
4501 Forbes Boulevard, Suite 200, Lanham, Maryland 20706
www.rowman.com

10 Thornbury Road, Plymouth PL6 7PP, United Kingdom

British Library Cataloguing in Publication Information Available

Library of Congress Cataloging-in-Publication Data
The Obama presidency : promise and performance / [edited by] William Crotty.
   p. cm.
  ISBN 978-0-7391-7234-6 (cloth : alk. paper) — ISBN 978-0-7391-7235-3 (electronic)
  1. Obama, Barack. 2. United States— Politics and government— 2009– I. Crotty,
William
  E907.O228 2012
  973.932092—dc23   2012002274

Printed in the United States of America

Contents

Preface

This book is about policy and politics in the Obama presidency. In a time of national crisis Barack Obama came into the presidency. He had run an often brilliant and mesmerizing campaign, one that promised change. In office he faced a series of seemingly intractable issues, difficult choices and strong opposition to whatever option he chose to follow. For many observers, he was limited in real-world terms to what he could accomplish, if you will a prisoner of history. For others and especially his most ardent supporters in the campaign, the Obama who was president was not the Obama who ran for office.

This book examines these issues from a wide variety of perspectives. The intention is to provide an evaluation of the Obama presidency in its first term and as full an understanding of the significance of the problems faced, the choices made and the varied reactions from different sectors of the society to these. To accomplish these objectives, we have assembled scholars with an established expertise in their representative areas and each with perspectives of significance to offer the reader.

The approaches and the evaluations are varied as was intended when the project was undertaken. Each however should add to an understanding of a presidency operating in a time of economic crisis, continuing wars and budgetary deficits, all to be addressed in an era of intense political polarization. The Obama presidency has been, as many have said, characterized by its unpredictability; it also has been one of the most contentious yet intriguing in the modern era.

The introductory chapter, "Representation and Counter-Representation in the Obama Presidency," presents an overview of the politics and major issue initiatives of the Obama administration. The approach is both descriptive and interpretive and is meant to provide a context and a point of reference for the individual chapters on specific policy areas to follow.

The thematic focus is on the changing dynamic in progress during the Obama years, both in the policy positions advanced and in the evolution of a style of presidential leadership. Obama's conception of his presidency and its role in policymaking was to set the agenda as best he could and in unusually broad terms the goals to be achieved. The specifics of legislative development on the most important of issues—the economy, unemployment, the housing crisis, health care, deficit reduction—were left to be argued out in the Congress. Once the parties and both houses of Congress had formulated their positions, Obama would step in to broker a compromise in line with centrist sentiments in the electorate. The intention was to appear nonpartisan and above politics, an advocate of civility and compromise and a consensus-builder. As he saw it, he would serve as the representative of all citizens.

This is not the dynamic role as the advocate of change and a progressive politics that he projected for himself in the election. As an exponent in Washington for a situation of maturity and reasonableness in policymaking, Obama increasingly came to embrace the perspectives and to adopt, although in considerably less strident terms, an agenda determined by his conservative opposition in the Congress.

Some argued that this was an acceptance of the political realities of the time. The Republican/conservative reaction to his initial agenda was too strong to be ignored and had to be accommodated. Others believed his centrist to conservative positioning of his administration reflected more accurately his own core values and past experience. Still others believed the connecting link in all that happened was the effort to better prepare himself for reelection and the campaign to come by appealing more forcefully to the moderate vote which would decide the outcome. The views are not antithetical and some combination of them may best explain Obama's first term in office. Meanwhile the economy continued to perform poorly, the recovery from the recession was slow and uncertain and unemployment stayed high, all while the administration's and the Congress's attention turned from economic stimulus and recovery to severe reductions in spending and the need for a balanced budget. These emphases were longtime Republican Party dogma and were positions that Obama had blamed for the economic collapse of 2008 and which he had campaigned against in his bid for election.

The concluding chapter, "Principles and Pragmatism in the Obama Presidency," emphasizes the themes of the book and provides summary perspectives as well as reactions to the directions taken by the president and explanations of these as put forward by observers. The range of views expressed during Obama's first term in these regards is extensive and the chapter can touch on only a select number. Nonetheless the intensity of the reactions invoked and the emotions exhibited give an idea why the Obama presidency has been such a focus of interest and contentiousness since its inception. The chapter also directs attention to severe structural issues facing the society and offers alternative explanations for what has occurred.

The intersection of policy and politics is the crux of governing in the American system. We explore this juncture in the context of Barack Obama's term as president. All in all the objective has been to offer a stimulating, informative and provocative evaluation of a presidency that has emerged as one of the most fundamentally important in establishing the direction of the nation and the future course of its political dialogue during an especially challenging era.

Chapter One

Representation and Counter-Representation in the Obama Presidency

William Crotty

Introduction

Two dynamics established the framework which Barack Obama encountered at the beginning of his presidency. The first and controlling force was the problems left by the Bush presidency for the in-coming president to deal with. These were formidable, resistant to quick resolution and demanding resources and a level of attention that would last throughout the Obama years.

The second was a reflection of Obama's own success in getting elected. His campaign for the presidency had been singularly effective and while run against as formidable odds as any in recent history, and he won an electrifying victory. In the process of his march to the presidency Obama committed to a broad range of programs from reintroducing a sense of trust, civility and integrity to politics and governing institutions to enacting a progressive policy agenda that would set the nation and its politics in a new direction.

First, the Bush legacy: these included a failed economy; constantly high employment; a home foreclosure crisis; and historic budget deficits. It was all subsumed under the label the "Great Recession." As Ben Bernanke, head of the Federal Reserve put it (in private), it was "the worst economic collapse since and including the Great Depression" (*National Commission on the Causes*, 2011).

This however was not the total. There were two elective wars in progress with no apparent resolution in sight, the longest running in American history;

1

the remnants of the "war on terror" and the legal and constitutional violations associated with it; the torture, illegal detentions, forced repatriations of targeted individuals to countries known for their abuse of human rights; CIA-maintained "black" (or secret) prisons worldwide, among a long list of other actions abetted by then Vice President Dick Cheney, in what he referred to as the "Dark Side" of the anti-terrorism effort (Mayer, 2008). America's claim to a moral superiority in international affairs was forfeited for a go-it-alone, anything-is-in-play administration approach during the post-9/11 years, the consequences of which the new president would have to deal with.

There was the most massive and expensive restructuring of American governing institutions since the immediate post-World War II period; a quantum leap in national intelligence agencies and in the expenditures and powers assigned them, some legal, some not; and an aggrandizement of presidential powers of a scope unseen in peacetime. One example of the expansion of executive prerogatives were referred to as "signing statements," the claim of the president to the extra-constitutional power to decide what in legislation passed by the Congress was constitutional and what was not and what he would choose to enforce and what he would refuse to (Savage, 2008).

Obama was effectively replacing what by any standard—constitutional, substantive policy outcomes or effectiveness in meeting the nation's needs and advancing its domestic or international interests—was one of the worst in modern history or for that matter all of American history. It also happened to be one of the least popular in recent times, benefitting Obama enormously in the election and should have been able to contain or reverse the damage inherited, a rare opportunity to strike out in a totally new direction. However he chose to approach them, the challenges would be fundamental in defining what the administration could do and how much it might achieve.

Secondly, Obama had run a campaign that held out a vision for the nation that was both moving and highly effective in motivating millions of Americans to support him in the election. It was a campaign full of promises and the hope for a brighter, better future. There were commitments to a modernized, more efficient and more globally aggressive economy, themes to resurface again later in his presidency; new approaches to international trade; the creation of jobs and a reduction in unemployment; efforts to deal with and moderate the income imbalance between the mass of Americans and the small percentage of the extremely wealthy; a reduction in the deficit and an effort to balance the budget; the reassertion of legality and a respect for human rights in foreign policy; an ending of the war in Iraq and a renewed emphasis on defeating al Qaeda in Afghanistan; and a commitment to diplomacy, negotiation and collaboration rather than military force as the weapons of first choice in dealing with international crises. There would be a repeal of the Bush tax cuts favoring the top one to two percent of the income hierarchy at the expense of the rest of society; an end to the mortgage foreclosure crisis; investments in technology that would secure the nation's leadership in the world; new environmental initiatives in clean air and water standards, efforts to reclaim the oceans and protect and expand national parks and public lands, reduce carbon emissions, meet the challenge of a warming planet, find new sources of energy; introduce a new mass transportation initiative and a high speed rail system that would compete with the world's best; and create a new national health care plan. In the international arena the emphasis would be on "peace"; in domestic politics it would be on a revived, expanded and vital economy, one competitive in the world marketplace.

It was a lengthy and exceptionally ambitious agenda. The list of pledges was extraordinarily comprehensive, even for a presidential campaign (see the chapter by John C. Berg in this volume). It was all brought together with the promise of "change" and "change you can believe in," which did little to dampen enthusiasm or set reasonable levels of expectation as to what the new president could achieve. It was questionable whether any administration could begin to realize such a richness of objectives and it raised concerns among some observers as to whether Obama was underestimating, or choosing to ignore, the full extent and severity of the problems faced by a nation in economic distress and what he would be forced to deal with on entering the presidency.

It is not possible to review all of these issue areas as to the nature of the problems encountered or the actions taken. Rather the following focuses on the most significant of these, the ones that received the most attention: national health care, President Obama's first priority; efforts at economic recovery, the nation's primary concern; the home mortgage/foreclosure crisis; and the battle over the budget, the most basic of statements as to the government and the opposition forces ideology, policy positioning and the interests in the electorate to be served.

First then the effort to establish a national health insurance program.

The National Health Insurance Plan

Introduction

In signing the bill on March 21, 2010, President Obama told the nation: "We have answered the call of history. We are a nation that faces its challenges and accepts its responsibilities. We are a nation that does what is hard. What is necessary. What is right . . . in this country we shape our own destiny. This is what we do. This is who we are. That is what makes us the United States of America." In earthier tones, Vice President Joe Biden whispered to Obama in a comment picked up by television microphones and replayed extensively on YouTube and cable: "This is a big f---ing deal." It was.

It was a proud moment for the President and an accomplishment no other Chief Executive had managed to achieve. The new plan represented a comprehensive, omnibus act that remade health care delivery and would affect every American. The new legislation "instantaneously took its place as a landmark in

U.S. social legislation, comparable to Social Security legislation enacted in 1935, Civil Rights legislation enacted in 1965 and, of course, Medicare" (Jacobs and Skocpol, 2010, p. 3; see also Morone, 2010; and Blumenthal and Morone, 2010).

The Case For Reform

The need for health care reform was not the question. Yet attempting to restructure health care touches on issues, and more significantly emotions, of fundamental importance to the society and to the individual. James A. Morone explains:

> Heath reform taps issues that stretch far beyond health care policy. Each effort to pass national health insurance becomes an argument about what kind of nation we are . . .
>
> Health care in the United States certainly raises the deepest communal questions: Who are we? What are our bedrock values? (Morone, 2010; see also the chapter by James A. Morone in this volume)

The system in effect was expensive and discretionary as to who would receive treatment and the level of attention they could expect. The United States was often championed as a model for the world, with the best doctors, medical specialists, hospitals, technological development and the leader in health research. In actuality the United States ranked well below other advanced democracies in the quality of care received, in fact lower than many developing nations. Additionally, and this was the main point of criticism for many, tens of millions of working-age Americans and their families who lacked insurance coverage were not eligible for treatment.

The system in place was based on a free-market, pay-as-you-go model for consumers and practitioners alike. It was very expensive. The country spent more per capita on health care than other advanced industrial nations and even some emerging nations. No other country came close to the level of expense encountered by Americans. They paid double the amount or better than citizens in any other advanced democracy and 50 percent more than the next highest nation's cost. The investment in health care increased faster than the GDP (Gross Domestic Product) and it was argued unduly burdened the economy. These costs were projected to consume 20 percent and more of the nation's productivity in the coming decades, again well out-of-line with comparable industrial nations (Jacobs and Skocpol, 2010, pp. 21-22).

In addition, unlike the United States, other industrial democracies provided health care to their entire populations and did a far better job in keeping costs down.

The United States ranked last among advanced democracies in quality of care in infant deaths per one thousand births and in preventable deaths per one million population. Increasingly fewer employers offered health care benefits to workers due to the costs. The pool of the uninsured continued to grow from an estimated thirty-eight million to forty-six million in the course of one decade alone. The nonpartisan Congressional Budget Office predicted that if the rate of cost inflation continued at present levels that within two decades or less the total would consume 25 percent of the economy and would continue to increase to where it would approach one-half before the end of the century. President Obama was to argue that beyond providing universal care, a reform of the system was critical to the nation's economic future and its ability to compete globally. He was to frame his policy proposals increasingly in these terms as his presidency went on.

Barriers to Reform

The argument for reform was persuasive. This was a point of agreement by all of the factions involved. Where they differed, fundamentally and seemingly uncompromisingly, was over what needed to be done. The proposals ranged from establishing a single-payer national plan or the extension of Medicare benefits or the government-sponsored health care plan available to those in public office and the federal bureaucracies to limited cost cutting measures or restrictions on the services provided as well as access to diagnostic technology and more expensive medical procedures. There appeared to be little room for agreement. Added to this was the opposition of Big Pharma, a heavy contributor to election campaigns, hospital corporations and most of the medical industry. The prospects for passage for any basic restructuring of the nation's health care delivery system appeared remote.

To add substantially to the degree of difficulty in achieving health care reform, or any change of breadth or consequence in the society, was the nature of American political institutions and the process of policy-making. These factors can be said to include the ideological polarization of the nation's politics; the failure of administrations (given the outcomes of previous efforts) to make it the priority effort of their programs; the extreme wealth and political resources of the health care industry, their effective targeting of elective public officials and ability to mount national media campaigns that proponents of reform could not equal; the conservative balance of political representation in recent decades, including the presidency, the Congress and the courts; and the failure to come up with any definitive plan that addressed both citizen needs, could relate to the capitalist structure that dominated the economy and would satisfy the interests of most sectors of the reform constituency. Add to this a policy decision-making process built on an incrementalist approach in a system of shared power and consciously created with the objective to delay or avoid major efforts at change and the difficulties to be faced become starkly clear.

Any proposal sent to the Congress would have to take its place among the thousands of prospective pieces of legislation introduced in any given session and faced hearings and positive action by no less than eight committees and subcommittees, plus floor debate and a vote in both chambers and then the president's signature of approval. To allow it to receive the attention necessary issue groups in favor of the legislation would have to be mobilized and an intense public relations marketing campaign launched to build mass support. It would take time, commitment, a sense of urgency and, not least of all, extensive resources.

It was in this context that opponents to health care reform held significant advantages. There were a large number of permanently organized associations (over forty by one count), sensitive to the implications of such an issue and its potential consequences and with the political expertise and financial resources to respond to any challenge to the status quo that might arise. The professional groups that tracked such developments in one multi-year period (1990-2004) as recorded by the Center for Responsive Politics had representatives consistently among the top twenty contributors to federal campaigns (Weissert and Weissert, 2006, p. 170). The money went to candidates for federal office and to the incumbents who held key positions at pressure points in the legislative process.

Opponents had the ability to put together highly effective media campaigns to convince a public with limited information of the dangers to them and their health care delivery of efforts to replace the system in effect. A classic example of the approach was the "Harry and Louise" television commercials that contributed to a broad-based skepticism about the Clinton health plan proposals in the 1990s. It was not by chance that prior administrations had been unable to bring basic change to the health care industry.

There were other problems. In the tense atmosphere surrounding the prolonged controversy over passage of a bill, angry charges were to be made. Obama was called a "socialist," was compared to the worst of totalitarian dictators, as advocating unconstitutional extension of government authority, as threatening the "liberty" and "freedom" of the nation and its citizens, and so on. The attacks were broad in scope, heated, repeated indefinitely and at times could be quite personalized.

There was another source of resistance that the administration did not anticipate and did not deal with well. It came from Obama's own party in Congress. At one point Speaker Nancy Pelosi told the president he simply did not understand how the House of Representatives operated, to their embarrassment an exchange captured by television microphones. Others caught in the legislative fight might expand the charge to the Congress as a whole (see the chapter by Arthur C. Paulson in this volume).

Obama's leadership in the effort was openly challenged by the Democrats in the Congress, feeling he left the burden of both framing the legislation and ensuring its passage on their shoulders. Many believed the president's use of the authority of his office on the issue was weak. He seemed unsure of what he really wanted or the contents of the legislation or the direction it should go in as well as unwilling to stand and fight when confronted by the opposition. They further believed they would pay a high price at the polls for their efforts and they were right.

A sampling from the debate in the Senate as examples: Senator Carl Levin (D, MI): "What is it? What exactly is the plan? What is the strategy?" Senator Bill Nelson (D, FL): "The President needs to be more hands-on with the health-care bill" (Obama while over-reacting to the Bill Clinton experience chose to let the Congress rather than the White House decide the legislation, a strategy it would often call on in policy battles). And in an unusually angry attack even for such an emotional issue, Senator Al Franken (D, MN) told his Senate colleagues (and the nation) he was "just livid. Goddamn it, what's the deal here?" And, targeting the White House and Obama's senior advisor, David Axelrod "You're talking platitudes and we have to go home and defend ourselves. We're getting the crap kicked out of us" (Staff of the *Washington Post*, 2010, pp. 54, 53). The frustration with events and the president's contribution to these was evident and it is hard to say they were wrong in their evaluations.

There was another dynamic at work. Republicans and many other opponents believed in a neo-liberal, free market, small government ideology forcibly advocated by Presidents Ronald Reagan and George W. Bush. It opposed any expansion of federal authority and in this case its extension to medical areas believed to be the province of private markets. The ideological resistance was to be fierce and unyielding.

Health care was to be an explosive political issue and one with powerful economic forces, well represented in both parties, unequivocally opposed to anything that might weaken their role in and benefits they received from the system in place. As Carol S. Weissert and William G. Weissert point out: "Despite its complexity and fragmentation . . . few issues have the personal, social and economic significance of health policy. . . . And few have so persistently demanded public action from presidents, congresses, legislatures, bureaucracies, and courts, and the interest groups that want to influence their decisions. This . . . reflects the reality that health policy problems are never really solved . . ." (Weissert and Weissert, 2006, p. 2). And it could be the differences added provided little middle ground on which to build a consensus.

The obstacles to passage then were enormous and the exchanges on both sides of the issue, much like the road to passage itself, highly charged. The stakes involved and the depth of the challenge to the existing practices were historic and even revolutionary in attempts to dismantle one system and replace it with another.

It was in this context that Obama's advisors unanimously and repeatedly warned against making health care reform the signature issue and initial legislative goal of his presidency. The fear was that it would divide the Congress and the country, ensure prolonged and likely effective opposition, take attention away from other issues arguably deserving of more immediate concern (the economy and unemployment), exhaust the aura of goodwill with which Obama had begun his presidency and set the tone and mood for the legislative battles to come. Nonetheless, and despite the potential costs to his presidency, Obama was determined to proceed.

Passage of the Act

It turned out that President Obama did not have any particular plan in mind when he proposed the health industry reforms and left the substance of the legislation (as indicated) to be worked out by the parties in the Congress. He then planned to come in during the final stages of deliberation to mobilize the necessary congressional and public support. The approach did not work well.

It took a year of divisive and polarizing debate before the Congress could come up with a bill most Democrats (the Republicans remained opposed) could agree on. It all took place in an atmosphere of great uncertainty fostered by constant changes of direction; additions and deletions, shifting coalitions of supporters and continuing (and unsuccessful) efforts to win a handful of Republican votes; sustained opposition from most sectors of the health care industry; side deals with pharmaceutical and selected other association representatives; and the abandonment of any hope for framing a bipartisan plan. Ultimately all of the persuasive power and resources the president could muster was required to pass any legislation.

The nature of the obstacles—political, financial, institutional, partisan and interest-group-based—which had to be overcome then were enormous. With great effort they were overcome. A bill (formally known as "The Patient Protection and Affordable Care Act") passed the Congress in March of 2010. The vote was 269 to 212 in favor in the House; 56-43 in favor in the Senate, Democrats broadly supported it, Republicans opposed the plan.[1]

The intensity of disagreements over the legislation and the closeness of the final vote foretold the nature of the debate to come.

The Plan

Overall, and curiously given the fight over its adoption, the health care legislation passed was less liberal than the one proposed by Richard M. Nixon in the early 1970s and in fact was principally based on two sources, a plan first proposed by the conservative Heritage Foundation put forth as a Republican Party alternative to Clinton's health care proposal and the Massachusetts law signed by then-Governor Mitt Romney in 2006 that extended coverage to all citizens of the Commonwealth through an individual mandate requirement and the channeling of market demand through private insurance corporations.

The law had become a cross Romney had to bear in seeking the Republican Party's presidential nomination. Running for president in 2008, Romney had reversed himself and disavowed any support for the plan he had designed, believed to be a necessity for any serious Republican candidate. In running for president in 2012, Romney chose to defend his Massachusetts plan while placing the emphasis on what he saw as the differences with what he has referred to as ObamaCare. Nonetheless whatever his views what was referred to as the "Romney Plan" served as a basis for the national act.

Among the National Health Insurance Plan's features as passed by the Congress and signed into law by the President were:

- a ban on exclusion for previous health problems
- a ban on lifetime caps for insurance costs or treatments
- the inclusion of older children in a family's plan
- the addition of tens of millions of new people to the insurance rolls (although Physicians for a National Health Plan estimated that twenty-three million would remain uninsured)
- health care costs in time would be substantially reduced
- the program would help reduce the deficit and would make the nation more globally competitive economically
- it was the first fully comprehensive national health care plan ever adopted in the United States (in contrast to other economically developed nations)[2]

Among the objections:

- it was "socialistic," or worse in nature
- it was an unwarranted expansion of federal authority
- it represented one more extension of Big Government
- it was unconstitutional
- its costs were unreasonably high
- it would place an undue economic burden on business
- it would add to the federal deficit
- government "death panels" would determine end-of-life care
- the federal government could not run any program economically or efficiently
- it violated the free-market philosophy that underlay American society and government
- and so on (see the chapter by R. Lawrence Butler in this volume)

Political, legal and electoral opposition developed quickly. The Republican/Tea Party candidates in the 2010 midterm election vowed to repeal the legislation if elected (and the Republican majority attempted to do so in the new House, voting 245 to 189 for repeal). All of the House Republicans and three Democrats voted in favor of repeal. The Senate, still with a Democratic majority, killed the effort. The Republicans also vowed to cut funding for implementing provisions of the act and on a more piecemeal basis repeal portions of it or change them enough that they and the act would be ineffective. They also promised to promote a more friendly-to-business, free-market alternative.

The Reaction

Both parties had problems with the bill. Liberals were put off, as they had been in the debate on the legislation, by what they saw as a failure by the Obama administration to include them in meaningful decision-making regarding the substance of the bill. They objected to the refusal to include the single-payer proposals or a public option, both advocated by Obama in the primaries, and the unwillingness to even debate or seriously consider such alternatives or to fight to extend Medicare to the entire population. They had opposed a mandate to funnel health care through the private insurance industry and thus subject the public's welfare to its profit-making imperatives. They feared the consequences ultimately would not be significantly dissimilar in practice from what they had been asked to replace. The liberal objections were not given much weight by the White House or the media, basically the assessment was where could they go and what could they do politically to change the substance of the legislation and that had the support of a president of their own party. They would have no reasonable alternative. The controversy did contribute to the growing divide between party and president.

The public reaction ranged from tepid support to aggressive opposition. Mostly people were confused and were sensitive to changes that might disrupt their current care. Few at any level read or really understood the act. The division in support for the legislation as measured by public opinion polls stayed steady with a slight plurality supporting the reforms. Three-quarters or more of Republican Party identifiers opposed the legislation and the reverse was true for Democrats. An indication of both parties' core strength support groups in the electorate.

Thomas R. Marshall has compared public support for health care proposals by various presidents with that for Obama's plan and the partisan divisions in the patterns of support. His conclusion is that the partisanship divide over the Obama legislation was greater and more intense than in previous presidencies and as also was the party polarization over the issue. Calling on a variety of sources for the years 2009-2010, Marshall uses the Gallup polls to evaluate the public reaction (table 1.1). Of interest, the overall level of public support remains basically constant at 50 percent or a little less, as does Democratic and Republican endorsements of the plan or their opposition to it. What changes the most is the fall-off among Independents. Also, as would be indicated by the extensiveness of the partisan debate, the gap in levels of support between party members was extreme (70 percent in 2009) and largely stayed in much the same range. There is in fact little change in the patterns of acceptance over time. Attempting to build a consensus under these conditions or to bring in significant Republican support whatever the concessions that had been made was a losing strategy.

Table 1.1. Percentage Who Favored the Obama Health Care Plan, Gallup Polls, 2009 and 2010

Poll Questions and Dates	All	Repub-licans	Indepen-dents	Demo-crats	R-D Gap
"Would you advise your member of Congress to vote for or against a health care bill this year, or do you not have an opinion?" IF UNDECIDED: *"As of today, would you say you lean more toward advising your member of Congress to vote for a health care bill, or lean more toward advising your member of Congress to vote against a health care bill?"* Gallup: 9/11-13/2009	50%	13%	48%	83%	70%
Same: 10/1-4/2009	51%	24%	45%	82%	58%
Same: 11/5-8/2009	43%	18%	37%	71%	53%
Same: 11/20-22/2009	44%	12%	37%	76%	64%
Same: 12/11-13/2009	46%	14%	43%	80%	66%
Same: 1/8-10/2010	49%	12%	35%	80%	68%

Source: Thomas R. Marshall, "Health Care Reform and the Two Faces of Public Opinion: ObamaCare in Perspective," A paper presented at the Midwest Political Science Association meeting, Chicago, 2011, table 1, p. 2. Reprinted by permission of author.
Note: Table one allocates Independents who lean toward one party or the other according to their partisan leanings.

Table 1.2. Percentage Who Favored the Obama Health Care Plan, various polls, 2009 and 2010

Poll questions and dates	All	Republicans	Independents	Democrats	R-D Gap
"Do you think it is a good idea or a bad idea to raise income taxes on households and businesses that make more than $200,000 a year in order to help provide health insurance for people who are not covered by health insurance?" CBS/*New York Times*: 1/11-15/2009**	57%	31%	54%	78%	47%
"Would you support or oppose a law that requires all Americans to have health insurance, either get-ting it from work or buying it on their own?" ABC/*Washington Post*: 9/10-12/2009	51%	36%	47%	64%	28%
"Would you support or oppose a law limiting the amount of money someone can collect if they win a lawsuit after being injured by bad medical care?" Same*	67%	69%	64%	66%	-3%
"In order to help pay for health care reform, would you support or oppose a federal tax on insurance companies when they sell high-cost health insurance policies with unusually high levels of benefits, known as Cadillac poli-cies?" Same	45%	35%	35%	59%	24%
"Would you advise your repre-sentative in Congress to vote for or against a healthcare reform bill similar to the one proposed by President Barack Obama?" Gal-lup: 3/4-7/2010	45%	9%	32%	80%	71%

"As you may know, a bill that makes major changes to the country's health care system became law earlier this year (2010). Based on what you have read or heard about that legislation, do you generally favor or generally oppose it?" CNN/ORC: 12/17-19/2010	43%	12%	35%	89%	77%
"Now here are a few provisions in the health care bill. Please tell me whether you favor or oppose each one . . . Preventing health insurance companies from dropping coverage for people who become seriously ill?" Same	61%	54%	54%	69%	15%
"Requiring all Americans who do not have health insurance to get it?" Same	38%	16%	37%	59%	43%
"Preventing health insurance companies from denying coverage to people with pre-existing conditions?" Same	64%	55%	55%	73%	18%

Source: Thomas R. Marshall, "Health Care Reform and the Two Faces of Public Opinion: ObamaCare in Perspective." A paper presented at the Midwest Political Science Association meeting, Chicago, 2011, table 2, pp. 3-4. Reprinted by permission of author.
*Medical malpractice limits were not included in the Obama health care plan, but are presented here for a comparison.
**The CBS/*New York Times* Poll did not allocate independent-leaners.

Secondly, Marshall looked at different issue positions in relation to the public acceptance of various health care-related proposals (table 1.2). The greatest polarization by party occurs in the acceptance of the plan eventually passed and whether voters would instruct their representatives to support or oppose the legislation (a 71 percent partisan divide) (Marshall, table 2, pp. 3-4).

Further, in polls of registered voters immediately prior to the 2008 presidential and the 2010 congressional elections in relation to party support, there was a difference, Republicans to Democrats, of 80 percent or better.

As a measure of the political climate, the Heritage Foundation now opposed legislation based largely on its own proposals. It mobilized along with other conservative think tanks and foundations and the medical industry. Among associated groups that had been actively opposing such changes were little-known but politically effective organizations like the American Legislative Action Committee (ALEC) funded by the billionaire Koch brothers. Its job was among other things to draft statutes for state legislatures to adopt modifying the act and to mobilize public support for these. A number of corporations such as Exxon-Mobil, Wal-Mart and Johnson & Johnson joined the fight.

Legal challenges were initiated. The drafters of the legislation had expected these and wrote a law based on Supreme Court precedents and rulings that they believed could withstand any constitutional assaults on the act's validity. Nonetheless a series of objections were raised in the courts. Early on two federal district court judges ruled part or all of the legislation unconstitutional, ensuring a long and contentious legal battle eventually to be resolved by decision of the U.S. Supreme Court.

In the final analysis, it may be the level of support and commitment to an appreciation of its benefits by the public that is likely to determine if this health care overhaul or any such federal program will prevail.

Evaluation: Health Care and Its Political Impact

The fight over the national health care insurance was significant in a number of regards. First, while mentioned it had not been the defining issue of the 2008 election campaign. The economy was. Obama decided to make it his major legislative goal, reordering the priority of voters. It was a decision he made on his own and according to his own conception of what was of the greatest immediate importance. He did this against the strong advice of his political advisors both from the campaign and in the Washington community. There could not be considered to have been an electoral mandate on the issue, making it exceedingly difficult to sell to the public or the Congress. His dependence on his internal compass as to what he needed to prioritize would continue to be a key to his tenure. He was to pay a high price for this particular decision.

Second, the long, exceptionally acrimonious fight over such a divisive issue would set the tone for the rest of his presidency (see the chapter by Bruce E. Caswell in this volume). His storehouse of goodwill was soon exhausted; he in actuality had no real health care plan, as both opponents and supporters quickly discovered; he was unprepared for the intensity of the fight and uncertain as to what his role in it should be; he was seen by those in Congress as vacillating and unable to mobilize his considerable majorities in the House and Senate (Democrats controlled the Congress and the presidency); he appeared unusually sympathetic to the views of opponents (some believed overly responsive), often conceding points before they became major issues of debate; he was unwilling to stand and fight for his programs, if it could be discerned as to what these actually might be; and through all of the concessions, short-term changes in direction and the divisions over who should be represented and how in the legislation, he remained distant from both his party in the Congress and from his core support in the electorate.

His conception of his role was to stay above the fray, let the parties in the Congress battle it out. There would be little help from the White House until the final stages necessary to push for the compromises and concessions essential to getting the legislation passed. The president then would declare victory for the middle class, regardless of the substantive outcome, praising the Congress and both parties for their good work and willingness to compromise in the public interest (not indicative of the severity of the fight or of the tenor of Washington politics). This was believed to be a good position if not to promote a legislative agenda then to win support from the moderate centrists needed for reelection. The political transfiguration was slow to evolve and did little to increase his appeal to conservatives. It did serve to make his programmatic commitments fluid and difficult to predict, creating a division between him and his party, all of which would characterize his presidency.

These tendencies came to be associated with the Obama style of governing, setting the tone and context for each of the policy fights to come. In the process, Obama would undergo a transformation of sorts, from the progressive and inspirational leader of a political movement to a less certain, more tentative and ultimately highly flexible proponent of issues and approaches. He moved closer to embracing in office the policy agenda he had run against in the campaign. All in all it was a surprising political transformation, one that was slow to be recognized (see the chapter by Shayla C. Nunnally in this volume). It did little if anything to increase his appeal to conservatives, made his programmatic commitments fluid and difficult to predict and fed a division between the president and his party. These would come to characterize his decision-making and in time his presidency.

The Economic Initiatives

Whatever the divisions over health care policy, it was the economy and in particular the need for jobs that dominated the public consciousness (figure 1.1). It was the economic failure that elected Barack Obama and the expectation was that he would move quickly and effectively to provide an economic recovery to get the nation moving again. It is difficult to over-estimate the level of national concern in this regard. The depths of the economic meltdown and its consequences were again not in debate. What was considerably less certain would be the adequacy of the government's response to and effectiveness in meeting the challenge of a national economy that had failed.

Figure 1.1. Unemployment Levels

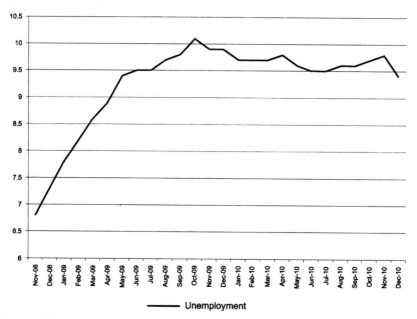

Source: U.S. Bureau of Labor Statistics

Barack Obama has been compared in some quarters to Franklin D. Roose-velt in the immensity of the economic problems to face his administration and in the call for government-based, comprehensive economic plans to put the country back to work and return it to economic stability. Some called for programs along the order of the Works Progress Administration (WPA) and the other New Deal initiatives. This was not Obama's intention as it soon became clear. The new president as it turned out was nowhere near as bold or aggressive as Roosevelt and in reality favored more limited and selective programs and where possible a greater reliance on spurring investments by the private sector. He also gave pri-mary attention to a financial industry recovery, believing it necessary for the nation's economic well-being and a weapon to provide funding for a revival of the job market. Unlike Roosevelt who gloried in attacking his opponents, using them as a foil for building public support for the programs he favored, Obama was much more sympathetic to the opposition and its calls for deficit reduction and limited financial investments in the economy. Such calls by opponents of federal programs over the decades from FDR to Lyndon B. Johnson and Bill Clinton had been successful in bringing to an end liberal/progressive efforts to, in particular, equalize the distribution of wealth in the country and the benefits that accompanied it.

The Recovery Plan

The first indicator of the approach to be followed by the new administration came when president-to-be Obama returned to Washington to vote in favor of the Bush bailout plan for the financial sector. For supporters this was something of a surprise given candidate Obama's criticisms of Bush's economic favoritism (as he saw it) and its consequences, including a consistent railing against Wall Street and its contributions to the nation's economic collapse. It might have been less of a surprise to voters had they realized that Obama had been in contact with Henry Paulson, the Secretary of the Treasury, during the presidential campaign, the major influence on the Bush administration's economic strategizing. Obama had quietly pledged to give his support to the administration's recovery efforts.

The principal economic stimulus programs included: TARP, the Troubled Asset Recovery Plan, initiated in the closing days of the Bush presidency and supported and implemented by President Obama; the job/economic stimulus package; the foreclosure relief legislation; and, over a broader period of time, the efforts to reduce the budget deficits. Each would receive intensive public and critical attention.

TARP did revive Wall Street and the financial industry. They regained profitability in a short period of time and returned to their former ways. Once the banks repaid their federal loans, the bonuses and salaries on Wall Street returned to levels approaching the pre-crash period. Obama had not insisted on stringent basic regulatory reforms as a precondition for government aid. There were measures along these lines later but the immediate urgency had passed and the proposed restrictions were milder than they might have been at an earlier stage. The stock market gained strength, improving by 50 percent or better from its lowest levels and approaching where it had been prior to the crash. In an ironic note, the banks and financial institutions were accused of using the public funding they received to lobby against congressional restrictions on their business practices.

The economic job stimulus program passed in 2009 and did have an impact. Economists Alan S. Blinder and Mark Zandi report that "without the government's response, GDP . . . would be about 11.5% lower, payroll employment would be less by some 8 ½ million jobs, and the nation would now be experiencing deflation" (Blinder and Zandi, 2010, p. 1).

President Obama later did call for a second economic stimulus package in a speech on Labor Day, 2010. It drew little attention. The time for such legislation had passed and the Congress and the nation were moving on to other concerns. Meanwhile opponents continually attacked the administration for its "failed economic stimulus program," an argument that was to prove persuasive to many Americans.

Evaluating the success of TARP and the economic stimulus plan is a relatively straightforward exercise. By relying on economic indicators the differentiated results as to their impact are clear. The recovery was two-tiered. Those who directly benefitted in the financial industry did extremely well; those who lost jobs in the Great Recession or their homes to foreclosures or were in danger of doing so continued to struggle.

The Financial Inquiry Report

A comprehensive and carefully documented evaluation of the causes and consequences of the nation's financial collapse was issued in early 2011 by the government commission created to assess the crisis (*National Commission on the Causes*, 2011). Its two major conclusions were that the crisis was preventable, the product of human design and would not have happened if the agencies involved in regulating the financial sector had exercised their responsibilities; and that unemployment and more generally the economy remained a matter of concern.

> . . . this financial crisis was avoidable. The crisis was the result of human action and inaction, not of Mother Nature or computer models gone haywire. The captains of finance and the public stewards of our financial system ignored warnings and failed to question, understand, and manage evolving risks within a system essential to the well-being of the American public. Theirs was a big miss, not a stumble. While the business cycle cannot be repealed, a crisis of this magnitude need not have occurred.

> Despite the expressed view of many on Wall Street and in Washington that the crisis could not have been foreseen or avoided, there were warning signs. The tragedy was that they were ignored or discounted. There was an explosion in risky subprime lending and securitization, an unsustainable rise in housing prices, widespread reports of egregious and predatory lending practices, dramatic increases in household mortgage debt, and exponential growth in financial firms' trading activities, unregulated derivatives, and short-term 'repo' lending markets, among many other red flags. Yet there was a pervasive permissiveness; little meaningful action was taken to quell the threats in a timely manner (p. XVII).

The *Inquiry Report* goes on:

> The prime example is the Federal Reserve's pivotal failure to stem the flow of toxic mortgages, which it could have done by setting prudent mortgage-lending standards. . . . The record of our examination is replete with evidence of other failures: financial institutions made, bought, and sold mortgage securities they never examined, did not care to examine, or knew to be defective; firms depended on tens of billions of dollars of borrowing that had to be renewed each and every night, secured by subprime mortgage securities; and major firms and investors blindly relied on credit rating agencies as their arbiters of risk (p. XVII).

The *Inquiry Report* documented the abuses:

- widespread failures in financial regulation and supervision proved devastating to the stability of the nation's financial markets.
- dramatic failures of corporate governance and risk management at many systematically important financial institutions were a key cause of this crisis.
- a combination of excessive borrowing, risky investments, and lack of transparency put the financial system on a collision course with crisis.
- the government was ill prepared for the crisis, and its inconsistent response added to the uncertainty and panic in the financial markets.
- there was a systemic breakdown in accountability and ethics (pp. XVIII, XIX, XXI, XXII).

And then the Commission in summation reemphasized its major point: [3]

> ... we clearly believe the crisis was a result of human mistakes, misjudgments, and misdeeds that resulted in systemic failures for which our nation has paid dearly ... specific firms and individuals acted irresponsibly ...

> We do place special responsibility with the public leaders charged with protecting our financial system, those entrusted to run our regulatory agencies, and the chief executives of companies whose failures drove us to crisis. These individuals sought and accepted positions of significant responsibility and obligation ...

> ... as a nation, we must also accept responsibility for what we permitted to occur. Collectively, but certainly not unanimously, we acquiesced to or embraced a system, a set of policies and actions, that gave rise to our present predicament (p. XXIII).

Mild regulatory reforms were introduced well after the economic recovery acts had been passed, but the fear was that they would do little to correct the structural weaknesses in the economy and in fact do little to avert another crisis. The assessment of one member of the commission echoed what some economists had been saying. That is, the financial system was "not really very different" than the one that brought on the collapse. He went on to say: "the concentration of financial assets in the largest commercial and investment banks is really significantly higher today than it was in the run-up to the crisis, as a result of the evisceration of some institutions, and the consolidation and merger of others into larger institutions" (Chan, 2011, p. 1).

Any sense of responsibility or accountability had been neglected by those charged with exercising controls in the name of the public and ignored by those interested in maximizing profits whatever the cost to the broader society.

A final note: The cost of any form of a broadly-based, government-sponsored economic recovery program would be substantial, most likely well beyond anything the contemporary political climate would accept. It also involved a revision of the "prevailing ideology and language," that is a neo-liberal economic Darwinism, to achieve a full recovery, something even more unlikely (Kuttner, 2008, pp. 177-178).

Mortgage Foreclosures

The dimensions of the home foreclosure crisis that struck in the wake of the financial collapse were extraordinary. Adding to the anger of a disaffected electorate, the Obama administration's response to the crisis proved to be ineffective. To be more specific, there were "a total of 3,825,637 foreclosure filings—default notices, scheduled auctions and bank repossessions—reported on a record 2,871,891 U.S. properties in 2010, an increase of nearly 2 percent from 2009 and an increase of 23 percent from 2008 . . . 2.23 percent of all U.S. housing units (1 in 45) received at least one foreclosure filings during the year, up from 2.21 percent in 2009, 1.84 percent in 2008, 1.03 percent in 2007 and 0.58 percent in 2006." Zillow Real Estate reported that real estate in the United States had been projected in 2010 to lose more than $1.7 trillion in value, a 70 percent increase of the $1.0 trillion that had been lost during the calendar year 2009 (Realty Trac Staff, 2011; Bun, 2010). The decrease in home values was expected to continue in 2011 and for the foreseeable future. The *Wall Street Journal* as an example predicted little improvement in future years. And, as with other forecasters, it was not sure as to whether the nation had "actually reached the trough in housing" or if the worst was yet to come (Wotapka, 2011).

Such figures begin to make clear the continuing dimensions of the problem. The Obama administration did propose and the Congress enacted a program intended to mitigate the effects of the foreclosures. The program was complicated and acceptance by the banks and other mortgage-holders was voluntary, not mandatory. Few chose to participate. The result was that it had a limited impact given the severity of the crisis it was intended to alleviate.

A later plan was developed with the intention of focusing on mortgage-servicing breakdowns, including a commitment from the largest banks to reduce the balance if the mortgage owed was more than the houses were worth. The speculators who invested in buying up such mortgages would not be penalized and the banks would either be fined $20 billion or required to fund loan modifications for distressed borrowers to the same amount. The plan required the cooperation of the banks, the administration, federal agencies, and regulators and the state attorneys general who had threatened to take legal action. It would be at best a partial solution and its implementation had proven difficult to achieve given the number of actors and constituencies involved and the strength of the opposition (Klan, 2010; Goldfarb and Cha, 2010).

As a bipartisan congressional panel reported: "The Government's Home Affordable Modification Program or HAMP [for relief of bank mortgage foreclosures] is on pace to prevent 700,000 to 800,000 foreclosure, a significant figure, but far fewer than the 3 million to 4 million struggling homeowners [Department of the] Treasury officials hope to help" (Dennis, 2010).

In a talk following the passage of the foreclosure legislation which included $275 billion to assist needy homeowners and $75 billion to subsidize the mortgage industry, President Obama repeatedly called attention to the exceptionally low home refinancing loans available from private banks, urged homeowners to take advantage of these and emphasized the creation of an administration website (http://makinghomeaffordable.gov) to discuss eligibility for such loans. He brought in a number of Washington, DC-area homeowners to attest to the value of such refinancing, the lowest rates in 35 years (at the time 4.78 percent). The message was to seek help from private industry sources, not a realistic option for those in financial trouble nor for those about to lose their homes. The president also said that a new housing plan would be offered soon. It was and it took a surprising turn.

The Obama administration when it returned to the problem in a long-awaited White Paper proposed programs to restructure the mortgage/home-owning market. In presenting the proposal, Secretary of the Treasury Timothy Geithner argued: "This is a place for fundamental reform—to wind down [the role of the federal government in home financing], strengthen consumer protection, and preserve access to affordable housing for people who need it." If the administration's original approach to the foreclosure problem could be considered timid, the new proposals were anything but. Obama planned nothing less than to reverse established American policy, ending all federal government subsidies and mortgage loan programs and to turn such financing over to private industry. Should it be enacted, this would bring to an end to home ownership programs dating back to the New Deal. The solution proposed by the Obama administration was that the emphasis should be placed on rentals.

An exhaustive two-year study of the financial and home market collapse and Wall Street's role in it was issued by the Senate Permanent Subcommittee on Investigations. It tells a disturbing story. Few were to be spared. Most damning, the government-financial sectors seemed to be in collusion, leading to a breakdown of the entire regulatory/investment/financing system. In fact, government regulators often chose to view those on Wall Street that they were charged to police in the public interest as "clients." They saw their role as promoting the profit-making of banks, corporations and investors. There were then no bounds as to what could be attempted and no fear of those pushing the limits of the law as to personal (or corporate) accountability. They also did not entertain thoughts of being held responsible for their actions (no one involved in the crisis was to go to jail).

The Senate report contains a comprehensive assessment of the causes and consequences of the financial industry's collapse, including the home mortgage crisis. It documents the lending and accounting practices of what were at the time referred to as "too-big-to-fail" (meaning too big to be allowed by the government to fail) financial institutions such as Goldman Sachs, Deutsche Bank and Washington Mutual Bank. It records the willful neglect of government agencies to investigate or curtail the worst of the lending activities and also notes areas in which the Congress by law had refused to allow regulators the power to supervise selected financial areas or institutions. The report's findings apply equally to concerns over mortgage foreclosures ànd to the broader national economic collapse. Among its conclusions:

> . . . no regulator was charged with identifying, preventing, or managing risks that threatened the safety and soundness of the overall U.S. financial system. In the area of high risk mortgage lending . . . bank regulators allowed banks to issue high risk mortgages as long as it was profitable and the banks quickly sold the high risk loans to get them off their books. Securities regulators allowed investment banks to underwrite, buy, and sell mortgage backed securities relying on high risk mortgages, as long as the securities received high ratings from the credit rating agencies and so were deemed 'safe' investments. No regulatory agency focused on what would happen when poor quality mortgages were allowed to saturate U.S. financial markets and contaminate . . . securities with high risk loans. In addition, none of the regulators focused on the impact derivatives like credit default swaps might have in exacerbating risk exposures, since they were barred by federal law from regulating or even gathering data about these financial instruments (United States Senate, 2011, p. 41).

The mortgage crisis was a critical part of the effort to achieve economic stability. The administration's response to it was belated and weak, depending more on private industry assistance and its assumed goodwill than government help. It proved to be largely a failure.

The Politics of a Balanced Budget

Deficit reduction is a political issue, as they say, that has legs. That is, it carries weight with the American public, it can be brought out at various times to counter reformist and progressive movements and it has electoral power as the Republican Party successes over the years show (including the election of 2010). The call for a balanced budget, ideologically as well as politically and pragmatically, is a central tenet of Republican Party (and now the Tea Party movement associated with it) orthodoxy.

It seems to have an intuitive appeal to voters, although the comparisons often made on balancing a home budget with that of the nation or for that matter to the bottom line of a corporation are a considerable stretch. Calls for deficit reduction in the 1930s effectively curtailed the New Deal's social engineering and left the movement toward a fully realized welfare state unrealized. It was called into action again to bring to an end Lyndon Johnson's "War on Poverty" and other mass-oriented social programming. Ronald Reagan emphasized a balanced budget in a small and limited government setting. Reagan in turn more pragmatic in office than in his ideological rhetoric managed to accumulate the highest budget deficit in peacetime history, a development overlooked by successive generations of conservatives. Bill Clinton took deficit reduction seriously in his "triangulation" approach to policymaking and in response to the Republican takeover of the Congress in 1994. Clinton succeeded in balancing the federal budget where others had failed. It did not last long. George W. Bush, heir to the Reagan legacy, managed to break the Reagan record with new highs in deficits.

The roots of the present debt are not difficult to trace:

> In January 2001, with the budget balanced and clear sailing ahead, the Congressional Budget Office forecast ever-larger annual surpluses indefinitely. The outlook was so rosy, the CBO said, that Washington would have enough money by the end of the decade to pay off everything it owed.

> Now . . . the national debt is larger, as a percentage of the economy, than at any time in U.S. history except for the period shortly after World War II (Montgomery, 2011).

And as to the Bush or Obama administration policies as contributing to the total debt: "Obama-era [policy] choices account for about $1.7 trillion in new debt . . . Bush-era policies . . . account for more than $7 trillion and are a major contributor to the trillion-dollar annual budget deficits that are dominating the political debate" (Montgomery, 2011).

Obama inherited a deficit of $1.4 trillion in 2009 (a Bush budget), and $1.3 trillion in 2010. The Congressional Budget Office projected a 2011 deficit of $1.5 trillion (some put it higher). The latter figure is an increase of $414 billion over previous estimates, in large part due to the reinstatement of the Bush tax cuts in late 2010. One consequence would be the need in turn to raise the nation's debt ceiling to account for the differences between income and outgo, always a point of partisan contention.

Deficit reduction is an important issue. It has an impact that goes well beyond a simple accounting of tax revenues and financial commitments. In truth it is a political issue of the first magnitude, a fundamental dividing point between Democrats and Republicans. It is used to decide, among other priorities, the future of social programs, the role of government in distributing the nation's wealth, the allocation chances and economic opportunities in employment, education, health and lifestyle opportunities. Timing alone is a major consideration. In the context of a fragile recovery underway from a severe national recession, it raises questions as to the most fundamental of national concerns should the economy be stimulated through enhanced federal spending to promote job growth, thus expanding the tax base and in turn government revenue. Or, is it more important to prioritize budgetary cuts in a period of economic shrinkage and recession on the assumption that money moved to corporate leaders and the wealthiest of Americans will result in an expansion of industry, more jobs and a stronger economy. The latter (combined with a reduction in taxes) is the dominant economic framework of conservatives and receives the greatest attention in actual debates over the economy in the contemporary era.

Domestic social programs bear the brunt of such attacks and once weakened or eliminated are unlikely to be reinstated during better economic times. The parties have much to lose or gain, outside of whatever the impact on balancing the budget might be, for their group base in the electorate and their future electoral support given the direction the budgetary debate takes.

President Obama had attempted to take the initiative by proposing what would turn out to be a painful if initially modest (by comparison) decrease in federal spending, especially in relation to social programs. His hope was to show goodwill, a commitment to deficit reduction and in the process lessen the intensity and comprehensiveness of his opponents' challenges to federal spending. Predictably, as he acknowledged in discussing his objectives, this was not likely to happen. The Republican Party in the House, pushed hard by its newly elected Tea Party members, took a far more aggressive stance, vowing to cut $100 billion for the current year's operating budget. The sum was later reduced to $60 to $61 billion with an additional $4 trillion to be cut from future budgets.

The $60 billion plus figure was later reduced to $40 billion and in the negotiations that followed ended with an agreement on $38 billion in operating budget cuts, a victory for the Republican/Tea Party deficit hawks. The negotiations were carried out largely by the House Republicans and Senate Democratic leadership, with Obama placing himself in the position of an above-the-battle mediator, not directly advancing one side or the other while recognizing the need for fiscal restraint. His objective was to enter the dialogue (again) late in the proceedings and facilitate its conclusion. This he did, while announcing his firm intention not to allow cuts in such programs as the Planned Parenthood and PBS federal subsidies, the last of the issues to be resolved. The amounts involved were small given what was on the table, but enough to allow the president to proclaim victory, both in relation to these programs and in succeeding to broker a budget deal. The cuts in expenditures would come from discretionary funding, a little more than 10 percent of federal operating expenses (12 percent to be precise).

The Tea Party caucus in the House claimed a full victory. Democrats in the Congress were less happy, although it took their votes to put the agreement into effect (59 Republicans in the House voted against it as not going far enough). The president endorsed the talks and the outcome as a success. He called a victory for the middle class and his administration as well as evidence that the two parties could work together to resolve important issues.

In a defense of the outcome he later said the American people would have to learn to live within their budgets, a disingenuous analogy of little relevance. He also said more severe cuts would be needed, in particular in entitlement programs, among the most expensive of federal programs, along with defense allocations, volatile political issues.

The Republicans in the Congress agreed and came up with their own recommendations. Their intention was to basically end the Medicare payment system and Medicaid, relying on block grants to states and set fees for medical services among other things. Such a restructuring would cut costs and service as intended. Party leaders also announced upcoming efforts to reshape Social Security. A privatization of the program had been attempted by the Bush administration and received little support. In addition, the nation's tax structure was to be reframed, cutting corporate and individual taxes and eliminating deductions for such things as home mortgages and funding for the national health insurance plan. President Obama agreed on the necessity for such basic measures and welcomed the efforts if not the extent of the proposed cuts.

Entitlement programs are popular with the public, among the handful of federal programs with support across party lines (table 1.3). There are serious risks, to the extent the public is aware of what is happening, in attacking programs that provide a safety net for the elderly and health care of various types to both the middle class and the most needy. The contemporary political climate favors a head-on assault of such programs while leaving the essential wealth and taxing discrepancies largely untouched.

Then there is a question as to whether anyone really fundamentally concerns themselves about a balanced budget. It is not something the general public understands or is interested in, Various interests can find it a useful tool to achieve other policy ends. Christopher Hayes writing in *The Nation* contends:

> . . . conservatives do not care about deficits or the national debt. Nothing they have done over the past several decades—from the record deficits of the Reagan and [George W.] Bush years to then party-line opposition to nearly every measure that would reduce the deficit—suggests otherwise. . . . What Republicans do care about is defending the incomes of the country's wealthiest, distributing income upward and cutting taxes in order to make progressive governance impossible (Hayes, 2010, p. 4).

An instance of what Hayes is talking about was the lengthy, party-divisive fight over extending the Bush tax cuts and increasing the 35 percent rate on estate taxes, the lowest in history. Both of these proposals favored the wealthiest of Americans. The Republicans committed early and uncompromisingly to a pledge to continue the rates put in place by the Bush administration. President Obama after severely and relentlessly attacking the tax breaks for the richest at the expense of the rest of society (over fifty times by one count) changed positions and supported their continuation. His argument was that overall the legislation would help middle class Americans. In turn Democrats in the Congress after bitter debate and substantial internal disagreements voted for them. In a broader context, it may represent the tenor of the times, an accurate portrayal of the balance of political power in contemporary politics.

The budget is in short the ultimate policy, and even more fundamentally ideological, battleground. Everything is in play. It reviews and assesses all aspects of government operations and services and their financing and consequently their future is in the balance. Nothing compares to it in demonstrating an administration's priorities or those of its opponents. Brought into relief are the contrasting conceptions of what government is, what it should do and who it should represent. There is little overlap, much less anything approaching a

Table 1.3. Support by Political Party for Budget Spending

Would you increase, decrease, or keep the same spending for:		Rep %	Dem %	Ind %	R-D gap
Unemployment aid	Increase	11	47	23	+36
	Decrease	50	11	29	-39
Health care	Increase	22	56	39	+34
	Decrease	47	8	25	-39
Aid to needy in the U.S.	Increase	24	57	37	+33
	Decrease	35	12	20	-23
Education	Increase	45	77	62	+32
	Decrease	15	4	13	-11
Environmental protection	Increase	16	47	41	+31
	Decrease	43	12	26	-31
Aid to the world's needy	Increase	7	32	22	+25
	Decrease	70	28	45	-42
Public school systems	Increase	42	65	58	+23
	Decrease	25	4	13	-21
Roads and transportation	Increase	22	44	43	+22
	Decrease	32	18	18	-14
College financial aid	Increase	30	51	47	+21
	Decrease	30	9	15	-21
Scientific research	Increase	28	46	35	+18
	Decrease	30	13	26	-17
Medicare	Increase	27	55	38	+18
	Decrease	20	5	14	-15
Energy	Increase	26	41	37	+15
	Decrease	28	18	22	-10
Social Security	Increase	33	45	40	+12
	Decrease	21	4	15	-17
Agriculture	Increase	29	37	31	+8
	Decrease	26	15	28	-11
Veterans' benefits	Increase	46	52	53	+6
	Decrease	8	6	5	-2
Combating crime	Increase	41	45	33	+4
	Decrease	19	13	20	-6
Terrorism defenses	Increase	38	32	30	-6
	Decrease	16	20	23	+4
Military defense	Increase	41	28	27	-13
	Decrease	18	36	33	+18

Source: Pew Research Center, Feb. 2-7, 2011. Q17a-s. P. 16. Percent Saying "keep spending about the same" now shown. http://people-press.org/files/2011/02/702.pdf

consensus, between Democrats/liberals and Republicans/conservatives, or in more immediate terms the Obama administration and its opposition in the Congress, as to what to fund or how much to cut. The problem is clear, although of less immediate urgency than Washington would have us believe. The resolution may be considerably less obvious.

Entitlement programs—Social Security, whose stability was not in question and not related to the budget debate, Medicare and Medicaid—were the principal federal funding priorities. These programs and other areas of domestic policy had been targets of prior administrations, most notably the Bush and Reagan presidencies, but given their popularity with the public and their core importance to what remained of the safety net, managed to avoid serious attacks. Finally and lost in the debate over the need for deficit reduction, the programs being proposed for cuts were in actuality supported by the public who while approving of a balanced budget also wanted an increase in government services (Pew Research Center, "Rethinking Budget Cutting," February 10, 2011).

Initially behind it all was the threat of a government shut-down for lack of funding. It had happened in 1995 when a Newt Gingrich-led Congress and President Bill Clinton came to an impasse over financing. Both parties said they did not want a recurrence, and went on to avoid it by enacting the $38 billion in budget reductions. The agreement between the parties was only a prelude to the fight to come over the nature of the proposed $4 trillion in budget cuts to take effect over the next decade.

President Obama more so than many Democratic Party members embraced deficit reduction. He demonstrated a willingness to consider opposition strategies and announced that he would weigh serious reductions in program expenditures at any level and in any area. One of the more prominent examples was community block grants, which as an organizer on the South Side of Chicago he had prized and which he announced in defending his budget proposals were close to his heart. He nonetheless indicated the necessity that the spending on these be reduced or eliminated. He also mandated a five year moratorium on discretionary federal domestic spending, not expected to have much impact on deficit reduction.

When the issue of budget deficits first arose President Obama decided to postpone giving serious attention to the issue by appointing a nonpartisan budget deficit commission to report back within a year with a recommended strategic approach to budgetary cuts. This is a favorite stratagem of Obama (and other presidents), allowing a Chief Executive to shield himself behind an appointed commission's recommendations in treating issues of great volatility. A president would appoint much of the membership of such a body, giving his administration a degree of control over the commission's recommendations and a degree of predictability as to the outcome of the deliberations. The (allegedly) impartial and nonpartisan nature of the proposals set forth by distinguished experts to promote the nation's well-being offers significant political advantages to a president with few drawbacks.

The deficit reduction commission reported back in late 2010. Its recommendations were harsh. The majority recommendations can be taken as presenting the point of view and representative of the interests of one sector of the society. One of the minority reports provides a contrast (the commission could not reach a consensus; there were a number of minority views presented). It acknowledged the value of deficit reduction but formulated a quite different prioritization of interests to be affected. Taken together, they provide as clear an indication of contrasting sides to the issue of a balanced budget and the targeting of who should bear the major burden of the sacrifices to be made as one is likely to find.

Among the commission recommendations to the Congress are the following:

- spending cuts that would account for 74 percent of the reductions and a reduction in tax breaks that would account for the remainder
- a payroll tax holiday for employees and/or workers as an economic stimulus measure
- a targeted reduction of the national debt to 40 percent of the economy by 2034 as against the 185 percent at the time
- government expenditures not to exceed 21 percent of GDP
- lowering the annual deficit to 3 percent of GDP by 2015. The commission recommendations in time would reduce it further to 2.5 percent
- capping federal health care spending, from Medicare to subsidies for health insurance and limiting it to the rate of economic growth plus 1 percent
- change the formulas for the payment of physicians, put in cost-sharing for Medicare beneficiaries, limit prescription drug costs and malpractice suits and court awards
- cap taxes at 21 percent of GDP
- make Social Security solvent over a 75 year period. It would reduce benefits for wealthy retirees and cost-of-living adjustments for all retirees
- increase the Social Security retirement age to 68 by 2050 and 69 by 2075. The age for early retirement would be increased to 64[4]

Predictably liberals, Democrats and those most affected by the proposed cuts in programs objected to the percent of the $4 trillion in estimated reductions to come from federal spending. Conservatives, the better-off, Republicans and Tea Party members criticized the proposed tax increases. For many pro-deficit hawks in the Congress, and whatever their objections might be to some of the proposals, the commission report would come to symbolize the "gold standard" for the budget debate. President Obama endorsed the deficit group's recommendations and later called on them in putting forth his comprehensive budget plan.

A budgetary alternative proposed by commission member Jan Schakowsky, a liberal Democrat from Illinois, illustrated the fundamental differences in approach in the identification of the programs to be protected, reduced or elimi- nated and in the groups most likely to be impacted. The difference in tone, tar- geted cuts, the nature of the financial sacrifices to be made and the individuals and economic sectors of the society to be most affected are pronounced.[5]

The battle lines were clearly drawn. Given the nature of fiscal and budgetary policy and how it is processed in the legislative system; the low priority and weight given to preserving much less extending domestic discretionary spending programs, most of which were underfunded initially; the inviting target this frac- tion of the budget presents for opponents to attack; the political appeal and cover (as was intended) of the recommendations made by an independent, nonpartisan commission; the conservative and some Democratic support voiced for most of the commission proposals for spending cuts, although not for the reduction in tax benefits; the composition of the Congress; and the endorsement of the com- mission plans by the President, indicated that the broad nature of the eventual outcome should be predictable.

Policymaking in Washington: The Debt Ceiling Crisis

The first term ideological debate over policy directions and the budget came down to a head in what ordinarily and in other presidencies was an innocuous, pro forma act, raising the debt limit so that the government could continue to function and to pay its bills. Most frequently this is a largely automatic affair, with both parties in agreement. In recent administrations it had been raised on a number of occasions without incident. Not so this time. The Tea Party and con- servative Republicans in the House decided to make a stand and force severe budget cuts before they would acquiesce to any increase in the debt ceiling. This faction of the Republican Party had the power to keep the Congress and the ad- ministration from acting and they used it.

The battle over the substance of the proposal to lift the debt limit was pro- longed. It went through a series of different stages, and included a series of compromise agreements to substantially reduce government spending. However these concessions continued to be seen by opponents as falling short of what was needed. One tentative agreement after another as negotiated by House speaker John Boehner, who had great difficulty in keeping his majority coalition together on the issue, and President Obama fell apart.

The ultimate threat was a government default on its obligations. The conse- quence would have been dire, from terminating government support for pro- grams to a reduction in its credit ratings that would be expensive (to be affected as it turned out by the process in itself).

A bipartisan deal of course was agreed to at the last minute, precluding a government shutdown. The stakes were too high, the anticipated public reaction that would result too severe and the Clinton-Gingrich experience too recent to ignore for a resolution not to emerge. The budget would be reduced by $2.1 to

$2.4 trillion over ten years, resulting in as the president said "the lowest level of domestic spending since Dwight Eisenhower was president." There would be no raise in taxes for corporate America or the ultra-wealthy, Democratic Party priorities. In addition a congressional committee would be formed, a bipartisan "Super Committee" or "Super Congress," to decide on further cuts in spending and to consider potential increases in revenue from a modified tax code. Both houses of Congress would be required to vote on the committee's proposals. Unofficially the Bowles–Simpson debt commission reduction recommendations would serve as a starting point. Fifty percent cuts in both domestic and defense spending would automatically go into effect if the Congress or the committee could not agree on the programs to be targeted.

There was a broad relief that a default had been avoided. Beyond that the reaction was not positive. The consensus view was that the Tea Party/Conservative Republicans had gotten what they wanted (although some continued to argue that it did not go far enough). Obama believed he had removed the budget issue from the reelection campaign, one of his major concerns. The Democrats felt they received nothing in the bargaining and many questioned the president's leadership and political skills in negotiating with the opposition. He had removed himself from the talks and chose to sign the deal as agreed to by House Republicans and Speaker John Boehner, in talks with the Senate Democratic Party leader Harry Reid.

It was claimed that a small faction of the Congress had taken the nation to the brink of default to gain their objectives; that it was an ideological decision more than an economic one; that it represented a perversion of the legislative, and more broadly, governing institutional processes for conflict resolution; and that given the success it achieved it would be repeated in the future. Further, it was argued that the agreement would slow the recovery from the recession, already well behind projections; increase unemployment; reduce consumer spending; decrease government revenues; and ironically, add to the nation's debt.

Democrats in the Congress were frustrated and angry. They had again been called on to pass legislation and to provide a margin of safety for an agreement that went against their core beliefs. Beyond Senate leader Reid, they had not been part of negotiations and had been effectively left out of the loop by a president of their own party who had refused in their eyes to put forward a Democratic liberal agenda. They had been left to hear about it in the media. The president's passivity and willingness to accommodate what some believed to be extremist views was of deep concern to them.

Robert Kuttner provides one indication of the intensity of the liberal reaction. Writing for The Huffington Post he charged that the country had elected "a Democratic president who raises hope, but turns out to be a close ally of the same forces that caused the collapse":

> The United States has been rendered ungovernable except on the extortionate terms of the far-right. For the first time in modern history, one of the two major parties is in the hands of a faction so extreme that it is willing to destroy the economy if it doesn't get its way.

. . . The Tea Party Republicans have a perfect foil in President Barack Obama. The budget deal is the logical conclusion of Obama's premise that the way to make governing partners of the far right is to keep appeasing them. He is the perfect punching bag. He can be blasted both as a far-left liberal and as a weakling (Kuttner, 2011; see also Westen, 2011).

The *New York Times*, the nation's newspaper of record, editorially referred to the outcome as "arbitrary butchering," a "nearly complete capitulation to the hostage-taking demands of the Republican extremists," and the product of a "political environment laced with lunacy" (Editorial, *New York Times*, August 1, 2011, p. A16). Economist Paul Krugman, writing in his *Times'* op-ed column, argues that it would "take America a long way down the road to banana-republic status" (Krugman, 2011, p. A17). Ross Douthat, a more conservative columnist for the *Times*, contended that the "White House's tactics have consistently maximized President Obama's short-term advantage while diminishing his overall authority. Call it the 'too clever by half' presidency: the Administration's maneuvering keeps working out as planned, but Obama's position keeps eroding" (Douthat, 2011, p. A17). Jacob S. Hacker and Oona A. Hathaway, in the same edition of the *Times*, outlined what they referred to as "the democracy crisis":

Nobody wins when our constitutional system falters: not the president, who gains unilateral power but loses a governing partner; not Congress, which gets to blame the president but risks irrelevance; and certainly not the American people, who have to bear the resulting dysfunction (Hacker and Hathaway, 2011, p. A17).

The *Times* editorial was to refer to the agreement as "contrived as the artificial crisis that spawned it" and with the Super Committee "giving enormous responsibility . . . to a ridiculously small number of people chosen for ideological purposes . . . reduces Congress' most fundamental power of the purse to an undemocratic and untransparent huddle" (Editorial, *New York Times*, August 3, 2011, p. A22).

The projections across the board were especially bleak: the stock market experienced its worst trade-off since the financial crisis; the prospect of a second recession on top of one that had yet to recover (a double-dip as it was called) was predicted by economists and financial planners as likely to follow; and most fundamentally as indicated the basic functioning of the American governing system was called into question.

The polls indicated a disconnect between the citizenry and their elected representatives.

. . . poll after poll has showed that rank-and-file Americans of all political persuasions believe that revenues (the nice way to say taxes) should be a part of any deal to resolve our debt crisis. Seventy-two percent of Americans . . . said taxes should be raised on those making more than $50,000 per year, including 73 percent of independents and a stunning 54 percent of Republicans. Fifty-nine percent wanted taxes raised on oil and gas companies, including 60 percent of independents and 55 percent of Republicans. Yet Republicans refused to vote for a deal that included any revenues at all, and the Democratic leadership capitulated despite the fact that the position was exactly the opposite of what large majorities wanted (Hogue, 2011).

The public's principal concern, as it had been since the beginning of the Great Recession, was jobs.

Standard & Poor's reacted to the debt agreement by reducing the government's top credit rating, a first in American history. The corporation defended its action by calling the debt limit negotiations a "debacle." It made the point that "fiscal policy, like other government policy, is a political process." The White House responded by raising what it referred to as "fundamental questions about the credibility and integrity of S&P's ratings actions" (Schwartz and Dash, 2011, p. 1).

There had been no broad public debate over the budget or on spending priorities. And given the procedures for enforcing debt reductions that had been established, there would not be. One of the few certainties was that despite the one-sided results, up to this point in time, the economic/budgetary/ideological debate and the divide it fostered between the parties would continue to be at the center of American politics.

The Wars in Afghanistan and Iraq (and Libya)

Whatever the initial rationale for the wars in Iraq and Afghanistan once begun they took on a life of their own (see the chapter by Lawrence C. Reardon in this volume). Obama had kept on Robert Gates, Bush's Secretary of Defense, among others in the Pentagon, and broadly committed to a continuation of the Bush-Cheney-Rumsfeld policies. He did allow for some redirection of efforts while actively extending the military involvement in Afghanistan and targeting Al Qaeda/Taliban bases in Pakistan for more extended attacks. Neither administration had been able to define what would constitute a reasonably successful effort or "victory." In the process the war in Afghanistan began to threaten America's tenuous relationship with Pakistan, a nation that had been considered an ally and a recipient of generous amounts of foreign aid over the decades. The country had offered sanctuary to both the Taliban and Al Qaeda.

Candidate Obama had promised "peace" (not clearly defined). He also pledged to withdraw the troops from Iraq, turning that country's governance over to its people and to redirect attention to locating and defeating Al Qaeda in Afghanistan. It had been assumed early in the Bush administration that the Afghan war had been won. The military presence in the country was reduced and reallocated to Iraq. It was then assumed that with the defeat of the Iraqi army in 2003 (and the later capture and execution of Saddam Hussein) that this war had also been won ("Mission Accomplished" as George W. Bush proclaimed).

Neither outcome proved to be correct. The engagement in Iraq dragged on in a chaotic conflicting mix of forces: sectarian, ethnic and tribal, and regional divisions; a stronger than anticipated militia resistance; corrupt, inexperienced governments; the difficulty of establishing inclusive and pluralistic party systems and instituting free elections; the absence of a willingness to abide by election results; the economic, oil-based enrichment of elites; and charges of officially-sanctioned drug smuggling, all combined series of blunders and poor decision-making by the Americans in charge added to the problem. Nation-building and democratization, the announced objectives of the government, would prove harder to achieve than military victory.

Much the same situation would be encountered in Afghanistan, a nation that had never experienced an effective central government, much less a quasi-democratic one; and a country that had managed to defeat the Russian invaders in the 1980s.

Significant numbers of American troops were withdrawn from Iraq and reallocated to Afghanistan. A core group of approximately fifty thousand military personnel were to be left in Iraq on a permanent basis and later the administration indicated a like number of contingent troops would remain in Afghanistan post-withdrawal, joining the over 175 countries worldwide with a stationing of American soldiers.

The problems in Afghanistan were at least as severe as those encountered in Iraq. Initially the American military's campaigns were limited and directed at Al Qaeda, the group responsible for the 9/11 World Trade Center bombings. With the migration of Al Qaeda to the mountains of Pakistan victory was declared. However the war in Afghanistan never ended and in fact was expanded to a fight against the Taliban and its campaign to take control of the national government. It was expanded further with the influx of troops from Iraq under Obama and in a short period of time the number of military personnel committed to the war under Obama exceeded that at the height of military actions during the Bush years.

Afghanistan was a mountainous country, undeveloped, with a history of violence and tribal warfare and with a variety of cultures and different languages. It was an ideal location for guerilla warfare and poorly suited to conventional military tactics. It was also fiercely independent, Islamic, ethnically, tribally and regionally divided and resistant to foreign interventions of any kind. The government was unable to control territory outside of the capital, Kabul; it was known for its corruption; a novice at governing and especially in any type of representative, democratic-based system; and leading political figures including President Karzai's family members had been accused of involvement in the drug trade. Karzai was considered an emotional, unpredictable and untrustworthy ally. Yet the United States had chosen to deal with him as the nation's representative (given the limited choices available) in promoting its interests and presumably his.

Pakistan's permitting both the Taliban and Al Qaeda to use its territory for their base allowed them to strike at times and places of their own choosing in attacking American troops across the border. Both terrorist organizations were protected by a sympathetic Pakistani secret service that operated with little supervision from the nation's elected leadership. The result was the Americans found it difficult to take and hold large areas of Afghanistan while at the same time finding themselves unable to effectively on a mass level strike at the enemy's bases in northwest Pakistan.

The administration had not only increased the military presence in Afghanistan but given the nature of the situation encountered, Obama had significantly increased a reliance on pilotless drones, launched primarily from Washington, to target and kill Taliban and Al Qaeda leaders in Pakistan. A number of civilians continued to be killed in these raids, a point made by the Taliban that had a strong appeal to Afghans. Despite the increased military presence, the drone attacks and assassination efforts, the war, much less any effort to provide a permanent democratic structure and a level of competence to a government resistant to both, did not go well.

The wars became the longest in American history with no realistic prospect as to closure. A 2014 "soft" deadline for an American withdrawal from Afghanistan was set by the administration but few expected it to be realized.

A major review of government policy in Afghanistan (and to a lesser extent Iraq, a secondary concern at this point) was initiated by Obama in 2010. It was though, relatively lengthy and basically reinforced what had happened and what was in progress. The Pentagon and the field commander in Afghanistan appointed by Obama, General David Petraeus, emphasized the military successes, the changes in strategy and the prospects for success. Sixteen national intelligence agencies in a joint evaluation called any real victory unlikely given the conditions faced and the sanctuary provided the Taliban and other terrorist groups in Pakistan.

Obama chose to side with the military and to take an optimistic position as to its success. In a visit to the American troops in Afghanistan in late 2010, he said: "we can be proud that there are fewer areas under Taliban control and more Afghans have a chance to build a more hopeful future." This was a view many on the ground in Afghanistan or who followed the war from Washington did not share.

Curiously the Pentagon in an earlier report to the Congress appeared to disagree with its own later assessment. It said that insurgent attacks had increased 70 percent since 2009 and by a factor of three since 2007 and that the Taliban remained a threat to the Afghan government. It was also reported that President Karzai's government was intrinsically corrupt; could not account for much of the aid and funding delivered to it; was intent on enriching itself; that relatives of Karzai were involved in the drug trade (familiar charges at this point); that Kabul could not control most of the country it claimed to govern; and that its army remained poorly trained and was incapable of providing security for the country should the Americans leave. The NGO (Non-Governmental Organization) Safety Office in Afghanistan, which coordinated such activity in the country, reported that insurgent attacks were up 60 percent in 2010 over the previous year and presented a growing security concern for its affiliated organizations. "The country is dramatically worse off than a year ago, both in terms of the geographical spread and its [the insurgents'] rate of attacks." A United Nations' mapping of the situation showed "the focus of the [United States and its allies] coalition's military offensives . . . remained 'very high risks,' with no noted improvements. At the same time, the . . . 'low risk' districts in northern, central and western Afghanistan shriveled . . . upgraded to 'high risk' [were] 16 previously more secure districts" (Trofimov, 2010, p. A10). What was clear was that the Taliban would design their campaigns with a flexibility that guerilla operatives excel at, moving its primary focus of attention from one district to another if it came under attack, ensuring in the process that no area could presume to remain safe.

At a minimum such conflicting reports as these increased confusion over exactly what was happening and skepticism as to the results reported and to the chances for an acceptable resolution of the conflicts. The human and financial costs of the wars were considerable. The overly ambitious objectives, a failure to appreciate the cultures involved and the geographic and cultural nature of the countries and their tribal and regional divisions or to plan adequately beyond the initial military efforts were to take their toll.

Afghanistan and Iraq are "invisible wars" in remote parts of the world. There was no draft affecting all of the nation's youth. There was no surtax to pay for the wars. They did not receive the massive amount of attention for example focused on the Vietnam War and they did not bring forth street demonstrations and a resistance to involvement anywhere near as massive or effective as they did on the order of Vietnam. They received little media attention due to a number of overlapping events: the government's largely successful efforts to control access to the war zones; the nature of the countries involved; the personal danger involved for reporters attempting to cover them; the press of other world events; a lack of public interest; the complexity of the situations; the economy and health care that dominated domestic political debate; and the pull of calls to patriotism to protect the nation from terrorists. They were fought by a small percentage of the nation's youth (1 percent) and at that among its most disadvantaged and politically marginalized. And then there was simple inertia; no prominent public figures had led the fight (again in contrast to the Vietnam era) to bring them to an end.

To the unease of some over an international policy that often led to military intervention, others would see it as a display of the country's military strength and/or social consciousness in reacting, the Obama administration joined France and NATO in bombing strongholds of the embattled Libyan leader, Colonel Moammar Khadafy, in 2011. There was little public preparation for the attacks and the Congress was not consulted. The action appeared almost impulsive and was justified by the president, out of the country at the time the bombings were initiated, post-intervention as a humanitarian gesture. Little was known about the Libyan insurgency as to who the rebels were and what would likely occur if Khadafy was driven from power. There was little question that his forty-two-year reign had been brutally repressive or he was an unpredictable dictator prone to killing his own people. The public was caught unaware and the Congress left uninformed. An early disengagement from the war was promised.

The uprisings were part of the wave of such movements that had spread from Tunisia across North Africa to Egypt and beyond to the Persian Gulf states. The Obama reaction to these in general was cautious and while not overly assertive, with the exception of the Libyan case, tailored to each country's history and what was known of the demonstrators, their leadership and their chances for success. In the late spring of 2011, American commandoes stormed an enclave in what was reported as a "garrison town" with a Pakistani army base nearby not far from the capital of Islamabad and killed Osama bin Laden. The news of bin Laden's death was welcomed, at times exuberantly by crowds of Americans, although it did increase tensions with the Pakistani government which was not notified ahead of time of the raid.

There was evidence that the public had grown increasingly disillusioned and would like to see the wars terminated (figure 1.2). With bin Laden's death, the calls for a withdrawal from Afghanistan increased. There is also the issue of their financing, which had been given little systematic attention. The Afghani war cost $100 billion/year to keep one hundred thousand American troops in the country pursuing what was left of Al Qaeda, an estimated one hundred or less (the total was disputed); most had moved on to sanctuary in Pakistan. The war in Iraq was projected in total to cost in the vicinity of $3 trillion (Bilmes and Stiglitz, 2008). Such figures had begun to receive renewed attention. The Tea Party/Republican gains in the midterm election and the calls for a responsible budget accounting began to direct attention to the nation's financial investment in these areas. An argument for a serious reduction in defense and war-related expense may be hard to make given the memories from 9/11 and the calls to patriotic pride. However the budgetary battles more than most other concerns may serve to direct attention to the costs of such wars and to raise questions as to the necessity for such military engagements (figures 1.3, 1.4).

Figure 1.2. Public Support for the Wars in Iraq and Afghanistan

Do you think the United States made a mistake in sending troops to Iraq?

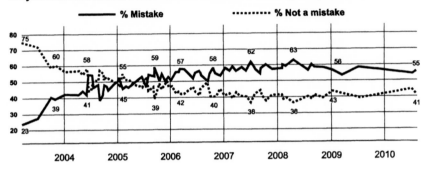

Thinking now about U.S. military action in Afghanistan that began in October 2001, do you think that the United States made a mistake in sending military forces to Afghanistan, or not?

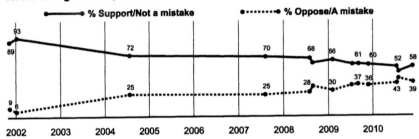

In general, how would you say things are going for the U.S. in Afghanistan [ROTATED: very well, moderately well, moderately badly, (or) very badly]?

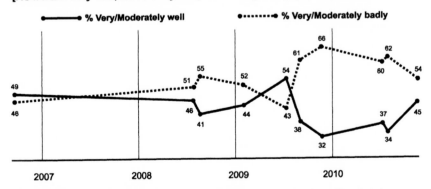

Source: Gallup, http://www.gallup.com/poll/144944/Americans-Less-Pessimistic-Progress-Afghanistan.aspx

William Crotty

Figure 1.3. The Financial Costs of the Wars in Iraq and Afghanistan

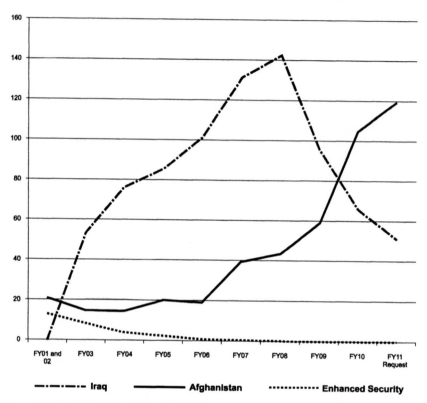

Source: U.S. Congressional Research Service,
http://www.scribd.com/doc/70020983/Congressional-Research-Service-Afghanistan-Iraq-War-Costs-July-2011

Figure 1.4. The Cumulative Costs of the Wars in Iraq and Afghanistan

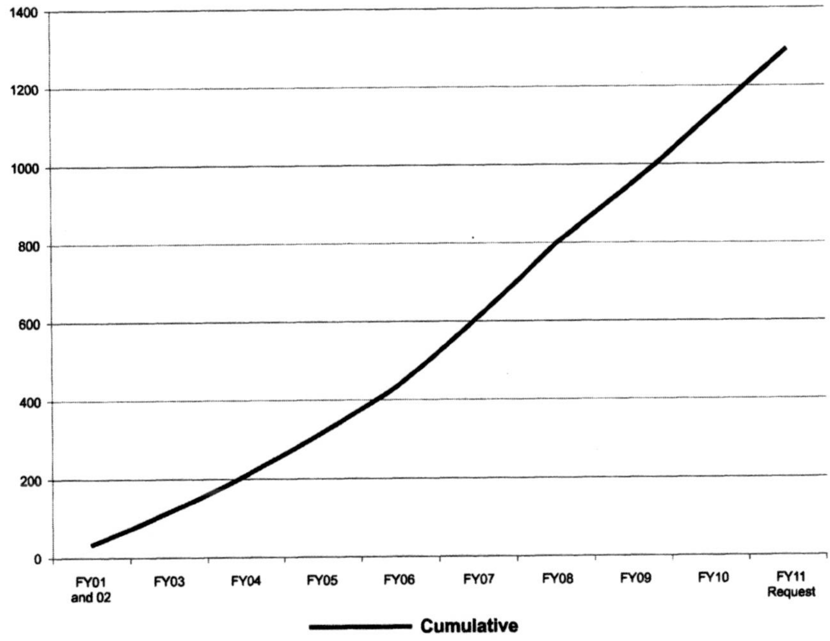

Source: Congressional Research Service, http://www.fas.org/sgp/crs/natsec/RL33110 .pdf

Conclusion

When it came to policy-making, the problems facing the incoming Obama administration were exceptional in terms of their scope and the immediacy of the attention demanded. In addition the president chose to initiate a long and nasty fight over health care and the federal government's role in it, an issue that had divided the nation for generations (Blumenthal and Morone, 2010). Eventually after a long and contentious fight the president got a bill he could support. The price was high, leading to divisions within his own party and an opposition that proved unyielding. It was a singular achievement but the cost paid in resources expended and the loss of goodwill that accompanies a new president into office, especially evident in the election of the nation's first African-American Chief Executive, were extensive. It is not possible to say that things might have been different should Obama have chosen to deal with the revival of the economy first (the likelihood was that they would not have been), but the acrimonious fight over the adoption of a national health insurance plan set the tone for the rest of Obama's term.

The president implemented the legislation originally introduced by George W. Bush on the bailout of the banks and Wall Street, justified as necessary to increase corporate investments in the economy and to stimulate job growth and a reinvigorated stock market. He supported a job stimulus plan passed by the Congress and efforts to provide relief through largely voluntary federal supplements to the banks to relieve the mortgage crisis.

The TARP program was highly successful and the banks and the stock market recovered quickly. The economic stimulus package did have an impact in avoiding a deeper recession but was not sufficient enough to relieve the nation's consistently high unemployment figures. The home mortgage crisis continued to worsen. Overall the recovery was both modest and discretionary, bringing little relief to those working Americans who had lost their jobs.

The continuous battle over a balanced budget demonstrated the competing policy and political agendas of the time and of the nation's politics. While the need for deficit reduction was generally recognized, the severity of the cuts in spending and those targeted to bear the greatest burden were subjects of intense debate. The debate served to illustrate the divisions in the population over the economy in terms of those to be rewarded and those to be penalized. It brought into clear relief the basic differences in approach, constituencies and values that separated the two political parties.

In his decision-making the president, who repeatedly said he was not guided by any ideological convictions, relied on a tightly controlled process. It called primarily on a few trusted White House advisors and even more so on Obama's own instincts and judgment as to the political climate. Few outsiders and a small number of select party members participated in the process in settling on the proposals to be put forth, the strategic approach to the negotiations to follow or whatever the concessions and modifications that might be needed to secure support. President Obama approached each policy domain, from the economy and health care to the START anti-nuclear treaty with the Russians and the repeal of the "don't ask, don't tell" gay policy in the military, as discrete, individualized assessments of the approach likely to result in the least opposition and in pragmatic terms result in some type of achievable policy outcomes.

What was less evident in such a decision-making calculus was the absence of long-term, distinctive policy agenda or the presence of a value-oriented substructure to framing and advancing policy objectives. More than the liberal/progressive that he might have appeared to be pre-election and despite frequent protestations as to where his sympathies lay (although it could be said these were more evident in lesser areas of public attention) there were few signs of such concerns in the pragmatic administration path that was followed. This approach it was argued was more central to the Obama persona, a surer reflection of his personality, his approach to life and to governing and a truer indication of his career prior to his assuming the office of the president.

Obama evidenced a greater receptiveness to the concerns of the business community and their needs and a reliance on private industry to meet and redress the problems facing the nation than was apparent in his campaign. It was to be a strain in the administration that became clearer and more public as his term progressed. His objective increasingly became the desire to appeal to the moderates in the electorate, the group critical to his re-election chances. Correspondingly he began early on and with increasing confidence a move to be seen as a centrist or possibly center/right politician and president, a perception that his support groups in the electorate might not have fully realized and one that his party in the Congress might not have found comfortable.

Overall the Obama presidency turned out to be largely unpredictable in policy-making, embracing a non-liberal programmatic agenda that few would have predicted on the eve of his election. He did face a unified and unrelenting Republican opposition in the Congress, one successful in setting the terms of debate and the framework for negotiations and one that enjoyed impressive gains in the midterm elections. Obama recognized their interests and showed a willingness to compromise, often well before the strength of their position could be established. He made an effort to meet their objections and to achieve some form of "consensus," an objective difficult to realize in a polarized Washington. For Democrats on the other hand, he appeared tentative in his decision-making, often distracted by a broad and frequently world-encompassing personal agenda seen by them as less relevant to the economic duress facing the nation. In this scenario he was pictured as unsure of himself, unable to set a clear set of priorities and then failing to communicate these effectively to the public at large or to the Congress or to fight consistently for their adoption. It was a quite different conception of the man and his potential role in the presidency than others believed they had seen in electing him to office. While this may have been a reasonable perspective from those on the left and the mainstream of his party, the Obama transiting to the centrist/business-sensitive president he chose to be increased his support among moderates and with it his chances for continuing in office.

One issue of concern however was that the basic structural problems that faced him when he entered the presidency and underlay the Great Recession collapse remained much as they had at the end of the previous administration. The economy recovery was slow and uncertain and the search for a "new normal" as it was referred to (and as unclear as the terminology might be) continued to be elusive; unemployment remained high, leading to the creation and acceptance of what could emerge as a new and permanent underclass of the jobless; the home foreclosure epidemic was unresolved, actually increasing in severity; the two wars continued with a venture into bombing Libya in support of those opposing Khadafy; and, virtually unnoticed, the Bush-Cheney anti-terrorism policies now supported by Obama (with modifications as to what would be considered permissible) remained in effect.

Notes

1. In addition there was the House-Senate reconciliation act passed by a vote of 220-207.

2. For a defense of the plan, see Blinder and Zandi, 2010.

3. For a more comprehensive account, see the full commission report: National Commission on Fiscal Responsibility and Reform, "The Moment of Truth: Report of the National Commission on Fiscal Responsibility and Reform." (Washington, DC: The White House, December, 2010). See also: National Commission on Fiscal Responsibility and Reform, "Member Statements for Fiscal Commission Report" (Washington, DC: National Commission on Fiscal Responsibility and Reform, January 31, 2011). www.fiscalcommission.gov/news.member-statements-finalcommission-report (accessed May 8, 2011).

4. Further information not contained in the published report can be found at www.fcic.gov/.

5. See Crotty, ed., 2011. For a related budgetary approach to Schakowsky, see "The People's Budget," Budget of the Congressional Progressive Caucus, Fiscal Year 2012, U.S. House of Representatives, released April 2011, grijalva.house.gov/uploads /The%20CPC%20FY2012%20Budget.pdf (accessed May 8, 2011).

References

Bilmes, Linda J. and Joseph E. Stiglitz. 2008. "The Iraq War Will Cost U.S. $3 Trillion and Much More." *Washington Post*, March 9. www.washingtonpost.com/wp-dyn/content/article/2008/03/07/AR2008030702846.html (accessed May 8, 2011).

Blinder, Alan S. and Mark Zandi. 2010. "How the Great Recession Was Brought to an End." July 27. www.economy.com/mark-zandi/documents/End-of-Great-Recession.pdf (accessed May 8, 2011).

Blumenthal, David and James Morone. 2010. *The Heart of Power: Health and Politics in the Oval Office*. Berkeley: University of California Press.

Bun, Yeng. 2010. "U.S. Homes Set To Lose $1.7 Trillion in Value During 2010." Zillow Estate Research, December 9. www.zillow.com/blog/research/2010/12/09/u-s-homes-set-to-lose-1.7-trillion-in-value-during-2010/ (accessed May 8, 2011).

Chan, Sewell. 2011. "Crisis Panel's Report Parsed Far and Wide." *New York Times*, January 28, p. 1.

Congressional Research Service, http://www.fas.org/sgp/crs/natsec/RL33110.pdf

Congressional Research Service, http://www.scribd.com/doc/70020983/Congressional-Research-Service-Afghanistan-Iraq-War-costs-July-2011

Crotty, William, ed. 2011. "Barack Obama and the Struggle to Survive." Boston, MA: Center for the Study of Democracy/Northeastern University.

Dennis, Brady. 2010. "U.S. Foreclosure-Prevention Program Fell Short, Congressional Oversight Panel Says." *Washington Post*, December 14. www.washingtonpost. com/wp-dyn/content/article/2010/12/14/AR2010121400203.html.

Douthat, Ross. 2011. "The Diminished President." *New York Times*, August 1, p. A17.

Editorial. 2011. "To Escape Chaos, A Terrible Deal." *New York Times*, August 1, p. A16.

Editorial. 2011. "Hiding Behind the Budget Act." *New York Times*, August 3, p. A22.

Gallup. http://www.gallup.com/poll/144944/Americans-Less-Pessimistic-Progress-Afgha

nistan.aspx

Goldfarb, Zachary A. and Ariana Eunjung Cha. 2010. "Rush to foreclosure by Fannie, Freddie helped feed problems with legal paperwork." *Washington Post*, December 22. www.washingtonpost.com/wp-dyn/content/article/2010/12/22/AR201012220582 8.html. (accessed May 13, 2011).

Hacker, Jacob S. and Oona Hathaway. 2011. "Our Unbalanced Democracy." *New York Times*, August 1, p. A17.

Hayes, Christopher. 2010. "The Bribery Model." *The Nation*, December 27, p. 4.

Herszenhorn, David M. 2011. "G.O.P. Bloc Presses Leaders To Slash Even More." *New York Times*, January 21, p. A1.

Hogue, Ilyse. 2011. "The Hidden Casualty of the Debt Deal." *The Nation*, August 3. www.thenation.com/article/162552/hidden-casualty-debt-deal (accessed August 22, 2011).

Jacobs, Lawrence R. and Theda Skocpol. 2010. *Health Care Reform and American Politics: What Everyone Needs To Know*. New York: Oxford University Press, Inc.

Klan, Anthony. 2010. "States Try to Force Mortgage Workouts." *Wall Street Journal*, December 31. online.wsj.com/article/SB100014240527487045430045760518431 40821936.html (accessed May 8, 2011).

Krugman, Paul. 2011. "The President Surrenders." *New York Times*, August 1, p. A17.

Kuttner, Robert. 2008. *Obama's Challenge: America's Economic Crisis and the Power of a Transformative Presidency*. White River Junction, VT: Chelsea Green Publishing Company.

Kuttner, Robert. 2011. "The Goons of August." *The Huffington Post*, July 31. www.huffingtonpost.com/robert-kuttner/the-goons-of-august_b_914518.html (accessed August 22, 2011).

Marshall, Thomas R. "Health Care Reform and the Two Faces of Public Opinion: ObamaCare in Perspective." A Paper Presented at the Midwest Political Science Association Meeting, Chicago, 2011.

Mayer, Jane. 2008. *The Dark Side: The Inside Story of How the War on Terror Turned Into a War on American Ideals*. New York: Doubleday.

Montgomery, Lori. 2011. "Running in the red: How the U.S., on the road to surplus, detoured to massive debt." *Washington Post*. April 30. www.washingtonpost.com/b usiness/economy/running-in-the-red-how-the-us-on-the-road-to-surplus-detoured-to-massive-debt/2011/04/28/AFFU7rNF_story.html (accessed May 8, 2011).

Morone, James. 2010. "Presidents and Health Reform: From Franklin D. Roosevelt to Barack Obama." *Health Affairs* 29 (6): 1096-1100.

National Commission on Fiscal Responsibility and Reform. 2010. "The Moment of Truth: Report of the National Commission on Fiscal Responsibility and Reform." Washington, DC: The White House, December.

National Commission on Fiscal Responsibility and Reform. 2011. "Member Statements for Fiscal Commission Report." Washington, DC: National Commission on Fiscal Responsibility and Reform, January 31. www.fiscalcommission.gov/news.member-statements-finalcommission-report (accessed May 8, 2011).

National Commission on the Causes of the Financial and Economic Crisis in the United States. 2011. "The Financial Crisis Inquiry Report." New York: Public Affairs

Pew Research Center. 2011. "Rethinking Budget Cutting: Fewer Want Spending to Grow, but Most Cuts Remain Unpopular." February 10. pewresearch.org/pubs/1889/ poll-federal-spending-programs-budget-cuts-raise-taxes-state-budgets

Realty Trac Staff. 2011. "Record 2.9 Million U.S. Properties Receive Foreclosure Filing in 2010 Despite 30-Month Low in December." January 18. www.realtytrac.com/con

tent/press-releases/record-29-million-us-properties-receive-foreclosure-filings

Savage, Charlie. 2008. *Takeover: The Return of the Imperial Presidency and the Subversion of American Democracy.* New York: Back Bay Books/ Little, Brown and Company/Hachette Book Group USA.

Schakowsky, Jan. 2010. "Schakowsky Offers Alternative to Simpson-Bowles Deficit Reduction Plan." Washington, DC: Office of Congresswoman Jan Schakowsky. November 16. schakowsky.house.gov/index.php?option=com_content&view=article&id=2777:schakowsky-alternative-to-simpson-bowles-deficit-reduction-plan&catid=21:2010-press-releases&Itemid=58 (accessed May 8, 2011).

Schwartz, Nelson D. and Eric Dash. 2011. "Amid Criticism on Downgrade, S&P Fires Back." *New York Sunday Times*, August 7, p. 1.

Staff of the *Washington Post.* 2010. *Landmark: The Inside Story of America's New Health-Care Law and What It Means for Us All.* New York: Public Affairs/Perseus Books Group.

Trofimov, Yaroslav. 2010. "U.N. Maps Out Afghan Security." *Wall Street Journal*, December 27, p. A10.

United States Senate, Permanent Subcommittee on Investigations. 2011. "Wall Street and the Financial Crisis: Anatomy of a Financial Collapse." Washington, DC: April 13, 639 pp.

Weissert, Carol S. and William G. Weissert. 2006. *Governing Health: The Politics of Health Policy.* 3rd Ed. Baltimore: The Johns Hopkins University Press.

Westen, Drew. 2011. "What Happened to Obama." *New York Times/Sunday Review*, August 7, p. 1.

Wotapka, Dawn. 2011. "UBS' 2011 Forecast Sees Little Improvement For Housing." *Wall Street Journal*, January 14. blogs.wsj.com/developments/2011/01/14/ubs-2011-forecast-sees-little-improvement-for-housing/ (accessed May 8, 2011).

Zeleny, Jeff. 2009. "Obama (as TV Salesman) Pushes Home Refinancing." *New York Times*, April 10, p. A15.

Chapter 2

Obama by the Numbers: A Comparison with Previous Presidencies

Bruce E. Caswell

Introduction

Candidate Barack Obama promised a departure from the partisan polarization of George W. Bush and other recent presidents and "a new kind of politics." He distinguished himself from the temporizing politics of William Clinton and by implication the politics of Hillary Clinton by offering the potential for "fundamentally transforming the United States of America." He distinguished himself from the routine political promise of "change" by promising "change we can believe in." Midway in his term, after years of legislative battles, continuation of many Bush defense policies, and only modest improvement in the economy, the talk of transformation has been replaced with expressions of disappointment and lower approval ratings. This chapter attempts an evaluation of the Obama presidency free of the media framing and political messaging that dominates short-term public opinion that places emphasis upon performance and historical context. The first two years of the Obama administration are analyzed using some of the criteria used by Obama to criticize the performance of his predecessor. The progress towards Obama's legacy based upon these criteria is analyzed, as well as what the first years of previous presidencies predicted about their ultimate standing on the basis of these same criteria.

The Obama Presidency in Perspective

He sounded transformational. Candidate Barack Obama promised a departure from the partisan polarization of George W. Bush and other recent presidents and "a new kind of politics." He distinguished himself from the temporizing politics of William Clinton and by implication the politics of Hillary Clinton by offering the potential for "fundamentally transforming the United States of America." He distinguished himself from the routine political promise of "change" by promising "change we can believe in" (Obama 2007; Obama 2008a; Obama 2008b; Skowronek 2011, 167-168). Whether candidate Obama's use of the "political time" reconstructive presidential vocabulary of Stephen Skowronek was intentional or merely accidental rhetorical flourish, a large number of political figures from the progressive left to the moderate Republican Colin Powell saw in Obama "transformational qualities" (Skowronek 2011, 1993; White 2009; Powell 2008). The general electorate reflected this enthusiasm as well. Some 56 percent of Obama voters were "excited" about the prospect of an Obama victory, as opposed to only 28 percent of McCain voters (CNN 2008). Talk turned to "realignment,"[1] a weighty term in political science (Davis 2008; Todd and Gawiser 2009, 42-43). Skowronek himself seems unconvinced (Skowronek 2011, 167-194). Midway in his term, after two years of nasty and divisive legislative battles, continuation of many Bush defense policies, only modest improvement in the economy, and low approval numbers, and in Obama's own words a "shellacking" (Obama 2010) in the mid-term elections, the talk of transformation has been replaced with expressions of disenchantment. Despite many significant legislative accomplishments, media coverage and commentary, substantially driven by effective oppositional messaging, have fallen into a fatalistic framing portending doom for Obama's policy agenda and reelection (DeGregorio, 1993; Faber and Faber, 2000; Felzenberg, 2008; Murray and Blessing, 1994; and Pfiffner, 2003).

This chapter attempts to keep the focus on measurable performance, to avoid as much as possible the pitfalls of framing and messaging that dominate contemporary political discourse. The first two Obama presidency years will be compared to other presidents since Harry Truman at the same point in their presidencies. The reader is forewarned, the focus on the first two years of presidencies requires making numerical comparisons one does not normally find in analysis. Evaluations of presidential performance typically look at a president's legacy, not a president's mid-term performance.

Evaluating and Ranking Presidents

Presidential rankings have become a familiar part of presidential commentary since historian Arthur M. Schlesinger, Sr.'s 1948 survey of fifty-five historians for *Life* Magazine (Schlesinger 1948). Schlesinger repeated his survey with seventy-five scholars in 1962 (Schlesinger 1966). In 1996 his son, Arthur M. Schlesinger, Jr., repeated the survey yet again for *Life* Magazine and made some useful methodological observations in *Political Science Quarterly* (Schlesinger 1996 and 1997). The Schlesinger model might be termed a scholar reputational method in that it does not provide criteria or ask for justification of rankings. Other scholars and organizations have attempted to improve upon the Schlesinger survey by expanding and diversifying the backgrounds of respondents and by developing multiple criteria for use in composite scores. In the interests of space, I won't review the literature here. This chapter is indebted to the review of the political science scholarly literature in Robert Maranto et al. (2009). Alvin Stephen Felzenberg and Ivan Eland provide some insights as well (Felzenberg 1997, 1-18; Eland 2009). Some ranking or evaluations of presidents attempt to improve upon Schlesinger's model by including scholars from law and political science as well as political commentators, politicians and even celebrities. Such surveys sometimes ask for the respondent experts to rank presidents in several categories and generate a composite score of the ranking. Generally these variations in elite reputation surveys produce large shifts in presidential rankings. (An exception is Dwight D. Eisenhower, who ranked 22nd in Schlesinger's 1962 survey but who has ranked at the bottom of the top ten in subsequent surveys.) The surveys of scholars and elites produce a kind of virtual Mount Rushmore "plus one," reflecting the historical stature of presidents Abraham Lincoln, George Washington, and Thomas Jefferson when Mt. Rushmore was conceived, plus Franklin D. Roosevelt who came later (Siena 2010). William J. Ridings, Jr. and Stuart B. McIver provide an interesting variation on the scholar reputational survey by making an effort to include female and African-American scholars in their 1989-1996 surveys. President Jimmy Carter fares a little better in Ridings and McIver's rankings and Ronald Reagan fares slightly poorer (Ridings and McIver 1997). Two polls commissioned by the *Wall Street Journal* attempt to eliminate the reputed liberal bias of academics by balancing the numbers of liberals and conservatives. The surveys did not produce significant differences in the traditionally highly rated presidents, but did produce lower rankings for Lyndon B. Johnson and John F. Kennedy as well as higher rankings for Ronald Reagan and George W. Bush (Gallup 2010).

As Alexis de Tocqueville might have predicted, in America's equalitarian culture it was inevitable that elite surveys would be replaced by public opinion surveys of presidential greatness. In public opinion surveys, historical reputation appears to be replaced by name recognition and recent presidents rank much higher than in scholar surveys. Asked "Who do you consider the greatest United States President?" by the Gallup Poll since 1999, the American public has consistently bunched three recent Presidents, Kennedy, Clinton and Reagan at the top along with the iconic Abraham Lincoln. Franklin Roosevelt and George Washington, who typically rank among the top two or three spots in scholar surveys, switch off between fifth and sixth. The first such Gallup Poll after the election of Obama, February 2011, finds Obama with 5 percent of the vote as the greatest American President ever (Gallup News Service 2011) (table 2.1).

Table 2.1. Percent Reporting President "Greatest," Gallup Poll 2011

Ronald Reagan	19
Abraham Lincoln	14
Bill Clinton	13
John Kennedy	11
George Washington	10
Franklin Roosevelt	8
Barack Obama	5
Theodore Roosevelt	3
Harry Truman	3
George W. Bush	2
Thomas Jefferson	2
Jimmy Carter	1
Dwight Eisenhower	1
George H.W. Bush	1
Andrew Jackson	*
Lyndon Johnson	*
Richard Nixon	*

Source: Gallup News Service 2011
*Less than 0.5 percent

While there is a robust scholarly literature of evaluating presidents retroactively, there isn't a literature of prospective evaluation of presidents. Skowronek tells us it is "the politics presidents make," but he provides few criteria for identifying "reconstructive" presidents before they assume office or early in their terms. The presidents known for great things are the presidents who find themselves facing great problems. In this sense, presidents don't create historical crises, presidents earn their places in history by responding well to crises. In recent history, we learned of Bill Clinton lamenting that history had not provided him an opportunity for greatness and G. W. Bush seizing upon the 9/11 terrorist attack as an opportunity to go down in history (Maranto, Lansford, and Johnson, eds., 2009). Without a momentous historical opportunity, Clinton could not distinguish himself; with such an opportunity, Bush failed to distinguish himself. Presidents without the opportunity to influence great events, as Clinton categorized himself, must perform under conditions that make distinguishing oneself difficult. Presidents labor under a separation of powers designed to limit their ability to act. Their short-term approval correlates strongly with the economic cycles of a free market over which they exert little influence. They face reelection and term limits more often than leaders of other democracies. As for defense and foreign policy, in which they have more power to shape events, the American public pays little attention. A president forced to make history through domestic legislation and foreign policy faces time constraints, procedural obstacles in the Congress, and indifference in the public without a crisis to hold the nation's attention.

This chapter uses data from the first two years of recent presidential administrations to determine if the first two years of an Obama administration can tell us about the ultimate fate of his presidency. By using empirical data, this chapter aspires to provide a perspective on the Obama presidency independent of the messaging of the political parties and the framing of the mass media.

Presidents and Partisanship

In his acceptance speech at the 2000 Republican convention, Bush promised to be a "uniter, not a divider," someone who could "change the tone of Washington to one of civility and respect" (Bush 2000). It is possible that Bush believed this himself as he had a good relationship with the Democratic legislature as governor of Texas, or it is possible that this promise was never more than a campaign tactic. Whatever Bush's original intention, Bush's governing style immediately began to contribute to the escalating partisan polarization of the American electorate (Jacobson 2008). Gary Jacobson uses as one indicator of polarization the difference between the president's party's approval of the president and the opposition party's approval of the president. Prior to Bush, the partisan differences in Gallup approval ratings had been rising for twenty years but had never exceeded 70 percent. By the second half of 2004, the difference never fell below 70 percent and remained that high or higher through the balance of his presidency. For comparison, the difference for Nixon peaked in the 40s during the Watergate scandal and investigation (Jacobson 2008, 6-8). Gary Jacobson documents the purposeful partisan polarization of George W. Bush's presidency. Yet, for whatever damage it did to national unity and civility, Bush's purposeful strategy of partisan polarization, of "mobilizing the base," combined with the 9/11 attack to enable Bush to achieve policy successes unimaginable in the aftermath of the close election of 2000—a huge tax cut for the rich and two wars.

Obama assumed the presidency promising bipartisanship and "a new kind of politics," but also in a Washington in which extreme partisanship was the proven model for legislative success. However sincere Obama might have been about bipartisanship, partisan polarization was the reality in both the legislative branch and the general electorate. The first quarter of a new president's first year has traditionally been a "honeymoon" period during which the new president receives a degree of bipartisan support (the following statistics derived from

Gallup polls are summarized in table 2.2). In the first quarter of his first year, Bill Clinton averaged 78 percent approval from Democrats and 28 percent approval from Republicans, a difference of fifty percentage points. This was ten points worse than Ronald Reagan, the most partisan president up until that time. Eight years after Clinton, George W. Bush received 89 percent and 40 percent approvals respectively from Republican and Democratic identifiers, a 49 percent difference. The polarization of Bush's first quarter followed the contested vote in Florida in the 2000 election as well as the Republican impeachment of Clinton in 1999. In his first quarter, Barack Obama received an average 89 percent approval from Democrats and 31 percent from Republicans, a difference of 58 percent. Thus, despite an historic election, Obama began his presidency with an electorate significantly more polarized than Clinton, Bush, or any previous president. By the end of two years, Obama faced as much partisan polarization in the electorate as G. H. W. Bush in the latter part of his fourth year in office. At the mid-term election in 2010, the difference between Democratic and Republican support for Obama was 70 percentage points, a level G. W. Bush took four years to obtain and which no other president had ever reached. Had it not been for unusually strong support in the African-American community, which despite being disproportionally affected by the economic downturn continues to support Obama at historically high levels, the partisan polarization over Obama's performance in the electorate would have exceeded seventy points in the summer of his first year.

Obama may suffer from the same partisan polarization as Bush because he took a similar political route to the presidency. Despite his appeals to unity and civility, Bush's campaign made pointed references to the morality and corruption of the previous Clinton administration (Crotty, ed., 2008). Obama campaigned against the failed policies of the Bush administration. Obama carried his forceful repudiation of Bush and Republican policies into his first state of the union and budget messages. Once in office, Obama found himself strategically in much the same situation as Bush—the desire to push a strongly partisan agenda with congressional party caucuses in his own party anxious to make up for years out of power. In 2001-2006, with Republican majorities in the House and some of the time in the Senate, Bush did not need support beyond the Republican caucus and did not seek it. Obama found himself in a similar situation in 2009-2010. Speaker of the House Nancy Pelosi and Senate Majority Leader Harry Reid did not need votes outside of their majority caucuses, and they soon discovered that an unusually cohesive Republican opposition was not going to provide any votes for Democratic initiatives. The unity of Republicans in opposition denied Obama even the few Republican votes he wanted to be able claim legitimacy for his signature policies—the stimulus package, health care reform, and financial regulatory reform. The stimulus package victory, won before Arlen Spector's party switch and Al Franken's eventual recount victory, acquired enormous concessions. These concessions weakened the recovery by forcing state governments into layoffs.

Table 2.2. First Two Years Of Presidential Term Approval Ratings

President	Years	Average 1st Quarter Job Approval	Approval by Political Party Id.			1st Quarter Pres. Party minus Opposition Party	Average 8th Quarter Job Approval	Approval by Political Party Id.			8th Quarter Pres. Party minus Opposition Party
			Dem	Ind	Rep			Dem	Ind	Rep	
Truman	1949-50	57	75	48	32	43	38	55	37	16	40
Eisenhower	1953-54	67	60	65	84	24	62	47	66	87	41
Eisenhower	1957-58	68	59	67	85	26	55	36	66	84	47
Kennedy/Johnson	1961-62	73	85	68	56	29	70	87	67	46	41
Johnson	1965-66	69	84	60	49	35	45	62	39	24	38
Nixon	1969-70	61	51	60	80	29	56	39	55	82	43
Nixon/Ford	1973-74	61	45	64	87	42	51	39	51	69	30
Carter	1977-78	71	80	68	55	25	51	62	48	32	30
Reagan	1981-82	55	39	57	80	40	42	21	42	79	58
Reagan	1985-86	61	35	60	89	53	55	35	54	80	46
G.H.W. Bush	1989-90	57	42	51	76	34	58	42	56	79	37
Clinton	1993-94	55	78	51	28	50	43	72	44	16	56
Clinton	1997-98	59	85	56	31	54	66	89	66	35	54
G. W. Bush	2001-02	73	40	55	89	49	64	40	60	93	53
G. W. Bush	2005-06	51	18	43	90	72	36	8	30	80	72
Obama	2009-10	64	89	61	31	58	45	81	41	10	71

Source: Gallup 2011, Presidential Job Approval Center

Thus did Obama begin his presidency in an environment of partisan polarization unprecedented in the modern presidency (table 2.2). Presidents Reagan, Clinton, and G. W. Bush also found themselves in highly polarized political environments and divided government and they managed to win significant policy victories and reelection nonetheless. Obama has already succeeded in passing the largest stimulus package in history, major new programs for clean energy, historic health care reform, and new financial market regulation. The very early onset of the extreme partisan polarization in Obama's presidency is unique, however, and there it remains to be seen what this portends for the balance of his policy agenda and his political party's prospects in 2012.

The Obama Baseline

Immediately following the President's 2009 "Budget Message" in the "Fiscal Year Overview Document" appears an unusual section entitled, "Inheriting a Legacy of Misplaced Priorities." The section begins with a recount of the "deep and destructive recession" which confronted the president when he assumed office. The opening detail compares job losses in the latest recession to job losses and housing starts in previous recessions, with emphasis upon manufacturing job losses and the high unemployment rate, and towards the end turns to the string of deficits accumulated in the previous administration. These are the traditional economic indicators of recession and recovery. What makes this statement unusual is the analysis of the decline of the middle class found amidst the statistics on jobs and deficits, and the linkage of the decline of the middle class to "policy failures of the last eight years." The administration's statement describes the economy as creating a "growing imbalance," as "accumulating wealth" while "closing doors to the middle class." The stagnation of real median household incomes is juxtaposed to the increasing income share of the top 1 percent of earners. The causes are further identified as the lack of quality elementary and secondary education for disadvantaged children and rising college costs and health care costs. The decline of the middle class is a result of a "failure to invest in the future," in policies to create long-term economic growth including education, infrastructure, and clean energy. The section concludes by noting the "fiscal irresponsibility" and "erosion of market oversight" that have been "eroding public trust" and an "unresponsive government."

Senior Advisor David Axelrod describes this analysis as a "baseline" (Brownstein 2009). The term baseline appears frequently in federal budgeting in different uses, in projections by the Congressional Budget Office, and as the starting point for legislative negotiation. Axelrod appears to use the opportunity of the budget message to document the economic, fiscal and policy hole from which the Obama administration begins. This could be merely political positioning, a variation on the "expectations game" with an eye towards Obama's 2012 reelection campaign. Most partisans and many serious scholars no doubt will see the Obama analysis of "failed priorities" lends itself to another interpretation. It could be taken as a continuation of the partisan attacks of the campaign and an intention to govern in a highly partisan manner, thus perpetuating the strong partisan polarization of the G. W. Bush era.

But the inclusion of the baseline analysis could have a strategic and visionary purpose. Ron Brownstein sees Obama's budget address as a strategy to realign the political landscape through the repudiation of the policies of the previous administration. Brownstein suggests the Obama administration is intuitively following the strategy of "reconstructive leaders" as described by Skowronek. Transformational or realigning presidents must be great communicators and "great repudiators" who arrive at the opportune "political time" of manifest political failure of the old regime. The old regime must be thoroughly discredited before it can be replaced.

The Obama measures of middle class opportunities and economic inequality echo the "full employment," homeownership, and health care promises of Franklin D. Roosevelt's New Deal and Economic Bill of Rights as well as Truman's Fair Deal and the War on Poverty of the Kennedy and Johnson administrations. In a sense, the Obama indicators are an attempt to revive the values of the liberal Democratic coalition. These values have been raised much by presidents since Carter. Together with Obama's emphasis upon building a clean energy economy, some good government measures, and the regulation of financial markets, the "Legacy" analysis sketches out a comprehensive and progressive domestic economic agenda. In suggesting that the Bush administration should be evaluated by these progressive standards, Obama invites the evaluation of his presidency by these criteria. This chapter uses some of these criteria here to evaluate the first two years of the Obama presidency and, by comparison, all modern presidencies. Because most of the measures used are short-term, there are some parallels to the *Wall Street Journal* short-term economic performance criteria for evaluating presidents (Eland 2009, 9). The difference is that the WSJ criteria focus on aggregate economic output. The Obama criteria focus on the condition of the middle class and the opportunities for expanding the middle class.

The lag in data for many of these measures makes it impossible to review the first two Obama years on all these criteria here and now. Since detailed economic data for many economic and social indicators does not exist before the passage of the Employment Act of 1946, comparisons are limited to presidents since 1948.

Employment

Since 2008, jobs and the economy have topped all opinion polls as the priority of the public. Table 2.3 compares job creation in the first two years of each presidential term and the full first term of each president since Truman using

BLS data. The figures represent the difference between the monthly non-farm employment in the January of a president's inauguration to the January after the mid-term election. Table 2.3 shows both the absolute job creation (or loss) and, because the size of the economy and the workforce grows so much over the six-decade period analyzed, job creation (or loss) as a percentage of total jobs.

Table 2.3 Monthly Job Creation (or Loss)
First Two Years and Full Presidential Term in Thousands (000's) and Percent (%) by President

		First Two Years (January - January)		Full Presidential Term (January - January)	
		New Jobs (000's)	New Jobs (%)	New Jobs (000's)	New Jobs (%)
Truman	1949-1953	2,527	5.7	5,311	12.0
Eisenhower	1953-1957	-706	-1.4	2,698	5.5
Eisenhower	1957-1961	-447	-0.9	612	1.2
Kennedy/Johnson	1961-1965	2,328	4.4	5,781	11.0
Johnson	1965-1969	5,878	10.0	9,933	17.0
Nixon	1969-1973	1,428	2.1	6,119	8.9
Nixon/Ford	1973-1977	1,576	2.1	4,927	6.6
Carter	1977-1981	8,110	10.2	10,291	12.9
Reagan	1981-1985	-2,115	-2.4	5,198	5.8
Reagan	1985-1989	4,278	4.5	10,679	11.2
G. H. W. Bush	1989-1993	1,675	1.6	2,313	2.2
Clinton	1993-1997	6,531	6.0	11,248	10.4
Clinton	1997-2001	6,191	5.2	11,164	9.4
G. W. Bush	2001-2005	-2,185	-1.7	-64	0.0
G. W. Bush	2005-2009	4,583	3.5	1,186	0.9
Obama	2009-{2011}	-3,372	-2.6	--	--

Source: United States Department of Labor, BLS Series CEU0000000001, Employment, Hours, and Earnings from the Current Employment Statistics survey.

Job losses in the first two years of the Obama administration amounted to 2.6 percent of all non-farm employment, or almost 3.4 million jobs lost. Since the U.S. economy grows about 1 percent per year, anything less than a 1 percent growth in employment represents a weakening of the overall employment picture. The only other administrations showing job losses in their first two years were Eisenhower in both terms, Reagan (first term), and G. W. Bush (first term). Eisenhower and Reagan also do moderately well in historical rankings of presidents. Three of these four were reelected. Eisenhower was ineligible for reelection in 1960 and his party's candidate, Vice President Richard Nixon, lost to John F. Kennedy in a close race. Five incumbents ran for reelection after job gains in their first term and of these, two lost, Jimmy Carter and G. H. W. Bush. Carter's loss followed an employment gain of over 10 percent in his first two years. A simple regression reveals no statistical relationship between a president's first half job performance and his political party's vote in the next presidential election. On the basis of this small universe, it would not appear that job creation or loss in a president's first term has much bearing on a president's place in history.

Table 2.4. Monthly Manufacturing Job Creation (or Loss)

First Two Years Presidential Term in Thousands (000's) and Percent (%) by President

		New Jobs (000's)	New Jobs (%)
Truman	1949-1950	1,083	7.8
Eisenhower	1953-1954	-1,033	-6.4
Eisenhower	1957-1958	-972	-6.1
Kennedy	1961-1962	682	4.6
Johnson	1965-1966	1,788	11.0
Nixon	1969-1970	-1,152	-6.3
Nixon/Ford	1973-1974	-932	-5.1
Carter	1977-1978	1,585	8.9
Reagan	1981-1982	-1,934	-10.4
Reagan	1985-1986	-544	-3.0
G.H.W. Bush	1989-1990	-726	-4.0
Clinton	1993-1994	470	2.8
Clinton	1997-1998	133	0.8
G.W. Bush	2001-2002	-2,247	-13.1
G.W. Bush	2005-2006	-252	-1.8
Obama	2009-2010	-941	-7.5

Source: United States Department of Labor, Bureau of Labor Statistics, Series CEU0000000001, Employment, Hours, and Earnings from the Current Employment Statistics survey.

The Obama administration has specifically raised the issue of manufacturing job loss. This is risky, but necessary, for Obama. Risky, because the forces diminishing manufacturing employment through automation and relocation of factories overseas appear irreversible. Even in the periods of economic prosperity and large employment growth of Reagan and Clinton, manufacturing employment did not expand. After eight years of Reagan, manufacturing employment was down over half a million jobs. After eight years of Clinton, a period of greater economic growth and greater focus on saving manufacturing jobs, manufacturing employment was down over two hundred thousand jobs. Following a loss of four and a half million manufacturing jobs under G. W. Bush, manufacturing employment continued to decline by almost a million jobs or 7.5 percent in Obama's first two years. Fortunately for Obama's future, loss of manufacturing jobs as occurred under Reagan and G. W. Bush does not appear to diminish chances of reelection, nor do large job gains such as occurred under Carter appear to ensure reelection (table 2.4).

Unemployment

Few economic statistics received more mention in the first two years of the Obama administration than the unemployment rate. Commentators often link President Obama's standing in public opinion polls and his chances of reelection to the unemployment rate. Table 3 shows the monthly unemployment rate at the end of the first two years and all four years, as well as the difference from the unemployment rate when the term began. The unemployment rate at Barack Obama's inauguration, 7.8 percent, was the highest unemployment rate inherited by any president from a previous administration. Only Reagan (7.5 percent), Clinton (7.3 percent), and Kennedy (6.6 percent) assumed office under similarly high unemployment rates. As with Reagan, the unemployment continued to climb in Obama's first two years although not over 10 percent as it did in the Reagan years. Reagan, Clinton and Kennedy's successor Lyndon B. Johnson all went on to win reelection easily.

The unemployment rate after a full term of office president presents a more nuanced picture. Many commentators have used the figure of 8 percent as a minimum for Obama's reelection. Of the four presidents running for reelection with the highest unemployment rates, Ford (7.5 percent), Carter (7.5 percent) and G. H. W. Bush (7.3 percent) lost close reelection races. Only Reagan at 7.5 percent unemployment at the end of his first term won reelection, and won in a landslide with 59 percent of the two-party vote. Two other presidents with high unemployment rates at the end of their second terms, Eisenhower (6.6 percent) and G. W. Bush (7.8 percent) saw their parties lose the presidency. While high unemployment rates usually mean defeat for the party in the White House, a simple regression finds no statistically significant relationship between unem-

Table 2.5. Unemployment Rate At Inauguration, Changes At Two Years, And Full Term

		First Two Years			Full Term	
		Unemployment Rate (%) at Inauguration (Jan.)	Unemployment Rate (%) at Two Years (Jan.)	Difference Two Years	Unemployment Rate (%) at Four Years (Jan.)	Difference Four Years
Truman	1949-1953	4.3	3.7	-0.6	2.9	-1.4
Eisenhower	1953-1957	2.9	4.9	2.0	4.2	1.3
Eisenhower	1957-1961	4.2	6.0	1.8	6.6	2.4
Kennedy/Johnson	1961-1965	6.6	5.7	-0.9	4.9	-1.7
Johnson	1965-1969	4.9	3.9	-1.0	3.4	-1.5
Nixon	1969-1973	3.4	5.9	2.5	4.9	1.5
Nixon/Ford	1973-1977	4.9	8.1	3.2	7.5	2.6
Carter	1977-1981	7.5	5.9	-1.6	7.5	0.0
Reagan	1981-1985	7.5	10.4	2.9	7.3	-0.2
Reagan	1985-1989	7.3	6.6	-0.7	5.4	-1.9
G. H. W. Bush	1989-1993	5.4	6.4	1.0	7.3	1.9
Clinton	1993-1997	7.3	5.6	-1.7	5.3	-2.0
Clinton	1997-2001	5.3	4.3	-1.0	4.2	-1.1
G. W. Bush	2001-2005	4.2	5.8	1.6	5.3	1.1
G. W. Bush	2005-2009	5.3	4.6	-0.7	7.8	2.5
Obama	2009-2011	7.8	9.0	1.2	--	--

Source: Department of Labor, Bureau of Labor Statistics, Labor Force Statistics from the Current Population Survey, Series LNS14000000, Unemployment Rate, 16 years and over, 1948-2011.

ployment at the end of a president's term and the two-party vote for the president's party.

Looking at actual workforce numbers, rather than at unemployment rates, produces a similar conclusion. Declines in the unemployment rate (expressed as a negative in table 2.5) occurred eight times in the first two years of presidential terms since Truman. In two of three instances where a president stood for reelection, Johnson and Clinton, the president won reelection. The exception was Carter. In all three instances in which the incumbent president was not running for reelection and the unemployment rate was declining in the first half, the incumbent president's party lost all three times—Stevenson following Truman, Humphrey following Johnson, and Gore following Clinton.

The Congressional Budget Office "Budget and Economic Outlook" of January 2011 projects an average annual unemployment rate of 8.2 percent in 2012. There is no post WW II precedent for a president running for reelection with such a high unemployment rate. Reagan proved that a president can be reelected with a high unemployment rate, but Reagan was the exception. An incumbent with an unemployment rate over 7 percent will probably find himself in a close race and the odds of winning are nominally one in four.

Fiscal Irresponsibility: Deficits and Debt

The first Obama budget message soberly projected the 2009 budget deficit to be the largest since WW II. The actual deficit was the largest in both nominal dollars ($1.4 trillion) and as a percent of gross domestic product (9.5 percent). Table 2.6 shows the two-year budget balances as surpluses or deficits for presidential administrations since Truman as both percentages of total federal outlays and the gross domestic product (GDP). As with employment and unemployment statistics, a visual inspection reveals an obvious pattern emerge between deficits and the success of presidents and a simple regression finds no statistical relationship. Eisenhower, Kennedy/Johnson, Reagan (both terms), and Clinton oversaw large deficit increases without consequence for their reelection or their historical reputation. There is no post WW II precedent, however, for magnitude of the deficit in Obama's first two years, 41 percent.

Through Obama's first two years to the mid-term election, the public generally placed the responsibility for the large deficit on the previous administration. The discussion of fiscal irresponsibility in the Bush "legacy of misplaced priorities" attempted to reinforce this attitude. The portion of the public so doing has gradually declined, however, and Obama will have difficulty escaping accountability for the continuing large deficits. As long as the legislative debate focused on the economy, health care, and financial regulation, Democrats had an advantage. As Obama begins the third year of his presidency, Republican control of the House of Representatives has enabled Republicans to shift the legislative agenda to the deficit and the debt, issues on which the public has more inherent confidence in Republicans.

Table 2.6. Deficits

First Two Years Presidential Term as Percent of Budget Outlays and GDP

	Years	Surplus (Deficit) as Percent Outlays	Surplus (Deficit) as Percent (%) GDP
Truman	1949-1950	(3.1)	(0.5)
Eisenhower	1953-1954	(5.6)	(1.0)
Eisenhower	1957-1958	0.5	0.1
Kennedy	1961-1962	(5.4)	(0.9)
Johnson	1965-1966	(2.1)	(0.4)
Nixon	1969-1970	0.1	0.0
Nixon/Ford	1973-1974	(4.3)	(0.8)
Carter	1977-1978	(14.9)	(2.7)
Reagan	1981-1982	(16.9)	(3.3)
Reagan	1985-1986	(28.8)	(5.1)
G. H. W. Bush	1989-1990	(18.4)	(3.4)
Clinton	1993-1994	(19.0)	(3.4)
Clinton	1997-1998	1.4	0.3
G. W. Bush	2001-2002	(0.7)	(0.1)
G. W. Bush	2005-2006	(12.5)	(2.2)
Obama*	2009-2010	(63.4)	(9.5)

*Preliminary
Source: *Budget of the United States Government* 2011a

The better measure of a deficit's effect on the economy is the deficit as a percentage of GDP, the last column in table 2.6. All three presidents who had surpluses, Eisenhower, Nixon and G. W. Bush, won reelection, although this group does not receive high presidential rankings as a whole. The four presidents (Truman, Johnson, Ford and G. W. Bush) who otherwise came closest to balanced budgets all lost the White House for their parties. Of these presidents, only Truman receives consistently high historical rankings and Truman's recognition came belatedly. Prior to Obama, the six largest deficits as a percent of GDP belonged to Carter, Reagan in both terms, G. H. W. Bush, Clinton in his first term, and G. W. Bush in his second term. Reagan and Clinton were reelected and Reagan was followed by a president of his party, G. H. W. Bush. Carter and the elder Bush lost reelection and the younger Bush's party lost the White House, overall a 3-3 record for presidential administrations with high deficits. Of these presidents, Skowronek rates only Reagan as a "reconstructive" president and Reagan's standing in ranking surveys is only mediocre. Looked at optimistically, these numbers might suggest a president with a big deficit in his first two years might have a 50-50 chance of reelection and a small chance of historical recognition. Obama's two-year deficit spending of 9.5 percent is so far and away larger than the comparative deficits of previous presidents, however, that even this limited optimism may not be warranted by the numbers.

The national debt presents a similar picture for the Obama presidency (table 2.7). By the end of Obama's second year, the debt had risen to 62.2 percent of GDP, the highest level since the first Eisenhower term when the United States was paying down the WW II debt. The growth in the debt as a percentage of GDP in Obama's first two years, 21.9 percent, is almost four times that of any comparable period since WW II. The projections for the future are not much better. The 2012 Obama budget message forecasts debt to escalate to 75 percent of GDP by the end of Obama's term and holding for several years at that high level. (As this book goes to press, the new Republican majority has successfully pressed for deficit reduction in the 2011 budget and Obama has responded with a long-term plan for reducing the deficit. These developments will change the debt outlook to an as yet indeterminable degree.)

Table 2.7. Publicly Held Debt As Percent (%) of Gross Domestic Product

		End Second Year Presidential Term	Change in Two Years	End Full Presidential Term	Change in Four Years
Truman	1949-1952	80.2	-4.1	61.6	-22.7
Eisenhower	1953-1956	59.5	-2.1	52.0	-9.6
Eisenhower	1957-1960	49.2	-2.8	45.6	-6.4
Kennedy/Johnson	1961-1964	43.7	-1.9	40.0	-5.6
Johnson	1965-1968	34.9	-5.1	33.3	-6.7
Nixon	1969-1972	28.0	-5.3	27.4	-5.9
Nixon/Ford	1973-1976	23.9	-3.5	27.5	0.1
Carter	1977-1980	27.4	0.4	26.1	-0.9
Reagan	1981-1984	28.7	2.6	34.0	7.9
Reagan	1985-1988	39.5	5.5	41.0	7.0
G. H. W. Bush	1989-1992	42.1	1.1	48.1	7.1
Clinton	1993-1996	49.2	1.1	48.4	0.3
Clinton	1997-2000	43.0	-5.4	34.7	-13.7
G. W. Bush	2001-2004	33.6	-1.1	36.8	2.1
G. W. Bush	2005-2008	36.5	-0.3	40.3	3.5
Obama	2009-2012	62.2	21.9	75.1*	34.8*

Source: *Budget of the United States Government* 2011b
*Projected

As with the previous economic indicators discussed, the recent historical record does not reveal any obvious relationship between federal debt and presidential success and a simple regression finds no correlation with future electoral success. Reagan, the president with the worst two-year debt record before Obama, was reelected in a landslide and is considered a transformational president by conservatives. Of the ten presidents who lowered the debt ratio in the first two years of their terms, four won reelection but six times these presidents lost the presidency for their party.

Income Inequality

In one of the most direct discussions of economic inequality from a presidential administration in a generation, the Obama budget narrative links the "misplaced priorities" of previous administrations to the "growing imbalance" in "accumulating wealth" and "closing doors to the middle class." Citing the latest Internal Revenue Service data, the Obama narrative finds "the Nation's top 400 taxpayers made more than $263 million on average in 2006, but paid income taxes at the lowest rate in 15 years in which these data have been reported." Using a figure depicting the income share of the top 1 percent of earners to illustrate the point, the narrative continues, "In fact, the top 1 percent took home more than 22 percent of total national income, up from 10 percent in 1980." The narrative continues, "these disparities are felt far beyond one's bank statement as several studies have found a direct correlation between health outcomes and personal income" (*Budget of the United States Government 2010*, 9). This analysis anticipates the critique of growing inequality in America and its roots in U.S. politics and public policy by Joseph E. Stiglitz, "Of the 1 percent, by the 1 percent, for the 1 percent" (Stiglitz 2011). The Obama analysis continues, in much the same manner as Stiglitz, by relating the rising share of income and wealth of the top 1 percent to the decline in opportunities for the middle class and rising poverty.

Unfortunately for purposes of this chapter, the lag in the availability of data on incomes and poverty limits our ability to evaluate the Obama administration's progress in lessening the effects of inequality. Table 2.8 provides the median family income in constant 2009 dollars for the second year of each presidential term. A second column shows the change in median family income of the first two years of each term. From Truman to Nixon, median family income showed healthy growth in the first two years of each presidential term. Eisenhower's second term is something of an exception, showing only 0.3 percent growth, but there was family income growth nonetheless albeit small. The Nixon term finished by Ford is the first of four presidential terms to show a decline in median family income at the front end. Reagan, G. W. Bush and Obama (first year only) also show a decline in family income in their first two years. The next two lowest performers are Eisenhower's second term and G. H. W.

Bush's one-term administration, which had nominal growth rates of 0.3 percent each.

Table 2.8. Median Family Income (Constant 2009 Dollars)
First Two Years Presidential Term

		Median Family Income Second Year	Two Year Change (%)
Truman	1949-1950	25,814	4.1
Eisenhower	1953-1954	29,040	5.5
Eisenhower	1957-1959	33,039	0.3
Kennedy	1961-1962	37,005	3.9
Johnson	1965-1966	43,614	9.8
Nixon	1969-1970	48,640	4.3
Nixon/Ford	1973-1974	50,612	-0.7
Carter	1977-1978	53,224	3.8
Reagan	1981-1982	50,009	-4.0
Reagan	1985-1986	55,005	5.8
G. H. W. Bush	1989-1990	56,243	0.3
Clinton	1993-1994	55,504	1.3
Clinton	1997-1998	61,419	6.7
G. W. Bush	2001-2002	61,617	-2.5
G. W. Bush	2005-2006	62,135	1.2
Obama	2009	60,088*	-2.0*

Source: U.S. Census Bureau, Current Population Survey, Annual Social and Economic Supplements, Table F-7. Type of Family, All Races by Median and Mean Income: 1947 to 2009 (Families as of March of the following year. Income in current and 2009 CPI-U-RS adjusted dollars (28))

*One-year (2009) only

Prior to G. H. W. Bush, no full presidential term witnessed a decline in real family income, and that was over one term. The only other president to preside over a decline in family income has been the son, G. W. Bush, who oversaw a total decline in real median family income of 3 percent over two terms. With only one year of data, Obama has overseen a decline of 2 percent in median family income. Data on personal disposable income, which is reported more quickly than family income, suggest that real family income was probably flat in 2010, with a growth or decline of no more than a few tenths of a percent.

One of the original features of Obama's "legacy of misplaced priorities" analysis is the linkage of income inequality to the shrinkage of the middle class. The decline in family income is coupled with a rise in the cost of opportunity in the form of higher education costs. As states have been forced to cut funding for higher education because of declining tax revenues, the out-of-pocket cost of higher education has skyrocketed. Table 2.9 shows the cost of tuition, fees, room and board at an average four-year public institution of higher education. The first two years of the Obama administration saw a 13.4 percent increase in college costs. Combined with a 2 percent decline in median family income in 2009, this presents a huge new burden for middle class families with children in college. From the beginning of the latest downturn in family income, 2006, median family income has declined 5.5 percent in constant dollars while the cost of a public college education has risen 17.4 percent.

Table 2.9. Avg. Tuition, Fee, Room and Board Charges at Four-Year Institutions, 1980-81 to 2010-11 (in Constant 2010 Dollars)

		Avg. College Costs ($)	Increase Two Years (%)
Reagan	1981-1982	7,146	6.3
Reagan	1985-1986	8,063	4.6
G. H. W. Bush	1989-1990	8,483	3.5
Clinton	1993-1994	9,725	7.4
Clinton	1997-1998	10,378	4.6
G. W. Bush	2001-2002	11,708	10.0
G. W. Bush	2005-2006	13,752	5.0
Obama	2009-2011	16,140	13.4

Source: College Board

The Obama administration's baseline analysis also draws the relationship between declining economic opportunities and rising poverty. Annual poverty rates are not available before 1960, but the data in table 2.10 show that economic growth and anti-poverty programs almost cut the poverty rate in half from Kennedy to Carter. Much of the decline in poverty came from lower rates among the elderly as Social Security payments were increased and Medicare provided health care coverage. The weak economy inherited by Reagan eroded gains against poverty. The economy that emerged after the restructuring of the Reagan years left many non-elderly poor behind. As a consequence, the economic recovery of the second Reagan term did not do as much to reduce poverty as the economic growth of the 1960s. The long Clinton prosperity lowered poverty rates, although not quite to the low levels of the 1960s, and these lower rates persisted through the G. W. Bush years. In the first year of the Obama administration, the poverty rate rose to 14.3 percent, the highest level since the mid-1990s. It will take years of a robust economy and possibly additional anti-poverty measures to return the poverty rate to the lower level of the Clinton and G. W. Bush years. The Obama administration identifies education and job creation as the means of lowering poverty, policies that take time to produce results, and Republican opposition in Congress will make funding of such policy initiatives difficult.

Table 2.10. Poverty Rate (%) First Two Years of Presidential Term

		End of Second Year	Rate (%) Change First Two Years
Truman	1949-1950	—	—
Eisenhower	1953-1954	—	—
Eisenhower	1957-1958	—	—
Kennedy	1961-1962	21.0	-2.0
Johnson	1965-1966	14.7	-1.9
Nixon	1969-1970	12.6	-0.7
Nixon/Ford	1973-1974	11.2	0.6
Carter	1977-1978	11.4	1.6
Reagan	1981-1982	15.0	-0.6
Reagan	1985-1986	13.6	-0.6
G. H. W. Bush	1989-1990	13.5	1.3
Clinton	1993-1994	14.5	-0.8
Clinton	1997-1998	12.7	-1.4
G. W. Bush	2001-2002	12.1	0.6
G. W. Bush	2005-2006	12.3	0.9
Obama	2009	14.3*	1.1*

Source: U.S. Census Bureau, Current Population Survey, Annual Social and Economic Supplements. Historical Poverty Tables—People, Table 2. Poverty Status by Family Relationship, Race, and Hispanic Origin: 1959 to 2009 (Accessed April 2011) http://www.census.gov/hhes/www/poverty/data/historical/people.html

* One-year (2009) only

The Obama Coalition

A transformational presidency requires a stable electoral coalition. The 2008 Obama coalition was a "surge" coalition rather than a "factional" coalition. Rather than bringing new groups into the Democratic coalition, Obama capitalized upon demographic trends and personal charisma to grow some of the existing components of the Democratic coalition. Specifically, the African-American, Hispanic and youth votes grew as shares of the electorate, and all these groups gave larger portions of their vote to the Democratic candidate. The speculation on the sustainability of this coalition rests on two observations: all three groups have been reliable components of the Democratic coalition for many election cycles and all three groups are growing demographically. African-Americans have voted Democratic since the 1930s and the margins African-Americans have given to Democratic candidates increased steadily with the passage of the Civil Rights and Voting Rights Acts, the presidential primary candidacy of Jesse Jackson, and finally the election of President Barack Obama. Hispanics have voted heavily Democratic since data has been available despite efforts by G. W. Bush to appeal to Hispanics, and the immigration and affirmative action policies of the Republican Party alienate most Hispanic voters. Younger cohorts have voted more Democratic for decades and Republican positions on issues such as gay rights and global warming are disaffecting to large majorities of younger voters. Each of these groups is growing as a share of the electorate at the expense of older white voters. The group that has given the Republican Party the strongest support in recent elections, older whites, is rapidly declining as a share of the electorate.

The historically large number of Republican gains in the House and Senate in the 2010 election brings the sustainability of the Obama coalition into question. To test whether the Obama coalition lost any members, table 2.11 compares Obama's vote in 2008 to the Democratic House Vote in 2010 by group. The overall decline in the Democratic vote was very consistent across race and age groups and all three of the groups identified as the Obama coalition, African-Americans, Hispanics and the 18-29 age group remained firmly Democratic. The decline of 11 percent in the 18-29 age group was perhaps slightly larger than the declines in other age groups. White voters in all the other age groups voted majority Republican in both 2008 and 2010. The evenness of the Democratic decline extended to the vote by gender. The major exception in the Democratic vote appears in partisan identification. Democratic candidates in 2008 received a nominally higher share of the partisan Democratic vote and a slightly smaller share of the partisan Republican vote. This is to be expected in a midterm election where activists form a larger portion of the electorate. The big loss for Democrats was among independents who gave Obama a narrow majority in 2008 and Republicans a landslide majority in 2010.

Conclusion

As for the question, "What Obama's first two years can tell us about the fate of his presidency," the answer to this is, "Nothing, or very little with any degree of

Table 2.11. 2008 Exit Poll Vote for Obama Compared to 2010 Exit Poll Vote for H. R. Vote

	2008 CNN Exit Poll Obama Vote	2010 CNN Exit Poll Dem. HR Vote	Difference
OVERALL	53	45	-8
GENDER			
Male	49	41	-8
Female	56	48	-8
AGE			
18-29	66	55	-11
30-49	52	46	-6
50-64	50	45	-5
65+	45	38	-7
RACE			
White	43	37	-6
Black	95	89	-6
Hispanic	67	60	-7
PARTY ID			
Democrat	89	91	+2
Independent	52	37	-15
Republican	9	5	-4

Sources:
CNN/Election Center 2008 Exit Polls http://www.cnn.com/ELECTION/2008/results/polls/
CNN/Election Center 2010 Exit Polls http://www.cnn.com/ELECTION/2010/results/polls/

certainty." Economic performance and presidential approval in the first two years of presidential terms have no nominal or statistical relationship to a president's subsequent standing. Given that the universe of modern presidents is small, the evidence is fairly strong. A president's economic performance or public opinion standing in his first two years bears no statistical relationship to the success of the president's political party in the next presidential election, nor does it appear to have any relationship to the ultimate historical ranking of the president either by elites or the mass public. Reagan, for example, experienced possibly the poorest economic numbers in his first two years, yet recovered to a landslide reelection, a respectable ranking in scholar surveys, and the highest score in the Gallup Polls latest presidential greatness survey.

To this strong caution against evaluating Obama's presidency on the basis of his first two years is added another layer of caution. The first two years of the Obama presidency is a statistical outlier by many measures. Obama came to office in the most polarized political environment in the history of polling and that unprecedented polarization has persisted. Obama inherited the highest unemployment rate in the modern history of the presidency and a national economy still hemorrhaging jobs, with the consequence that the Obama administration experienced the largest job loss in the first two years of a presidential term since the Great Depression. Obama inherited the largest deficits and debt since WW II and his attempts to correct the economic downturn and loss of jobs added hugely to those deficits and debt. In the 1990s the United States was able to recover from a similar deficit situation by virtue of the end of the Cold War and a booming economy. The slow recovery of the economy and the defense spending required for the United States many engagements across the globe preclude the kind of rapid shrinking of the federal spending and the sharp increase in federal revenues as occurred under Clinton. The costs in the American lifestyle are staggering. Since this Great Recession began in 2008, the number of Americans in poverty has climbed 6.3 million and the poverty rate jumped to its highest level in more than three decades. Family incomes are down 4.5 percent to $60,000. Job losses appear to have bottomed out in the summer of 2009, nonetheless the unemployment rate at the end of Obama's first term is projected to be over 8 percent, the highest of any president running for reelection since the Depression.

Yet the promise of Obama politics still exists for many. Despite facing worse economic and budget circumstances than Reagan and Clinton in the middle of their first terms, Obama's approval numbers are a few points better than Reagan and Clinton's at the same point in their presidencies (Gallup 2011). Indeed, Obama's job approval has consistently run a few points higher than what would have been expected from the economy (Cuzán 2011). And there is a significant record of legislative accomplishment including the stimulus package, health care reform and financial market regulation. It seems hope survives, if just barely.

Note

1. Todd and Gawiser, p. 28 and 47 and many others.

References

Brownstein, Ronald. 2009. "Repudiating Bush," *The Atlantic*, March 2.
Budget of the United States Government 2010, "A New Era of Responsibility. Renewing America's Promise." "Inheriting a Legacy of Misplaced Priorities," 5-15. February 26, 2009. www.budget.gov
Budget of the United States Government: Historical Tables Fiscal Year 2012 2011a. "Table 1.2—Summary of Receipts, Outlays, and Surpluses or Deficits (-) as Per-

centages of GDP: 1930–2016" and "Table 1.3—Summary of Receipts, Outlays, and
Surpluses or Deficits (-) in Current Dollars, Constant (FY 2005) Dollars, and as Percentages   of   GDP: 1940–2016."   Washington   DC: The   White   House.
www.gpoaccess.gov/usbudget/fy12/hist.html

Budget of the United States Government: Historical Tables Fiscal Year 2012 2011b.
"Table 7.1—Federal Debt at the End of Year: 1940–2016." Washington DC: The
White House. www.gpoaccess.gov/usbudget/fy12/hist.html

Bush, George W. 2000. Acceptance Speech to the Republican National Convention, August 3.

CNN Election Center. 2008. Exit Polls. www.cnn.com/election//2008/results/polls.main/

CNN Election Center. 2010. Exit Polls. www.cnn.com/election/2010/results/polls.main/

College Board, Advocacy and Policy Center, Trends in College Pricing, Table 5: Average Published Tuition and Fee and Room and Board Charges at Four-Year Institutions in Constant 2010 Dollars, 1980-81 to 2010-11 (Enrollment-Weighted)
trends.collegeboard.org/college_pricing/report_findings/indicator/Tuition_and_Fee_
and_Room_and_Board_Charges_Over_Time

Crotty, William J. ed. 2009. *Winning the Presidency 2008.* Boulder, CO: Paradigm Publishers.

Cuzán, Alfred G. 2011. "Obama and His Predecessors: How Does He Compare?" Paper
presented at the 2011 Annual Meeting of the Southern Political Science Association,
New Orleans, Louisiana, January 6. Davis, Lanny J. 2008. "The Obama Realignment. This could be the start of a lasting Democratic majority like that created by
FDR." *Wall Street Journal,* November 6, A19.

DeGregorio, William A. 1993. *The Complete Book of U.S. Presidents 4th ed.* New York:
Barricade Books.

Eland, Ivan. 2009. *Recarving Rushmore: Ranking the Presidents on Peace, Prosperity,
and Liberty.* Oakland, CA: Independent Institute.

Faber, Charles, and Faber, Richard. 2000. *The American Presidents Ranked by Performance.* Jefferson, NC: McFarland & Co.

Felzenberg, Alvin S. 2008. *The Leaders We Deserved (and a Few We Didn't). Rethinking
the Presidential Ranking Game.* New York: Basic Books.

Felzenberg, Alvin S. 1997. "There You Go Again: Liberal Historians and the New York
Times Deny Ronald Reagan His Due." *Policy Review* 82: 51–54.

Gallup 2010. "Bush Still Takes Brunt of Blame for Economy vs. Obama," by Linda Saad.
Princeton, NJ, September 16.

Gallup 2011. Presidential Job Approval Center. www.gallup.com/poll/124922/Presidentia
l-Job-Approval-Center.aspx

Gallup News Service. 2011, Gallup Poll Social Series: World Affairs, Timberline:
927890 G: 687 Princeton Job #: 11-02-003, February 2-5.

Jacobson, Gary C. 2008. *A Divider, Not a Uniter. George W. Bush and the American
People.* New York: Pearson Longman.

Maranto, Robert, Lansford, Tom, and Johnson, Jeremy eds. 2009. *Judging Bush.* Stanford, CA: Stanford University Press.

Murray, Robert K., and Blessing, Tim H. 1994. *Greatness in the White House: Rating the
Presidents, from Washington Through Ronald Reagan 2nd ed.* University Park, PA:
Pennsylvania State University Press.

Obama, Barack. 2007. Video address announcing the formation of presidential exploratory committee, January 16.

Obama, Barack. 2008a. Nomination Acceptance Speech, Democratic National Convention. Denver, CO, August 28.

Obama, Barack. 2008b. Campaign rally, Columbia, MO, October 30.

Obama, Barack. 2010. Press Conference by the President, White House, November 3.

Powell, Colin L. 2008. Endorsement of Barack Obama for president on NBC's "Meet the Press," October 19.

Pfiffner, James P. 2003. "Ranking the Presidents: Continuity and Volatility." *White House Studies* 3: 23. mason.gmu.edu/~pubp502/Pres.rating.mss.pdf

Ridings, William J., Jr., and McIver, Stuart B. 1997. *Rating the Presidents: A Ranking of U.S. leaders, from the Great and Honorable to the Dishonest and Incompetent.* Secaucus, NJ: Carol Publishing.

Schlesinger, Arthur M., Jr. 1996. "The Ultimate Approval Rating," *New York Times Magazine*, December 15, 46-51.

Schlesinger, Arthur M., Jr. 1997. "Ranking the Presidents: From Washington to Clinton," *Political Science Quarterly* 112 (2): 179–190.

Schlesinger, Arthur M., Sr. 1948. "Historians Rate U.S. Presidents," *Life*, November.

Schlesinger, Arthur M., Sr. 1962. "Our Presidents: A Rating by 75 Historians," *New York Times Magazine*, July 29.

Siena Research Institute 2010. "American Presidents: Greatest and Worst. Siena's 5th Presidential Expert Poll 1982–2010. Rushmore Plus One; FDR joins Mountainside Figures Washington, Jefferson, Teddy Roosevelt and Lincoln as Top Presidents." www.siena.edu/sri/research

Skowronek, Stephen. 1993. *The Politics Presidents Make: Leadership from John Adams to George Bush.* Cambridge, MA: Belknap Press of Harvard University Press.

Skowronek, Stephen. 2011. *Presidential Leadership in Political Time. Reprise and Reappraisal. Second Edition, Revised and Expanded.* Lawrence: University Press of Kansas.

Stiglitz, Joseph E. 2011. "Of the 1%, by the 1%, for the 1%," *Vanity Fair*, May.

Taranto, James, and Leo, Leonard. 2004. *Presidential Leadership: Rating the Best and Worst in the White House.* New York: Wall Street Journal Books.

Todd, Chuck, and Gawiser, Sheldon. 2009. *How Barack Obama Won. A State-by-State Guide to the Historic 2008 Presidential Election.* New York: Vintage Books.

United States Department of Labor, Bureau of Labor Statistics, Series CEU0000000001, Employment, Hours, and Earnings from the Current Employment Statistics survey.

United States Department of Labor, Bureau of Labor Statistics, Series Id. CEU0000000001, Employment, Hours, and Earnings from the Current Employment Statistics survey (National), Not Seasonally Adjusted, www.bls.gov/ces/home.htm (extracted March 16, 2011).

White, John Kenneth, "A Transforming Election: How Barack Obama Changed American Politics," in Crotty 2009, p. 185-208.

Chapter 3

Obama's Health Reform:
The Managerial President and the Political Storm

James A. Morone

As Franklin Roosevelt contemplated the end of World War II, he cast around for another crusade to lead. He alighted on "cradle to grave" national health insurance. Roosevelt tasked his long time aide, Sam Rosenman, with drafting a health plan and, more important, a political strategy with which to win it. By the time the plan was ready, Roosevelt had died and the Rosenman draft passed on to President Harry Truman who seized it with fervor. From Truman, national health insurance passed down through the Democratic generations—the last, elusive, social democratic bequest from the New Deal.[1]

Few ideas have been pursued as long—or opposed quite as ferociously—as national health care. The Obama administration's victory in March 2010 was no small achievement. Despite a significant Democratic majority in the House and (after Al Franken was finally declared winner in Minnesota in July, 2009) a filibuster proof majority of 60 in the Senate, the politics were extremely difficult. In this chapter, I trace the long, often surprising roots of the Obama health plan and reflect on the essence of the reform. Despite the thunder on the right and the despair on the left, the final legislation delivered real, significant reform. It is not, however, what Harry Truman had in mind.

Harry Truman: Dreams of Social Insurance

When Truman announced the Roosevelt plan, the American Medical Association (AMA) did something unprecedented. It hired a public relations firm to campaign against the legislation. Whitaker and Baxter did a legendary job. They hired thirty-seven associates who found all kinds of creative ways to shout "socialism!" in the middle of a red scare. Their propaganda campaign has become legendary.[2]

In an inspired move, the PR team lined up hundreds of groups (by one count, 1,829 of them) and scripted their indignation over socialized medicine. The Truman administration archives bulge with letters, memorials, and petitions from local VFW posts and Chambers of Commerce expressing outrage, all worded suspiciously the same.[3]

The Barking Dogs Don't Matter

Few political historians have noticed that all the sound and fury did not matter much. Congress was dominated by the conservative bulls who chaired the key committees. The chairman of the House Ways and Means Committee, Clarence Lea (D *and* R, CA) never bothered to schedule hearings on Truman's proposal; the chairman of the Senate Finance Committee was so hostile that the reformers stripped all finance provisions from the proposal to avoid his committee. No matter, Senator Robert Taft was ready for what he called "the most socialistic measure Congress has ever had before it." The media—*Time, Newsweek, The New York Times*—all commented that no one in Washington expected the bill to go anywhere. And all this before Whitaker and Baxter got down to work (Blumenthal and Morone, chap. 2).

One of the great culture stories about the United States suggests that the failure to win comprehensive health reform reflects American disdain for government. There is much truth to this view of the culture, but it cannot explain America's national health insurance exceptionalism. If the United States had been playing by Parliamentary rules, it would have had an NHI program when Truman first proposed it, in 1945-6 or when he featured it prominently in his long shot reelection bid in 1948. The voters did not seem panicked by socialized medicine when they returned him to office by two million votes (4 percent). It was not the culture or the health care lobby but the peculiarities of America's legislature that stymied Truman and the liberals.

Two Ideas

But that is not the end of the Truman legacy. The still-born Truman proposal produced two powerful ideas that would, in turn, influence future debates. An enduring liberal aspiration and a fierce (and equally) conservative reaction were forged, framed and ready to launch.

First, the idea of *social insurance*. Truman was entirely maladroit about getting his legislation through Congress. But he found his voice during the 1948 campaign and used it to push the health plan. Truman dispatched with speeches and simply pounded his talking points in an angry staccato, freely mixing arguments with insults. His idea was clear and simple: A just and modern society takes care of people when they are sick—even if they are "derelicts who . . . did not have any ambition" (Blumenthal and Morone, 66). Health care was not a question of merit or of markets. It was something we owed one another as fellow citizens. We were all together in the same boat—just as we had been during the great wars. The idea of mutual obligation became one of the Democratic Party's great canons—partially vindicated when the Lyndon Johnson Administration won Medicare. This is the idea that repeatedly fires up the Democratic base when NHI rises up the agenda. And it always raises the same dilemma: How to get it through Congress?

On the other side, what political scientists call *Lockean Liberalism* (or, in more descriptive terms, shouting *"Socialism!"*). The AMA campaign generated an unexpected dividend: A ready response to any Democratic health insurance proposal. Each time the debate warms up, Democrats are surprised by the ferocity of the opposition. And no wonder: The arguments seem so wild, the rhetoric so exaggerated. National health insurance may or may not have been wise policy, but it was not really going to deliver America to the Soviets (in the 1940s) or get a bureaucratic panel to weigh grandpa's fate. The wild arguments always seem to catch on. Why?

The angry argument against socialized medicine is a fine illustration of a truculent fear of government that first caught the eye of social scientists in the 1950s. Richard Hofstadter called it "a paranoid style in American politics." Righteous, overheated, oversuspicious, overaggressive, morally indignant, patriotically inspired Americans see in simple policy proposals an apocalyptic threat to their nation, their culture, and their way of life. In that simpler era Hofstadter pointed to "paranoid' individuals who feared gun control was "a further attempt . . . to make us part of one world socialistic government" (Hofstadter, 1965, 4-5).

Louis Hartz made the best-known analysis of the phenomenon. The early American experience, argued Hartz, shaped a ferocious, irrational, *"Lockean liberalism"* (a reference to John Locke's concern for private property) that provokes a gut deep aversion to socialism, redistribution, or expansions of government authority. Since there were no feudal restraints in early America any man could make it on his own. Government would only undermine the market test of virtue. Even American populists dither like Hamlet, wrote Hartz, at the prospect of redistributing income—even when it is in his own self-interest. The theory has come in for a great deal of criticism. It traces all American thought to one frankly dubious cause; it entirely ignores the great American binaries—race, gender, and religion. It can't explain how government grew. But for all that, it beautifully captures the conservative reaction to the Truman health proposal: the cries of socialism! What is more, it uncannily predicts the public reaction to health care proposals right down to the hot town meetings and Tea Party rallies in the summer of 2009 (Hartz, 1954).

In short, two overarching ideas emerged from the 1940s and—filtered through the epic 1948 election campaign—took on almost totemic power for future generations. When the base of either party hears the call to National Health Insurance, their notions are already formulated and ready to be primed.

Obama: Massive Incrementalism

Truman's Congress was simplicity itself compared to the legislature that Obama faced. As the latest effort wended its way through the legislature, the nation got an unsavory seminar with a simple take home: Congress may just be the most complicated, exasperating, unwieldy legislative body in the industrial world.

F'ing Ben Nelson

Consider the gauntlet this reform had to run. In the House, three different committees produced two quite different bills. Speaker of the House Nancy Pelosi (D CA) then hammered them into a single bill through long negotiations with different coalitions—the conservative blue dogs, the progressive caucus, the black caucus, the Hispanic caucus, abortion opponents, and the list goes on. Then—after going to the rules committee to set the terms of the debate—she brought the legislation to the floor where it squeaked by 220-215.

In the Senate, two committees produced two more bills. Majority leader Harry Reid (D NV) then renegotiated the package, not with blocks but with individuals, searching for the magic sixty votes that shuts off a filibuster. That sixtieth vote did not come easy and the Democratic staffers' mantra was "F'ing Ben Nelson" (the Democrat from Nebraska who negotiated long and hard). The Senate Bill finally passed on December 24 and then went to conference where substantial differences between the bills passed in House and Senate could be negotiated into still another bill—with, count 'em, three more filibuster opportunities on the Senate side. That conference committee would have been the *seventh* different health bill (produced by five committees, two chambers, and one conference). Then, just as the reform neared completion, a special election in Massachusetts yielded a Republican who had run on a striking platform: Stop this health reform. That, in turn, short-circuited the "direct" approach through conference and required fresh rounds of parliamentary maneuvering.

The sausage metaphor has been ubiquitous. But there is a more profound point: this is a uniquely tortured way to pass legislation. Some political scientists have been dubbing the Congress—and especially the Senate—"the broken branch" (Mann and Ornstein, 2006). Many observers have criticized the Obama administration for not sending a more robust plan to Congress. The criticism is naïve about congressional process. The crucial element lies not in the plan's details—which Congress will rewrite multiple times—but the clarity of its principles. And here lies the real question. Did Obama have a clear set of ideas? Or did he drift though the congressional gauntlet?

It will be years before interviews, archives and the results of the reform—if it is fully put in place—yield an answer. On its face, the reform looks like massive incrementalism: Expand Medicaid to cover every American up to 133 percent of poverty—an enormous expansion of the familiar program; tax breaks for individuals shopping the insurance markets; a mandate, first proposed by Republicans Bob Dole (KA) and John Chaffee (RI) in 1993, requiring that individuals buy health insurance (and large employers offer it) or face a tax penalty.

What's the core idea? The politics that swirled around the ObamaCare debate injected two very different ideas into the health care debate: the "technical fix" (from proponents) and the familiar cries of "socialism!" from Republicans.

The Technical Fix

On the campaign trail, candidate Obama competed with Hillary Clinton to sound the classic social insurance themes. He wrapped his campaign in the classic style and rhetoric of the classic social gospel: the moral call to feed the hungry, lift the poor, and care for the ill. The idea got plenty of play, for example, in the famous debate with Joe the Plumber—a large man with a goatee who challenged Obama about taxes and prompted a now famous comment from the candidate:

> My attitude is that if the economy's good for folks from the bottom up, it's gonna be good for everybody. If you've got a plumbing business, you're gonna be better off if you've got a whole bunch of customers who can afford to hire you, and right now everybody's so pinched that business is bad for everybody and I think when you spread the wealth around, it's good for everybody.

Republicans pounced on the last line—spread the wealth—and branded the Democrat a socialist. On the campaign trail, candidate Obama stuck to his position, articulating the social democrat's canon: "When you spread the wealth around, it's good for everybody."

After a fitful start through the first year of health reform, Obama finally seemed to go back to these philosophical roots. He rallied his party with the unabashed Harry Truman rhetoric of social insurance. Speaking at a fundraiser in February, 2010—a year into the process—the president hushed the audience with the story of an uninsured Obama volunteer from St. Louis who was dying from breast cancer. "She insisted she is going to be buried in an Obama T-shirt," the president continued. "How can I say to her, 'You know what, we're giving up'? How can I say to her family, 'This is too hard'? How can Democrats on the Hill say, 'This is politically too risky'? How can Republicans on the Hill say, 'We're better off just blocking anything from happening'?" "Yes we can," chanted the Democratic faithful, cheering the clarion call of the great social insurance principle (Pear and Herszenhorn, 2010 A9; Blumenthal and Morone, 2009, v).

However, social insurance leaked out of the proposal—the Democrats lost the public option, a weak form of single payer, and then a Medicare buy-in which was, in turn, a weak form of the public option.

What was left rested on an entirely different idea with its own long provenance: a neo-Progressive faith in managerial efficiency, a kind of technical fix. "There is no Democratic or Republican way to pave a street," cried the original Progressive reformers; let's work out a bipartisan solution to the health care mess echo their intellectual heirs.[4] The signature move of the new Democrat, embraced by Jimmy Carter, Bill Clinton, and Barack Obama, is to put aside the ambitious social insurance agenda; no more universal programs like Medicare in which the federal government pays health care bills for all beneficiaries. Instead, contemporary health reforms hunt for expert solutions that might lift the debate beyond partisanship and politics. Information technology, electronic medical records, lessons from health services research, and many other innovations might just render the system more efficient.

The neo-Progressive urge can be seen most vividly in the extraordinary implementation process of the Obama health plan, now well under way. By one count, the final legislation contains 1,563 *"Secretary shalls"*—that is, items that require rules from the implementing agencies. That dwarfs the count of any prior health care reform. These regulations affect the nuts and bolts of the medical system. While the debate focused on insurers, 974 (or 64 percent) of those called-for regulations focused on medical providers. The idea animating all those regulations is a faith that regulations can impose efficiencies on the health care system.

Was this result—not New Deal style social insurance but Progressive era managerial reform—inevitable? An inexorable result of the political process? Perhaps. The brute political necessity—sixty votes in the Senate—limited the Democrats' options.

Moreover, the seductions of technique seemed to wink across the aisle. A small knot of Republicans, led by Charles Grassley (IA) negotiated long and hard—underscore long—with Senator Max Baucus, the chair of Senate Finance. The subtext of their negotiations can be summarized like this: keep the social insurance out of this package and a couple of us Republicans might just support it. In truth, there is a thin area of agreement where the health care wonks of the center left and the center right find common ground. Beltway Republicans aim to unleash the power of markets on our health problems, the Democrats turn to regulation with a more cautious dose of competition. The mix of government regulation and health care market shades across party lines. However the solutions—whatever their technical merits—are politically unstable because the true believers in both parties despise them. In every generation, the Progressive impulse—fix the machinery—crashes into the unyielding politics.

This move to technique, however, reflected something more than the political exigencies of winning health reform or the allure of bipartisanship. It appears to be part of a larger pattern that marks the Obama administration. The managerial philosophy was vivid in the president's inaugural address.

The question we ask today is not whether our government is too big or too small, but whether it works . . . where the answer is yes, we intend to move forward. Where the answer is no, programs will end. And those of us who manage the public's dollars will be held to account, to spend wisely, reform bad habits, and do our business in the light of day, because only then can we restore the vital trust between a people and their government.

Candidate Obama's clarion calls to share, to spread the wealth and to lift the poor have vanished. In their place stands the dream of efficiency. The president promises to manage wisely; he calls for reforming—not the rampant inequality of a new gilded age but—government's "bad business habits."

The neo-Progressive faith in good management offers no broader philosophical umbrella for a Truman style social insurance. Still standing in the shadow of Ronald Reagan—an era celebrating individualism, markets, government bashing, and gilded age wealth—the Obama administration never reset the philosophical agenda in a way that would introduce and justify a more ambitious health care agenda.

Both the Washington consensus on health care and the administration's own broader vision pulled in the same direction: A careful, managerial, health reform heavy on technological solutions. It went light on social insurance (we're all in this together) and relied, instead, on regulation, technology and markets. In a less charged political season, a handful of Republicans might very well have negotiated an agreement and signed on to the legislation.

Cry Socialism

Perhaps this framing is what robbed Obama of his eloquent voice. His speeches on health care descended into the political weeds. They baffled the Democratic faithful—who could not find the connection between all the dull details and the simple idea they espoused. The Democratic Party base was eager for some version of social insurance. The Washington Democrats sought the Progressive style managerial solution that might manage to run through the congressional gauntlet—and perhaps even find some common ground with moderate Republicans. It was not till there was no chance of Republican support that Obama found his voice—speaking in bold social insurance rhetoric over a package that had, in fact, been negotiated with the aim of winning Republican votes.

The most dramatic turn in the debate came in the long hot summer of 2009—long before Obama started to call out to his base. Right-wing populists, self-styled Tea Party activists, roared into the health policy discussion screaming their familiar slogan: "socialized medicine." This time, they managed a new rhetorical variation on the idea of Lenin and the Soviet state: this plan would introduce government run death panels—a pungent, memorable, simple, and effective symbol of the evil state. The administration never found a way to recapture public attention or offer a simple counter to the charges. Like Truman or

Clinton before them, the Democrats tried denial (this is not socialized medicine, there are no death panels), backtracking (striking the counseling provisions in the House bill that had set off the media storm) and delving into the details (here is what is really in the bill). Once again—yet again—the opposition won the battle of popular perceptions.

In past debates, the opposition came from well-oiled, richly financed corporate lobbies like the physicians or the insurers. Reports suggest that conservative organizations richly funded the Tea Party activists too. However, it is generally a mistake to dismiss populist energy. The furious outbursts tapped a powerful idea that stretches back over time. They may have been well funded, but ordinary people responded to the health care proposals with their veins bulging.

The health care debate has turned into a debate about what kind of nation the United States is. It is no coincidence that the most deeply felt issues of our time—race, immigration, welfare, the role of government, and abortion—all roiled up with health reform. It was the issue of illegal immigration that moved Congressman Wilson to shout "You lie" as the president spoke before Congress; it was abortion that almost derailed the reform among then Democrats in the House. And, as always, there were plenty of hints that race and religion was roiling somewhere in the mix.

Perhaps every nation's health care system offers a snapshot of essential national characteristics, of the kind of community the nation aspires to be. It may be that health care in the United States raises the deepest communal question: who are we?

In this case, the right-wing populism grew so hot that even Charles Grassley turned and pandered. "You have every right to fear. You shouldn't have counseling at the end of life. . . . We should not have a government program that determines if you're going to pull the plug on grandma." Democrats in Washington, who thought they were prepared for the standard inflated rhetoric about socialism, were gobsmacked about death panels. Where was *this* coming from?

There is no reason to be surprised. It comes from a venerable national wellspring. It is the familiar, rightist fear of government. The same passionate idea that Louis Hartz and Richard Hofstadter identified a half century ago. It is the same idea, for that matter, that confronted the health care proposals made by Harry Truman and John F. Kennedy.

Echo and Difference

Perhaps the strangest aspect of the Obama reforms lies in its echo of the George W. Bush administration experience in adding prescription drugs to Medicare. Like the Bush administration, the Obama administration cut a deal with the major corporate actors (pharmaceutical and insurance industries respectively). Like the Bush administration, the Obama team set out broad guidelines and left the details to Congress. Both administrations lost core principles in the legislative process; Bush had aimed to privatize Medicare (always known as "modernization"), Obama to introduce social insurance principles at least for Americans who wanted it. In both cases the opposition grew furious about the congressional process (with the ire focused, respectively, on Tom DeLay and Nancy Pelosi). In both cases, the administration appeared to rouse the opposition while alienating its base. In both cases, allies wanly suggested that this was a good start while polls suggested that public opinion on the issue had swung to the other side. The similarities running between such different administrations suggest powerful structural constraints on the political process.

For all the similarities, however, there is a striking difference. Conservatives, defeated in Congress, vow to keep fighting. They promise to repeal the legislation in Congress, sue to upend key features in the courts, and compile a "hit list" of regulations to "kill" in the bureaucracy.

Health care has always been jarringly partisan. Perhaps that is because it has always stretched beyond public policy and stirred up questions of national identity, of who we are as a nation. The health care debates always go on. However, despite all the drama of past debates, there are not many precedents for a conflict that rages on after the final congressional votes are taken and a bill is signed.

Only one Republican in the House of Representatives voted for the Social Security package in 1935. Only ten Republicans in the House voted for Medicare. However, once the parliamentary maneuvers were over and victory assured, most Republicans crossed sides and voted for the final package (in the words of Democratic presidential candidate John Kerry, they voted against it before they voted for it). In short, even very fractious issues in the past—Social Security, Medicare, the Civil Rights Act, the Voting Rights Act, and even Medicare's prescription drug coverage (part D)—found rough closure in definitive Congressional Action. It is unusual—perhaps unprecedented—to see the debate simply roar on unabated after major entitlement reform (Johnson, 2010).

The similarities between George W. Bush and Barack Obama intimate a Washington centric politics cut loose from either political base. The continuing uproar, on the other hand, suggests a whole new level of partisan ferocity. We may very well be facing a rising right-wing populist—with the latest recrudescence of the cry against socialism—for a long time to come. If that is so, both Democrats and Republicans may be well advised to return to first principles—perhaps at the price of bipartisanship and even the kind of ambitious incrementalism that won substantial health reforms in both the Bush and Obama administrations.

Affordable Care Act

The politics have been so boisterous that it is easy to overlook the act itself. Like any health care legislation, this one is complicated, technical, and obscure. However, the rhetoric on neither side reflects the dull details. Republicans vastly exaggerate its failures: No, there are no death panels. In fact, the cost containment measures are weak enough that there is not likely to be any serious motion toward rationing care in new ways. Compared to Medicare or even Medicaid, this is a quite modest "government takeover of health care." The Democratic reaction is more difficult to understand for, even running for office, they appear to vastly underestimate the legislation's potential to achieve classic Democratic goals.

The bill itself turns on four general principles:

Private Insurance Rules. It changes the rules of private insurance coverage. Today, the incentives facing private insurance companies are simple: seek the healthy, shun the sick. The Affordable Care Act changes the ground rules. Insurance companies are proscribed from refusing to cover preexisting conditions; from denying coverage after the onset of an illness or condition; from placing caps on the amount they will pay (so that very sick or chronically ill patients simply run out of benefits); or from charging different premiums to different populations (though, within limits, different age groups will pay different premiums).

Affordable Coverage. For liberals, the most dramatic effect is—or ought to be—the Act's effort to extend insurance coverage to the poor and middle class. Today, Medicaid is an extraordinary patchwork—with generous coverage and eligibility criteria in some places, very limited coverage in others. In Texas, for example, an adult making more than $188 a month (yes, that's $1,250 a year) does not qualify. The legislation sets universal Medicaid standards: any American making less than 133 percent of poverty would qualify for Medicaid. For the first years, the significant expansion of Medicaid budgets would be borne entirely by the Federal budget. Here's the irony: the northern states, with their historically generous Medicaid programs, would be sending their tax dollars to the southern states, with their historically limited Medicaid programs, which are, in turn, suing to block the transfer. The programmatic bottom line, if the act is fully implemented, would be a dramatic expansion of health care coverage: for the first time, there would be a health care program that covers most low income Americans.

Other mechanisms for making health insurance more affordable include a large tax expenditure—a tax deduction—to help people between 100 percent and 400 percent of poverty buy private health insurance. And an expanded use of statewide high-risk insurance pools.

Each of these mechanisms will help individuals negotiate insurance coverage. An estimated thirty-two million Americans would win coverage (again, if the plan somehow runs the gauntlet of courts and state governments and goes fully into effect).

Mandates. Along with the expansion of Medicaid, insurance pools, and tax subsidies, the program includes a mandate on both individuals and businesses to buy health insurance—or pay a fine.

Provision of Care. A great many regulations are aimed at making the provision of health care more efficient. The administration is pushing the industry to move toward electronic medical records, to adopt new quality standards and—in general—to adapt to the quality and efficiency findings being generated by health services research.

Of course, there is much more detail. However, the dull details of the legislation make one piece of the political fallout puzzling: Why have Democrats not defended their long sought legislation? While, as we have seen, it does not conform to the classic social democratic model, it manages far more than one would imagine just listening to the debates: Reining in the abuses in the insurance markets, creating a national Medicaid program that covers adults as well as children, rendering the hospitals more efficient—it is not Medicare for all, but it moves decisively towards long held Democratic Party goals.

The great political fact about this round of health care reform is most strange: The Democrats held together to win legislation, achieved many (by no means all) of the goals they claimed to be seeking, and then skulked away from the results and declined to defend (never mind celebrate) what they had achieved. Only one side showed up to the debate and, with practice honed by sixty years, it shouted "socialism."

Learn to Lose, Learn to Win

Harry Truman never came close to winning health reform. But he never gave up the ideal. Even after he left office he continued to write, and speak, and pound away. He kept the issue alive for a future generation of reformers. When President Lyndon Johnson won Medicare, in 1965, he announced that he would sign the bill in Independence, Missouri, in front of Harry. Some aides tried to dissuade him, wary of being tarred by "socialized medicine" but LBJ was adamant. As he signed the bill he said, "It was Harry Truman who planted the seeds of compassion and duty which have today flowered . . ." Few people, he went on to say, have the guts to keep on fighting for a cause that few people share. Truman kept fighting for the hopeless cause and, as a result, helped keep it alive.

Contrast President Bill Clinton. He was eloquent about his own health reform: "Our grandchildren will find it unthinkable that there was . . . a time in this country when hard working families lost their homes, their savings, their businesses, lost everything simply because their children got sick . . ."

The Republicans worried that if the plan won it might—in the words of one internal memo—reconnect the Democratic Party to the middle class. The Republicans heaped scorn on the effort, defeated it, and made sure, as Senator Bob Packwood (R-PR) put it, that their "fingerprints [were] not on the body." They controlled the historical spin in part because President Clinton walked away. In the end, the president wanly concluded, "I felt bad that Hillary and Ira Magaziner were taking the rap for the failure." In retrospect, he mused, he should have done health reform first (Clinton, 621, 631). Where, in the end, were the families that "lost everything"?

Truman had continued to fight. Clinton walked away from the reform. The lesson appeared to be clear: *Learn to lose.* Keep the issue alive and your coalition together by fighting for your principle regardless of how it comes out. Somewhere between Truman and Clinton, health reform changed. For Truman it was a principle to believe in and fight for. For Clinton it became a tactical issue that could rally support. When it lost its political power, he jettisoned it.

In contrast to Clinton (or, for that matter, Carter) the Obama administration and the Democrats did not lose their reform. Having won it, however, they acted more like Clinton than like Truman. They jettisoned their success. The lesson for the 2010 Democrats is a strange one: Learn how to win.

Throughout the debate, the president seemed reluctant to articulate the great principles that underlay the health reform effort. When the reform was won, both administration and party were even more reluctant to explain what they had won, how the long quest for health reform achieved many—though certainly not all—of the Democrats' long sought goals. Why? How is it that the Democrats did not know how to win?

Two possibilities suggest themselves. First, the Democratic faithful—in and out of government—still reserve their faith for Harry Truman's reform. What they believe is the social insurance idea. The Affordable Care Act may achieve some of the same goals. But it falls short of the great principles that Democrats believe in.

The alternative is more painful for the party to contemplate: Perhaps the Democrats no longer share overarching principles. Harry Truman's great faith, shared by President Obama, no longer resonates with the party. Perhaps the problem is not that health reform falls short of the great Democratic principles, but that those principles no longer exist.

Notes

1. Truman later called his failure to win national health insurance the greatest regret of his life (Truman, 1955, Vol. 1: 19).

2. See Max Skidmore: *Medicare and the American Rhetoric of Reconciliation* and Richard Harris, *A Sacred Trust* for examples of the rhetoric and symbols.

3. Details in David Blumenthal and James Morone, *The Heart of Power: Health and Politics in the Oval Office.* California. 2009.

4. On the original Progressive Tradition, see James Morone, 1998, chapter 3.

References

Blumenthal, David and James Morone. 2009. *The Heart of Power: Health and Politics in the Oval Office*. Berkeley and Los Angeles: University of California.

Clinton, Bill. 2004. *My Life*. New York: Knopf.

Harris, Richard. 1966. *A Sacred Trust*. New York: New American Library.

Hartz. Louis. 1954. *The Liberal Tradition in America*. New York: Harcourt, Brace and World.

Hofstadter, Richard. 1963. *Anti-Intellectualism in American Life*. New York: Knopf.

Hofstadter, Richard. 1965. *The Paranoid Style in American Politics*. New York: Knopf.

Johnson, Jeremy. 2010. *The Republican Welfare State*. PhD Dissertation, Brown University, Providence, RI.

Mann, Thomas and Norman Ornstein. 2006. *The Broken Branch: How Congress Is Failing America and How to Get It Back on Track*. New York: Oxford University Press.

Morone, James. 1998. *The Democratic Wish*. New Haven, CT: Yale.

Pear, Robert and Herszenhorn, David M. 2010. "Democrats Ask, Can This Health Care Bill Be Saved?" *New York Times*, February 6.

Skidmore, Max. 1970. *Medicare and the American Rhetoric of Reconciliation*. University Park: University of Alabama Press.

Truman, Harry. 1955. *Memoirs*. New York: Doubleday.

Chapter 4

Environmental Policy: The Success and Failure of the Obama Presidency

John C. Berg

Introduction

In *The Success and Failure of Picasso*, the art critic John Berger argues that Pablo Picasso achieved rapid success soon after launching his career in France because as a Spaniard he was a "vertical invader," from a different cultural tradition (Berger 1989). The insight gained from this outsider position combined with Picasso's natural talent to fuel his rise to the top of the art world. That was the success; the failure was that, in Berger's view, Picasso then felt no pressure to pursue further artistic development during the remaining decades of his life.[1]

Whether or not Berger was right about Picasso, I think his approach is useful, albeit on a radically accelerated time scale, for considering the presidency of Barack Obama. As our first African American president, Obama was a vertical invader. In addition he had another great advantage, *viz.*, that he was not George W. Bush. These two characteristics combined with Obama's talents as a speaker to bring him into office with tremendous popularity and support, which led in turn to early success in passage of the American Reinvestment and Recovery Act. However, this early success was not sustained, arguably because the president failed to develop his political skills beyond the point at which he won election.

Here the similarity ends. Berger was writing at the end of Picasso's career, but Obama has completed only two years of his presidency. Moreover, Picasso retained his artistic reputation for the rest of his life, despite the limitations that

85

Berger thought he saw, while Obama's ratings began to plummet halfway through his first year in office. On the other hand, Obama now has the opportunity to learn from his experience, which includes experiencing the Republican gains in the Congressional election of 2010. As of the late 2010 lame-duck session of Congress, Obama 1, who combined great talk with weaker action, seems to have been replaced with Obama 2, who is repackaging environmentalism as job creation and competitiveness. But before turning to an examination of the Obama environmental record, we need to decide what criteria we will use to evaluate that record. Three possible sorts of criteria spring to mind. We might evaluate the extent to which Obama delivered on his environmental campaign promises; his ability to move forward on his environmental policy priorities; or his success in solving the environmental problems that confront our planet. Let us consider each of these in turn.

One simple criterion might be to start with Obama's campaign promises. The "Politifact" website of the *St. Petersburg Times* has carefully collated all such promises and classified them by issue in its "Obameter"; fifty-seven of these are "promises about the environment." These promises are categorized as *kept, in the works, compromised, stalled,* or *broken.* As figure 4.1 shows, 28 percent of Obama's environmental promises have been kept, with a further 52 percent "in the works"; only 6 percent are stalled or have been broken. From this strictly numerical point of view, Obama has done well (Promises About Environment on the Obameter).

Figure 4.1. Fulfillment of Environmental Campaign Promises

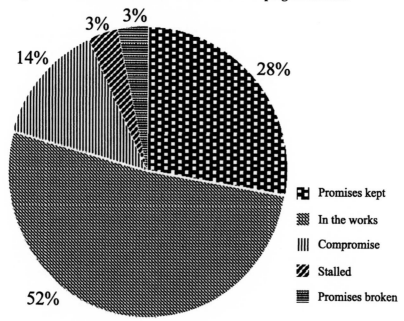

However, there are some problems with this simple statistic, since the promises are not of equal importance. They range from "Create cap and trade system with interim goals to reduce global warming" (No. 456) and "Work with UN on climate change" (No. 455) through "improve water quality" (No. 263) and "restore the Great Lakes" (No. 265) to "More controlled burns to reduce wildfires" (No. 279) and "Provide more funds to educate young hunters and anglers" (No. 285), and on to such anti-environmental goals as "Expedite oil and gas drilling from domestic shale formations" (No. 451) and "Create clean coal partnerships" (No. 453). Without a weighting scheme, the percentages are not particularly meaningful.

A second method might be to limit our evaluation to those environmental goals which appeared to be genuine priorities for the Obama administration during its first two years. While this method is more subjective, it allows us to assess how well the administration did in its own terms. Here we can consider three categories: moderately important environmental priorities; major environmental priorities; and priorities that were bad for the environment.

The Obama Agenda

Moderately important priorities of the Obama administration included regulation of arsenic in drinking water, preservation and restoration of ocean fisheries, restoring the environmental health of the Great Lakes, supporting the development of a national high-speed rail network, and promoting the concept of "green jobs." At the midterm point he had been relatively successful in attaining these priorities, although some of them are threatened in the budget for fiscal year 2012.

On March 20, 2001, during the George W. Bush administration, the Environmental Protection Agency (EPA) had announced that it was withdrawing a Clinton-era regulation tightening the standard for arsenic in drinking water from 50 to 10 parts per billion (ppb). The stricter standard had been based on a study by the National Academy of Sciences that had found that the looser standard could lead to a 1 percent chance of cancer, and was identical to the standard in use by the European Union and the World Health Organization; then-EPA Administrator Christie Todd Whitman had asserted that the stricter standard was not supported by the best available science (Jehl 2001). The loosening of the standard was criticized widely. The director of the Duke University Center for Hydrologic Science asserted that "when it comes to drinking water standards, our president and Environmental Protection Agency administrator are more concerned with pleasing special interests than with saving lives" (Rojstaczer 2001), and the Natural Resources Defense Council challenged the decision in court (National Briefing, EPA Sued on Arsenic 2001). Obama pledged during the campaign that he would restore the old standard. This could not be done immediately, due to the need for the EPA to first solicit and consider public comment, but that process is now complete. The EPA issued the new standard of 10 ppb on January 22, 2011 (*Federal Register* January 22, 2011).

The Obama administration has also strengthened regulations for protecting and restoring the stocks of ocean fish. The National Oceanic and Atmospheric Administration (NOAA) has moved to adopt a catch-share policy, which went into force in November 2010. Under this policy, each year fishermen are allocated a specific quantity of fish, a percentage share of the total permissible catch for that year; previously the catch had been regulated by limiting the number of days of fishing, rather than the amount of fish caught. By directly regulating the size of the catch, rather than the number of days fished, NOAA is able to hold the catch to sustainable levels more reliably, while relieving the pressure on fishermen to fish in dangerous weather if they wish to make maximum use of their allotted fishing days. During the current administration NOAA has placed strict limits on the catch for a number of important fish species, which has led to howls of protest from both fishermen and the politicians who represent them. Massachusetts Governor Patrick, for example, has decried "Commerce's intransigence and disrespect toward the working men and women who harvest our seafood, and their representatives in elected office" (Urbon 2011). Such a reaction can be taken to indicate the stringency of the regulation in question.

Obama also pledged to implement an important program to improve the environmental health of the Great Lakes, similar to existing programs for Chesapeake Bay and the Everglades. Such a program had been formally created during the George W. Bush administration, but had received only minimal funding. The Great Lakes contain 21 percent of the world's fresh water, and 84 percent of the supply in North America. Approximately 10 percent of the population of the United States, and 30 percent of the population of Canada, lives in the Great Lakes Basin. Historically the region has had enormous ecological problems, symbolized dramatically when the Cuyahoga River caught on fire, not for the first time, in 1952, and when Lake Erie became a biological dead zone as its lower level became depleted of oxygen (Environmental Protection Agency. Great Lakes National Program Office 2001). There has been considerable improvement since that time, but much remains to be done.

The Great Lakes program creates a council of sixteen federal agencies, in collaboration with the states and Canadian provinces that border the Great Lakes, to administer the plan. The plan calls for action in several "focus areas," including toxic substances, invasive species, ecologically degraded areas, nearshore pollution, and wildlife habitat. Obama included $475 million for this program in his first budget, and $300 million in his second. The administration had pledged to seek $475 million for each of the next three budget years; however the cuts proposed by the Republican leadership of the House would reduce this amount to $225 million for fiscal year 2012 (Egan 2009; Landers 2010; Melzer 2010).

Support for high-speed rail has been one of the environmental high points of the Obama administration. Railroads are considerably more efficient at moving people than either automobiles or airplanes. This efficiency alone means that both greenhouse gas emission and other forms of air pollution will be reduced to the extent that more people travel by train. In addition, it is feasible to power trains entirely by electricity, while this is not currently the case for automobiles, and probably never will be for airplanes. Electric power is only environmentally desirable if it is generated by non-polluting methods, such as wind, water, and solar. Moving to these methods is a challenge, but at least the replacement of automobiles and airplanes by trains makes it possible.

At present, passenger trains are too slow and too expensive to compete effectively with air travel, and do not cover enough routes to displace automobiles for interurban travel. However, a network of high-speed trains has the potential to be competitive. While trains cannot achieve the speed of airplanes, their routes start and end in central cities, and on journeys of up to 500 miles the door-to-door time for a train trip can be less. Obama has taken important steps to develop such a network. The American Recovery and Reinvestment Act (ARRA) included $8 billion for high-speed rail projects (White House). Then in February 2011 Vice President Biden announced that the administration would seek to dedicate $53 billion over six years in order to achieve the goal of having high-speed rail transportation accessible to 80 percent of the population in twenty-five years (White House. Office of the President 2011). If this pledge survives the budget process it will be a very significant environmental achievement indeed.

A fifth intermediate environmental priority of the Obama administration was to popularize the concept of "green jobs." The basic idea of green jobs is to counter the frequently-heard view that protecting the environment hurts the economy, and thereby eliminates jobs, because it is more expensive to produce commodities if the producer is prevented from discharging pollutants into the air, water, and soil. Green jobs advocates argue that environmental programs can create jobs, rather than destroying them, as more workers are needed to insulate houses, install solar collectors, build and operate windmills, and build railroad and mass transit lines, for example. In order to promote this idea, on March 9, 2009, Obama appointed Van Jones, a green jobs advocate, to a special position as advisor on green jobs, enterprise, and innovation within the Council on Environmental Quality (Burnham 2009).

Jones was an African American community organizer, the child of schoolteachers from Tennessee and a graduate of Yale Law School. He had published a book on the green jobs idea in 2007 (Jones and Conrad 2008), and had been promoting the idea effectively both during the 2008 campaign and before (Mufson 2008). However, Jones soon became the recipient of heavy public criticism for forthrightly radical political statements he had made in the past, when he had been a member of Standing Together to Organize a Revolutionary Movement (STORM), a revolutionary Black Marxist organization. Obama, following the course he had set during the controversy over Rev. Jeremiah Wright during his campaign, backed away from Jones, who resigned under pressure in September 2009 (Wilson and Franke-Ruta 2009). Jones's resignation was regarded as a setback by environmentalists; however, since his actual position was advisory, it has not prevented the Obama administration from continuing to push the idea of green jobs. Green jobs were an important part of the ARRA, and Obama continued to promote the concept in the 2011 State of the Union address, as discussed later in this chapter.

Priorities and Performance

These five programs are examples of the new pro-environment mindset that Obama has installed in the government. Perhaps the biggest effect of this mindset is that career employees were more likely to feel empowered to take strong environmental action within the parameters of their jobs. This should count as a very positive accomplishment.

However, the record on Obama's major environmental priorities and actions is more mixed. These included both a priority he chose, pursuing strong action against climate change, in contrast to the Bush administration's posture of denial, and a priority that was forced upon him, coping with the Deepwater Horizon oil spill. Each of these was characterized by a combination of strong talk with weak or failed action.

The administration pursued action on climate change through two channels, domestic legislation and international treaties; a third potential channel, the power of the Environmental Protection Agency to regulate carbon dioxide as a pollutant, was deferred initially, but is now being developed more seriously. Domestically, the administration called for major legislation to reduce carbon emissions. Internationally, Obama pledged to return to the international process of negotiating a successor to the Kyoto Protocol of the United Nations Framework Convention on Climate Change (UNFCCC), which will expire in 2012.

The administration supported major legislation on climate change, the Waxman-Markey bill (HR 2454), which passed the House on June 26, 2009, by a vote of 219-212. The bill contained a number of provisions, of which the most important were a requirement that utilities provide 20 percent of electricity through a combination of renewable sources and savings by 2020 and a cap-and-trade system for carbon dioxide emissions; it also authorized funds to help adapt to climate change, since it is generally agreed that a rise in global temperature of between 2 and 4 degrees Celsius can no longer be prevented.

The bill was problematic from the environmentalist standpoint, both in its definition of "clean coal" as a clean energy source, and its reliance on the cap-and-trade approach to reducing carbon emissions (more on both of these below), but it was still the most significant initiative on climate change ever undertaken by a U.S. president. Unfortunately, the bill went nowhere in the Senate, as Majority Leader Reid could not find enough votes to overcome a threatened filibuster. Senators Kerry (D-MA) and Lieberman (I-CT) introduced a different climate change bill on May 12, 2010. This bill still included cap-and-trade, but on an industry-by-industry basis, rather than for the economy as a whole; it also provided for subsidies for three less environmentally desirable energy sources, offshore oil drilling, "clean coal," and nuclear power. Many (but not all) environmental groups denounced the bill, which failed to pass in any case (Davenport 2010; Koss and Scholtes 2010). As of midterm, the president has failed to obtain action on climate change through the domestic legislation channel.

The International Context

A second channel for possible action on climate change was the international negotiations being conducted under the auspices of the UNFCCC, a treaty signed in 1992 at the Rio de Janeiro Earth Summit. As a framework convention, this treaty does not contain substantive provisions for the reduction of greenhouse gases, it simply provides a framework (periodic meetings of the parties to the treaty, and a secretariat) for working out such substantive agreements. The first such agreement, the Kyoto Protocol, was signed during the Clinton administration, in December 1997, but never ratified by the United States. In March 2001 President George W. Bush had withdrawn the United States from the Kyoto Protocol, but not from the UNFCCC (Eisner 2007:235–237; Keohane and Victor 2011:9–12). This withdrawal had been widely criticized, particularly by Democrats, and a pledge to return to the process was part of the Obama campaign (Promises About Environment on the Obameter). Although the administration did attempt to take a more serious role in the UNFCCC negotiations, this attempt ultimately failed, culminating with a whirlwind personal appearance by President Obama at the Copenhagen conference in 2009 that was perceived by many environmentalists as undermining the process he had pledged to rejuvenate.

Since Obama knew that he could not obtain the two-thirds vote in the Senate required to ratify the Kyoto Protocol, which will expire in 2012, he chose to focus on the successor treaty. The UNFCCC's plan was for this treaty to be signed at a conference in Copenhagen in December 2009, following a number of preparatory conferences at which the details would be worked out (United Nations Framework Convention on Climate Change).

However, as the date for the Copenhagen conference drew near it seemed increasingly less likely that a significant agreement would be reached. Neither the United States nor China was willing to make a binding agreement to reduce its greenhouse gas emissions by enough to prevent a damaging increase in the global temperature. Although many heads of state were present for the conference, Obama, perhaps seeking to evade the taint of failure, did not appear until the last day, when he gave a speech that David Corn characterized as "clearly venting," adding that "This was not a speech of persuasion; it was one of positioning" (Corn 2009). Rather than continuing the attempt to reach a formal agreement within the parameters of the UNFCCC, the United States, China, Brazil, India, and South Africa announced at the end of the conference that they had signed their own agreement, the Copenhagen Accord, and invited other countries to sign on to it (McKibben 2009). Obama then left the conference and returned to the United States.

The Copenhagen Accord simply stated that the signatories (of which there eventually came to be 114 as other countries signed on after the fact) were committed to making meaningful reductions in the emissions of greenhouse gases. Specifically, it declared that the parties to the Accord sought to limit the increase in average global temperature to 2 degrees Celsius. However, it did not contain targets for specific countries, a date by which the concentration of greenhouse gases should stop increasing, or a schedule for the negotiation of a binding treaty (Karaim 2011:3).

Obama presented it as a step forward, a "meaningful breakthrough" toward a binding agreement; others, including many of the environmentalists present at the conference, saw it as a weakening of the UNFCCC process that did nothing to advance action on climate change (Loven 2009). Bill McKibben referred to it as a "non-face-saving pact" among a "cartel of serious coal-burners [that] laid out the most minimal of frameworks" (McKibben 2009). The 15th Conference of the Parties (COP 15) of the UNFCCC decided formally to "take note" rather than endorse the Accord. In the year since the conference there has been no significant progress toward an agreement to replace the Kyoto Protocol when it expires.

One could debate whether Obama's pursuit of the Copenhagen Accord was the best course available to him at that moment. However, the situation looks very different if we adopt a slightly longer-term perspective. As Eric Pooley puts it:

> COP 15 was never going to produce a strong agreement; a binding global deal was out of reach because the U.S., as Obama conceded during his grueling fifteen-hour visit on the summit's final day, "was coming with a clean slate." America still hadn't passed a bill to cap and reduce greenhouse gas emissions. It had kept the world waiting a decade since walking away from the Kyoto Protocol. U.S. negotiators liked to talk about the "lesson of Kyoto," not agreeing to anything in the U.N. that they couldn't sell to the Senate. But other nations had a Kyoto lesson of their own: not agreeing to anything real until the U.S. proved it was serious by passing a climate bill (Pooley 2010:424).

A third possible channel for climate action is the regulation of carbon dioxide as a pollutant by the Environmental Protection Agency (EPA). Action through this channel had been deferred while the administration pursued legislation and international agreements; however, EPA is now moving ahead with the cumbersome process of setting regulations. As this is written there is a possibility that the budget bill, at least as passed by the House, will specifically prohibit use of funds for the purpose of regulating greenhouse gases. If Obama and the Senate Democratic majority are able to keep this provision out of the final budget, it is possible that more effective action on climate change will ensue, once the issue has worked its way through the regulatory process.

The BP Disaster and Its Ramifications

Obama's third major environmental priority was thrust upon him on April 20, 2010, when the Deepwater Horizon oil drilling platform exploded, breaking open the oil well named "Macondo" and letting more than two hundred million barrels of crude oil gush into the Gulf of Mexico until the well was permanently sealed on September 19 (Quigley and McNiff 2010). Here again the President talked tough, chastising the company responsible, BP, stating in a TV interview on June 8 that if he had been running BP he would already have fired the company's chief executive Tony Hayward, and declaring that he wanted to learn "whose ass to kick" (Lauer 2010). He ordered a freeze on new deep-water oil drilling on May 27, 2010, only to have his order lifted by a federal judge on June 22 (Wild 2010). (The judge in question, Martin Feldman, was later found to own stock in Transocean, the owner of the Deepwater Horizon (Freudenburg and Gramling 2011:59)). In the end, however, BP was left to deal with the problem on its own terms.

Although BP was forced to pledge at least $20 billion in compensation for damages from the spill, payout of those funds depends on determination of liability. Unresolved issues from the spill include the amount of missing oil in the ocean, the environmental consequences of the dispersants used to break up big concentrations of floating oil, and the long-term effects on marine life, including larval fish and shellfish (Borenstein 2010; Freudenburg, et al. 2011:157; Harris 2010).

The problems in coping with the spill may have been less a sign of ineffectiveness by the Obama administration than of the lack of government capacity. This was true both in the immediate sense that the government had to rely on BP itself to attempt to stop the spill, because only BP possessed the needed equipment and expertise, and in the deeper sense that the Minerals Management Service had proved incapable of effective regulation of drilling. The real test for Obama was whether he would be able to reform the relevant agencies so as to make them more competent to regulate drilling and cope with spills in the future. Early progress in this area has not been promising; despite Obama's pledge to reform the Minerals Management Service, that agency has continued to grant exemptions to underwater drilling regulations at the rate of one per day, including an exemption from full environmental studies for BP exploratory drilling at a depth of 4,000 feet, and for an exploration plan by Anadarko—one of BP's partners in the Macondo well—at 9,000 feet (Mezey 1979:56–57).

In addition, it has to be said that some of the Obama administration's stated environmental priorities are contrary to environmental preservation. These include what is being called "clean coal," the expansion of domestic energy exploration and drilling, and the choice of carbon trading as a mechanism for reducing the emission of greenhouse gases.

In February 2010, Obama issued a presidential memorandum laying out a federal strategy on carbon capture and storage. The memorandum began:

For decades, the coal industry has supported quality high-paying jobs for American workers, and coal has provided an important domestic source of reliable, affordable energy. At the same time, coal-fired power plants are the largest contributor to U.S. greenhouse gas emissions and coal accounts for 40 percent of global emissions. Charting a path toward clean coal is essential to achieving my Administration's goals of providing clean energy, supporting American jobs, and reducing emissions of carbon pollution. Rapid commercial development and deployment of clean coal technologies, particularly carbon capture and storage (CCS), will help position the United States as a leader in the global clean energy race (Obama 2010).

This is not the place to explore the origins of the phrase "clean coal." Suffice it to point out that the concept is meaningful if we are referring to low sulfur coal, the use of which decreases acid rain, but it is not meaningful when referring to climate change. Since carbon dioxide is the most abundant greenhouse gas, coal could only be "clean" if it contained no carbon—in which case it would not be coal at all, but some sort of nonflammable rock. What is really meant is not "clean coal," but "clean coal technology." This is another term for carbon sequestration or "carbon capture and storage" (CCS), capturing all the exhaust fumes from a coal-burning electricity plant and storing them somewhere permanently, so as to keep them out of the atmosphere. This is feasible technically, but only at great expense. It is hard to see how it could ever be cheap enough for practical use; yet Obama consistently advocates spending money to develop clean coal technology as a means of combating climate change. He has argued that such technology is needed because the nation cannot get by without the use of coal; however, it is hard to see this as anything except a sop to the coal industry. Unfortunately, given the generally low level of public understanding of climate science, the repeated references to "clean coal" by the President are likely only to sow confusion, and to delay progress toward replacing coal with energy sources that do not produce greenhouse gases.

From the environmental point of view, the Obama administration has been inconsistent in the area of oil and gas extraction, where he has endorsed potentially conflicting goals: greenhouse gas reduction on the one hand, and energy independence and job creation on the other. In February 2009 the administration approved going ahead with leasing for oil shale development, then reversed course partially, imposing more restrictions, in February 2011 (Associated Press 2011). Similarly, Obama announced in March 2010 that the government would open 167 million acres of ocean to oil and natural gas drilling, reversing a long-term ban on drilling from Delaware to Florida, an action that environmentalist Jacqueline Savitz described as "a wholesale assault on the oceans." Obama defended this policy change with the assertion that it was "time to move beyond the tired debates" over the desirability of offshore drilling (Broder 2010). Then in December, the administration announced that it would not allow new leases in the Atlantic or the eastern Gulf of Mexico from 2012-2017, a move described by Interior Secretary Salazar as "adjusting our strategy" (Eilperin 2010). While the policy change was commendable from the environmental point of view, the

President seemed to be operating without a larger vision of combating climate change, so that increasing the availability of oil and gas and limiting their use, while logically contradictory, appeared as equally important policy goals.

Obama's commitment to carbon trading, or "cap and trade," as his preferred method for greenhouse gas reduction is also problematic. Under a carbon trading regime major greenhouse gas emitters, such as coal and oil-burning utility plants, are given permits that limit the quantity of greenhouse gases they can release into the atmosphere. The permits are tradable. That is, a firm that does not emit its full quota of greenhouse gases can sell the right to emit them to someone else; and a firm that does not want or is not able to reduce its emissions to the required limit can instead purchase the right to emit an additional amount from someone who has an excess available. The amount of permitted emissions would be reduced every year in order to meet the eventual goal.

The advantage of cap and trade is the supposed flexibility of the market. The system creates an incentive for a firm to reduce its emissions more than required; if unused permits can be sold, firms have an incentive to invest in more efficient technology. At the same time, the system allows less efficient plants to stay in operation as long as they are willing to pay what is required to buy permits. However, as proposed in the Waxman-Markey bill, the cap-and-trade system has two serious drawbacks: free permits and offsets. Because of these drawbacks most climate activists prefer either a carbon tax or straightforward command-and-control regulation of greenhouse gases to carbon trading.
Although Obama had proposed that carbon-emission permits should be sold at auction, the bill as written provided that they would be given away to those needing them. Since permits are valuable, giving them away constitutes a subsidy to the polluters. As Alan Viard of the American Enterprise Institute put it, "A cap-and-trade system with freely allocated permits is equivalent to a carbon tax in which the tax revenue is given to stockholders" (Viard 2009). The permit giveaway cannot be blamed entirely on Obama, since the initiative came from Congress; however, he did little to oppose it, and the cap-and-trade system is prone to such abuses.

Giving away permits creates a corporate windfall, but does not affect the amount of greenhouse gas reduction achieved. Carbon offsets are another story. The basic idea of offsets is that instead of actually reducing carbon emissions, the emitter can pay someone else for an activity that removes carbon from the atmosphere. The problem with offsets is that it has proven extremely hard in practice to assure that the promised offsetting actually occurs. Offsets are already being traded among the parties to the Kyoto Protocol, with scandalous results. For example, the Sinar Mas corporation in Indonesia received carbon offset credits for planting a palm oil plantation, despite their having previously clear-cut an indigenous forest to make room for it (Fogarty 2009); in other cases, companies have claimed offset credit by claiming that they had planned to expand their operations, and would agree not to (Macalister 2009). Carbon offset payments are for future activity, not for something that has occurred already.

They have to be, since otherwise they would have no effect. However, this makes them essentially unverifiable, and therefore inherently open to fraud.

Ironically, "cap-and-trade" became the shorthand label used by conservatives to name what they objected to in Obama's approach, and in the Waxman-Markey bill. In 2008 Representative Michelle Bachmann (R-MN) declared that "cap-and-trade would be more aptly called 'tax and trade' or 'tax and spend,'" and that it amounted to "unilateral economic disarmament" (Bachmann 2008). By 2009, with Obama in office, she said on a Minnesota radio station that "I want people in Minnesota armed and dangerous on this issue of the energy tax because we need to fight back" (Galbraith 2009). On the other side of Capitol Hill, Senator Mitch McConnell (R-KY) was more forthright; cap-and-trade was a threat to jobs in the coal industry, he told the East Kentucky Independent Oil and Gas Association. "Think of it as a light switch tax, every time that you turn on a light, you would be paying this tax" (Rees 2009). However, it was clearly the cap, relabeled as a tax, that aroused the objections, rather than the trade. Since the permits were to be given away, there was actually no tax involved. Nevertheless, this rhetorical attack on the cap-and-trade concept contributed to the death of the Waxman-Markey bill in the Senate.

To sum up, during the first half of his term the President had followed what I have called the "Obama 1" approach. This approach began with open advocacy of strong policy measures, such as national health care, the stimulus bill, and a strong climate bill. The stimulus passed quickly, national health care passed with great difficulty and public acrimony, and the climate bill, made to wait on the other two, bogged down and died. As of the lame-duck session of Congress in December 2010, Obama 1 seemed to have been replaced by Obama 2, the compromiser and seeker of middle ground who worked with the Republicans in the House to extend the Bush-era tax cuts.

Obama 2 was on display for the 2011 State of the Union address. The President gave little mention to the environment as a policy goal, and none to coping with climate change. He jocularly cited the protection of salmon as an example of excessive red tape.[2] And, as Andrew Cohen points out, he presented environmental initiatives under the headings of job creation and competitiveness, rather than on environmental protection. Obama pledged to have one million electric cars in operation by 2015, and said:

> . . . clean energy breakthroughs will only translate into clean energy jobs if businesses know there will be a market for what they're selling. So tonight, I challenge you to join me in setting a new goal: By 2035, 80 percent of America's electricity will come from clean energy sources. Some folks want wind and solar. Others want nuclear, clean coal and natural gas. To meet this goal, we will need them all—and I urge Democrats and Republicans to work together to make it happen (Obama 2011).

Cohen argues that "These energy goals, when coupled with EPA's regulation of greenhouse gasses under the Clean Air Act, are the Obama climate policy. While it is less comprehensive than cap and trade or a carbon tax, it is a real, operational policy" (Cohen 2011). It is simply a policy that is presented as job creation. Obama 1 liked to talk about environmental job creation as well; the difference is that Obama 2 does not talk about anything else.

Conclusion

This brings us to our third sort of evaluative criteria, the adequacy of the Obama administration's actions to the environmental problems we face. Here the situation is very grave. The consensus of climate scientists is that the rise in average global temperature must be held to 2 degrees Celsius, and that doing so will require maintaining the atmospheric concentration of greenhouse gases at no more than 350 ppm (Pooley 2010:9–10). "Transgressing these boundaries will increase the risk of irreversible climate change, such as the loss of major ice sheets, accelerated sea-level rise and abrupt shifts in forest and agricultural systems." The current greenhouse gas concentration is about 390 ppm, already too high; the Global Humanitarian Forum has estimated that climate change, with the resulting natural disasters, is already resulting in about three hundred thousand deaths per year, and about $125 billion in economic loss (Karaim 2011:6). The GHG concentration is now increasing by about 2 ppm per year (Rockstrom 2009). Climate scientist James Hansen and others, in a recent paper, have concluded that a level of 450 ppm, long the target of government policy, "would push earth toward the ice-free state" (Hansen, et al. 2008).

There is a strong need to reduce GHG emissions in order to bring GHG concentration back to 350 ppm. Stealth approaches, such as presenting climate policies as job creation, are not adequate to the task, because they do not address the main barrier to effective climate action, namely public opinion. On the one hand, Americans have a high level of awareness of climate change compared to other nations. In 2009 the Gallup organization found that 97 percent of Americans were aware of climate change, 63 percent thought it would be a personal threat to them, and only 35 percent of those aware did not consider it a threat; this placed the level of climate awareness in the United States behind that in Japan, but ahead of those in Russia, China, and India among the top greenhouse gas emitters (Pugliese and Ray 2009). However, even the perception that climate change was a personal threat did not transfer completely into policy support. When asked a year later if Congress should "regulate energy output from private companies in an attempt to reduce global warming," only 56 percent were in favor, with 40 percent opposed (Saad 2010), and only 55 percent had favored signing a binding climate treaty in Copenhagen in December 2009 (Saad 2009).

These slight majorities in public opinion might still be converted into stronger public policy. However, the problem is that the positive opinions are not rooted in understanding of the problem. Climate-change denial, the belief that climate change is not actually happening, has faded away, although it took far too long to do so. What we have now is climate confusion, a situation where the public wants action on climate, but does not know which actions are appropriate. "Clean coal" is the best example of that. Most climate activists believe that we need to immediately begin to phase out the burning of coal, with a view to completing that phase-out as rapidly as possible. Carbon capture and storage, or "clean-coal technology," might be acceptable once it is available, but it is not available now, and if we wait until it is it will be too late to prevent catastrophic climate change.

Biofuels and biodiesel are another example. They sound green, they let us keep using automobiles as much as we want, and they are profitable for the agricultural industry. However, they have major flaws. They don't actually reduce carbon dioxide emissions; biofuels are carbohydrates, after all, and burning them produces carbon dioxide. The only advantage of biofuels is that they are made from newly-grown plants, so growing the plants takes carbon out of the atmosphere, which is then put back in when they are burned. That is an advantage over fossil fuels, which dig carbon out of the ground and spew it into the atmosphere. But biofuels are still much worse than solar, wind, or water power, which do not emit carbon dioxide at all.

Biofuels have a second major flaw: they divert land from food production. The increase in acreage for biofuel growth has contributed to the current high level of food prices, and to world hunger. Moreover, in some areas biofuel crops are grown on land which was formerly forested, so that they make a net positive contribution to atmospheric carbon dioxide.

The "lesson of Kyoto," discussed above, is that there are not enough votes in the Senate to ratify a strong climate treaty. The lesson of the Waxman-Markey bill is that there are not enough votes for strong climate legislation to overcome a filibuster, either. If that situation does not change, the United States will not take effective action on climate change; and if the United States does not act, the global problem will not be solved.

This political situation will change only if public opinion changes; so what is needed from the President is an intensive campaign of public education. It may well be the case that effective climate action would create jobs, develop new technology, and make the United States more competitive in the world market. Unfortunately, if the President talks only about the economic benefits, he is unlikely to develop political support for any policies that may be costly. From this perspective, President Obama's leadership on environmental issues has been poor.

Notes

1. The author would like to thank Kristen Hughes, a graduate student at Suffolk University, who contributed substantially to the research on which this chapter is based.
2. He cited as his "favorite example" of out-of-date bureaucratic organization that "the Interior Department is in charge of salmon while they're in fresh water, but the Commerce Department handles them when they're in saltwater. And I hear it gets even

more complicated once they're smoked." Of course, salmon are regulated by different agencies because they are treated in the context of their total environment, which changes during their life cycle (Obama 2011).

References

Associated Press. 2011. "Obama to Reexamine Shale's Role of Oil Shale [Sic]." *Standard-Examiner*, February 15. www.standard.net/topics/business/2011/02/15/obama-re-examine-shales-role-oil-shale

Bachmann, Michele. 2008. "'Cap and Trade?' More Like 'Tax and Spend'." StarTribune.Com, June 9. www.startribune.com/opinion/commentary/19678679.html?page=1&c=y

Berger, John. 1989. *The Success and Failure of Picasso*. New York: Pantheon.

Borenstein, Seth. 2010. "Major Study Charts Long-Lasting Oil Plume in Gulf." *Atlanta Journal-Constitution*, August 20. www.ajc.com/news/nation-world/major-study-charts-long-595511

Broder, John M. 2010. "Obama Oil Drilling Plan Draws Critics." *New York Times*, March 31. www.nytimes.com/2010/04/01/science/earth/01energy.html

Burnham, Michael. 2009. "Author-Activist Tapped as White House 'green' Jobs Adviser." *New York Times*, March 10. www.nytimes.com/gwire/2009/03/10/10greenwire-authoractivist-tapped-as-green-jobs-adviser10055.html?scp=7&sq=van%20jones&st=cse

Cohen, Steven. 2011. "The Transition from Environmental Politics to Sustainability Politics." *Huffington Post*, January 31. www.huffingtonpost.com/steven-cohen/the-transition-from-envir_b_816198.html

Corn, David. 2009. "Obama's Copenhagen Speech: The Collapse of a Deal?" *Huffington Post*, December 18. www.huffingtonpost.com/2009/12/18/obamas-copenhagen-speech_n_397152.html

Davenport, Coral. 2010. "Carbon-Cutting Bill Aims at 'Grand Bargain.'" *CQ Weekly*, May 17. 0-library.cqpress.com.library.law.suffolk.edu/cqweekly/weeklyreport111–000003664055

Egan, Dan. 2009. "$475 Million in Plan for Great Lakes." *Milwaukee Journal-Sentinel*, February 26. www.jsonline.com/news/wisconsin/40357712.html

Eilperin, Juliet. 2010. "Obama Administration Reimposes Offshore Drilling Ban." *Washington Post: Post Carbon*, December 1. voices.washingtonpost.com/post-carbon/2010/12/obama_administration_will_ban.html

Eisner, Marc Allen. 2007. *Governing the Environment: The Transformation of Environmental Protection*. Boulder, CO: Lynne Rienner.

Environmental Protection Agency. Great Lakes National Program Office. 2001. *Great Lakes Ecological Protection and Restoration: Great Lakes Ecosystem Report 2000*. Chicago: Environmental Protection Agency. epa.gov/greatlakes/rptcong/2001/index.html

Fogarty, David. 2009. "Indonesia Forest Projects Target 13 Mln CO2 Offset." *Reuters*, July 21. www.reuters.com/article/latestCrisis/idUSSP436960

Freudenburg, William R., and Robert Gramling. 2011. "Blowout in the Gulf: The BP Oil Spill Disaster and the Future of Energy in America." Cambridge, MA: MIT Press.

Galbraith, Kate. 2009. "Michele Bachmann Seeks 'Armed and Dangerous' Opposition to Cap-and-Trade." *New York Times*: Green, A Blog About Energy and the Environment, March 25. green.blogs.nytimes.com/2009/03/25/michele-bachmann-seeks-armed-and-dangerous-opposition-to-cap-and-trade/

Hansen, James, et al. 2008. "Target Atmospheric CO2: Where Should Humanity Aim?" *The Open Atmospheric Science Journal* 2(1) (December): 217-31.

Harris, Richard. 2010. "Scientists Find Thick Layer of Oil on Seafloor." All Things Considered, September 10. National Public Radio. www.npr.org/templates/story/story.php?StoryId=129782098

Jehl, Douglas. 2001. "E.P.A. to Abandon New Arsenic Limits for Water Supply." *New York Times,* March 21.

Jones, Van, and Ariane Conrad. 2008. *The Green-Collar Economy: How One Solution Can Fix Our Two Biggest Problems.* New York: HarperOne.

Karaim, Reed. 2011. "Climate Change." In Global Environmental Issues: Selections from CQ Researcher, CQ Researcher. Washington, DC: CQ Press.

Keohane, Robert O., and David G. Victor. 2011. "The Regime Complex for Climate Change." *Perspectives on Politics* 9(1) (March): 7-23.

Koss, Geof, and Jennifer Scholtes. 2010. "Senate Puts Off Broad Climate Change Bill; Vote on Narrow Version Expected This Week.*" CQ Weekly,* July 26. 0-library.cqpress.com.library.law.suffolk.edu/cqweekly/weeklyreport111–0000037093 22

Landers, Jay. 2010. "Federal 'Action Plan' Sets Ambitious Goals for Great Lakes Restoration." *Civil Engineering* 80(4) (April): 26-29.

Lauer, Matthew. 2010. "I Would Have Fired BP Chief by Now, Obama Says." Video interview with Barack Obama, June 8. www.msnbc.msn.com/id/37566848/ns/disaster_in_the_gulf/

Loven, Jennifer. 2009. "Copenhagen Deal Achieves 'Meaningful Breakthrough,' Obama Says." *Huffington Post,* December 18. www.huffingtonpost.com/2009/12/18/copenhagen-deal-achieves-_n_397872.html

Macalister, Terry. 2009. "Britain's Big Polluters Accused of Abusing EU's Carbon Trading Scheme." *Guardian,* January 27. www.guardian.co.uk/business/2009/jan27/industry-abusing-ets-carbon-trading

McKibben, Bill. 2009. "Copenhagen: Things Fall Apart and an Uncertain Future Looms," December 21. e360.yale.edu/feature/copenhagen_things_fall_apart_and_an_uncertain_future_looms/2225/

Melzer, Eartha Jane. 2010. "Great Lakes Spending Reduced in Obama Budget." *Michigan Messenger,* February 2. michiganmessenger.com/34213/great-lakes-spending-reduced-in-obama-budget

Mezey, Michael L. 1979. Comparative Legislatures. Gen. ed. Lloyd D. Musolf. Publications of the Consortium for Comparative Legislative Studies. Durham, NC: Duke University Press.

Mufson, Steven. 2008. "The Green Machine: Promoting the Future, Van Jones Has No Shortage of Energy." *Washington Post,* December 9. www.washingtonpost.com/wp-dyn/content/article/2008/12/08/AR2008120803569.html

"National Briefing-Washington: E.P.A. Is Sued on Arsenic Standard." 2001. *New York Times,* June 29.

Obama, Barack. 2010. Presidential Memorandum: A Comprehensive Federal Strategy on Carbon Capture and Storage. Washington: White House, Office of the Press Secretary, February 3. www.whitehouse.gov/the-press-office/presidential-memorandum-a-comprehensive-federal-strategy-carbon-capture-and-storage

Obama, Barack. 2011. Remarks of President Obama in the State of the Union Address—as Prepared for Delivery. Address. Washington: White House. Office of the Press Secretary. www.whitehouse.gov/the-press-office/2011/01/25/remarks-president-barack-obama-state-union-address-prepared-delivery

Pooley, Eric. 2010. *The Climate War: True Believers, Power Brokers, and the Fight to Save the Earth.* New York: Hyperion.

"Promises About Environment on the Obameter." Politifact.Com. *St. Petersburg Times.* www.politifact.com/truth-o-meter/promises/obameter/subjects/environment/?page=1

Pugliese, Anita, and Julie Ray. 2009. "Gallup Presents: A Heated Debate: Global Attitudes Toward Climate Change." *Harvard International Review* 31(3) (Fall): 64-68.

Quigley, Dana J., and Catherine McNiff. 2010. "2010 Gulf of Mexico Oil Spill Timeline." Infoplease. Pearson Education. www.infoplease.com/world/disasters/2010-gulf-oil-spill-timeline.html

Rees, Dara. 2009. "McConnell Speaks Out About Cap and Trade." *WYMT News,* August 12. www.wkyt.com/wymtnews/headlines/53085962.html

Rockstrom, J. Steffen. 2009. "A Safe Operating Space for Humanity: Identifying and Quantifying Planetary Boundaries That Must not Be Transgressed Could Help Prevent Human Activities from Causing Unacceptable Environmental Change, Argue Johan Rockstrom and Colleagues." *Nature* 461(7263) (September 24): 472-75.

Rojstaczer, Stuart. 2001. "Arsenic in water: how much is safe?" *New York Times,* March 21.

Saad, Lydia. 2009. "Americans Favor U.S. Signature on Copenhagen Treaty." *Gallup Politics,* December 15. www.gallup.com/poll/124712/Americans-Favor-Signature-Copenhagen-Treaty.aspx

Saad, Lydia. 2010. "Americans Back More Stimulus Spending to Create Jobs." *Gallup Politics,* June 17. www.gallup.com/poll/140786/Americans-Back-Stimulus-Spending-Create-Jobs.aspx

United Nations Framework Convention on Climate Change. The United Nations Climate Change Conference in Copenhagen, December 7-19, 2009. unfccc.int/meetings/cop_15/items/5257.php

Urbon, Steve. 2011. "Patrick Asks Obama to Intervene in Fishing Regulations." Southcoasttoday.Com, January 31. www.southcoasttoday.com/apps/pbcs.dll/article?AID=/20110131/NEWS/110139981

Viard, Alan. 2009. "The Cap-and-Trade Giveaway." *The American: The Journal of the American Enterprise Institute,* June 26. www.american.com/archive/2009/june/the-cap-and-trade-giveaway

White House. Office of the President. 2011. Vice President Biden Announces Six Year Plan to Build National High-Speed Rail Network. Washington: White House, February 8. www.whitehouse.gov/the-press-office/2011/02/08/vice-president-biden-announces-six-year-plan-build-national-high-speed-r

White House. "DOT Awards $2.4 Billion to Continue Developing 21st Century High-Speed Passenger Rail Corridors." www.whitehouse.gov/blog/2010/10/28/dot-awards-24-billion-continue-developing-21st-century-high-speed-passenger-rail-c-0

Wild, Matthew. 2010. "Gulf Drilling Freeze Lifted as Oil Disaster Worsens," June 23. peakgeneration.blogspot.com/2010/06/gulf-drilling-freeze-lifted-as-oil.html

Wilson, Scott, and Garance Franke-Ruta. 2009. "White House Adviser Van Jones Resigns Amid Controversy Over Past Activism." *Washington Post,* September 6. voices.washingtonpost.com/44/2009/09/06/van_jones_resigns.html

Chapter 5

Shifting Global Paradigms and Obama's Adaptive Foreign Policy

Lawrence C. Reardon

Introduction

During his inaugural address to the U.S. nation in January 2009, Barack Obama noted that the U.S. people were faced with a fundamental crisis of confidence, characterized by "a nagging fear that America's decline is inevitable, that the next generation must lower its sights" (Obama, 2009a).

The United States also was facing a crisis of legitimacy, as foreign countries questioned the preeminent U.S. role in global strategic and economic affairs enjoyed since the end of WWII. While initially garnering strong global support following the 9/11 attack on the World Trade Center, the Bush Administration planted the seeds of crisis with its adoption of the "war on terror" and the Bush Doctrine of preemptive war. These decisions led to the 2003 Iraq invasion and occupation as well as the abusive detentions at Abu Ghraib and Guantanamo Bay, all of which undermined U.S. moral authority (Cassin, 2006). The crisis also was rooted in the lack of U.S. economic oversight in mortgage-backed securities originating from U.S. banking and mortgage institutions. The bursting of the U.S. housing bubble in 2007 reverberated throughout the global economy and resulted in the greatest economic crisis since the global depression of the early 1930s (IMF, 2011a). Thus by the time President Obama was sworn into office, countries questioned the legitimacy of the U.S. use of force, its moral authority, and its global economic stewardship.

In less than one year, Obama transformed the international perception of crisis into one of hope and change. According to a survey conducted between May and June 2009 by the Pew Research Center's Global Attitudes Project, there was a dramatic increase in U.S. favorability ratings, especially in Western Europe and Latin America. People around the world strongly believed that the newly elected president would right the wrongs of the Bush administration by closing the Guantanamo military prison, withdrawing troops from Iraq, treating Middle East countries in a fair manner, and rejecting unilateral action to embrace multilateral cooperation (Pew, 2009). Perhaps the best indication of this transformation was the unanimous vote of the Nobel selection committee to recommend Barack Obama for the Nobel Peace prize. According to the selection committee chairman, Thorbyorn Iagland, Obama was responsible for a noticeable improvement of the international climate that had occurred between February and October 2009 (Erlanger and Stolberg, 2009). During this short period of time, Obama had changed the course of U.S. foreign policy to emphasize mutual interest and mutual respect, rejected unilateral actions that went against international norms of behavior, and emphasized the use of diplomacy and multilateral cooperation.

This hope for transformational change would dim by Obama's midterm, as the U.S. administration confronted growing difficulty in achieving its long-term political and economic policy objectives around the world. While no longer confronting a crisis of legitimacy, President Obama has adapted many Bush administration policies and experimented with new strategies to confront several long-term structural problems, including the growing U.S. debt, the strategic threats from Asia, the Middle East, and international terrorism, and the instability in the international economic regime.

Long-Term Structural Problems: The Debt

The most ominous structural problem facing the Obama administration was the U.S. deficit and its impact on the long-term U.S. debt. While the U.S. government enjoyed four successive years of budget surpluses during the 1990s Clinton administration, the $3.1 trillion in government outlays spent during FY2000 and FY2009 exceeded the $2.1 trillion in government revenue (figure 5.1); the 2009 debt figure totaled 53 percent of U.S. GDP. For the first half of FY2011, the U.S. government budget deficit totaled $830 billion (Delisle et al., 2011, 1), which prompted the International Monetary Fund (IMF) to issue an unusual public criticism of the United States for increasing fiscal outlays, which was "projected to contribute to an increase in the general government deficit to 10¾ percent of GDP, the largest among advanced economies this year [Note: 2011]." The IMF called upon U.S. leaders to adopt "credible measures to reduce debt ratios" (IMF, 2011b, x, 2). While maintaining the U.S. credit rating at triple A, the credit rating agency Standard & Poor's downgraded the U.S. outlook from

Figure 5.1. Total Outlays and Revenues as a Percentage of GDP

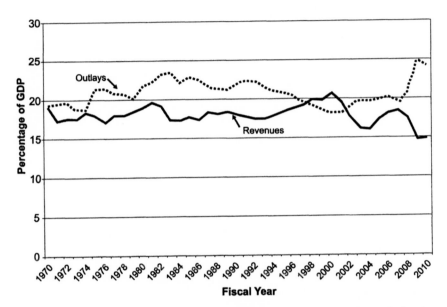

Source: Mindy R. Levit, *The FY2011 Federal Budget*, Congressional Research Service, August 4, 2010, p. 3.

"stable" to "negative," which "means there is a one-third chance of a downgrade in the next two years" (Harding, Politi, and Mackenzie, 2011).

In light of the IMF call for the United States to adopt "credible measures," President Obama and Congressional leaders initiated discussions on budget cutting measures in spring 2011. Republican House members focused on the growing costs of entitlement programs such as Social Security, Medicare, and Medicaid. In FY2010, outlays for these three entitlement programs totaled $695 billion; by FY2011, the Congressional Budget Office (CBO) estimated that total cost would rise to $728 billion (Delisle et al., 2011, 2). They also sought to reduce non-military discretionary spending, which included outlays for job creation, long-term benefit extensions, etc.

However, the president and the Congress continued to be fairly silent about financing discretionary expenditures related to the Iraq and Afghan wars, which were considered emergency funding for "overseas contingency operations" and thus exempt from the various caps and budget rules. Between FY2000 and FY2009, the military-related discretionary budget increased 5.3 percent in real terms per year, versus 3.6 percent growth for the non-military discretionary budget (Levit, 2010, 5). Between FY2000 and FY2010, funding for Operation Iraqi Freedom ($750.8 billion) and Operation Enduring Freedom in Afghanistan ($336 billion) totaled $1.087 trillion. Since President Obama's February 2009 decision to withdraw U.S. troops from Iraq, costs for the Iraqi military operation have dropped from $95.5 billion (FY2009) to $51 billion (FY2011). However, these savings were offset by the decision to expand operations in Afghanistan, which resulted in an increase from $59.5 billion (FY2009) to $119.4 billion (FY2011) (see figure 5.2). Partly as a result of the Afghan operation, the CBO estimated that there was an overall 1.7 percent increase in military expenditures between FY2010 ($335 billion) and FY2011 ($341 billion) (Delisle, et al., 2011, 2). As the financing of the decade-long conflicts is "off the books," the U.S. still must confront the long-term hidden financial costs of war, including the willingness of U.S. and foreign investors to invest in future federal debt issues (Cashell, 2010, 10).

Figure 5.2. Estimated War Funding: FY2001-FY2011 Request

Operation and Source of Funding	FY01 and FY02	FY03	FY04	FY05	FY06	FY07	FY08	FY09	FY10	FY2011 Request	Cum. Enacted: FY01-FY10	Cumulative Total: FY01-FY10 Including Request
IRAQ												
Department of Defense	0	50.0	56.4	83.4	98.1	127.2	138.5	92.0	61.1	45.8	706.7	752.5
State/USAID	0	3.0	19.5	2.0	3.2	3.2	2.7	2.2	3.3	3.9	39.0	43.0
VA Medical	0	0	0	0.2	0.4	0.9	0.9	1.2	1.5	1.4	5.1	6.5
Total: Iraq	0	53.0	75.9	85.5	101.6	131.2	142.1	95.5	65.9	51.1	750.8	802.0
AFGHANISTAN												
Department of Defense	20.0	14.0	12.4	17.2	17.9	37.2	40.6	56.1	99.5	113.5	314.8	428.4
State/USAID	0.8	0.7	2.2	2.8	1.1	1.9	2.7	3.1	4.9	4.6	20.2	24.9
VA Medical	0	0	0	0	0	0.1	0.1	0.2	0.5	1.2	1.0	2.1
Total: Afghanistan	20.8	14.7	14.5	20.0	19.0	39.2	43.5	59.5	104.9	119.4	336.0	455.4

Source: Amy Belasco. 2010. "The Cost of Iraq, Afghanistan, and other Global War on Terror Operations since 9/11." September 2, Washington, DC: Congressional Research Service, No. RL33110, p. 14.

Long-Term Structural Problems: Strategic Competitors

By the end of World War II, the great powers initially agreed to establish the United Nations Security Council, whose membership included the five victorious powers as permanent members (P5) and ten non-permanent members chosen from various regional groupings. Although responsible for maintaining international peace and security, the Security Council was essentially superseded by the two global superpowers during the Cold War. While the G4 nations (Brazil, Germany, India, and Japan) have called for changes among the permanent membership in the post-Cold War era, the current ability of the UN Security Council to maintain world peace ultimately depends on the cooperative actions of the unipolar power and the international security and economic community, which includes the second tier powers of the European Union and Japan. As the unipolar power, the long-term goals of the United States have been "to prevent the rise of a peer competitor but also to stamp out terrorism, maintain an open economic system, spread democracy throughout the world, and establish a high degree of cooperation among countries that remain juridically equal" (Jervis, 2009, 210).

To remain the unipolar power, the United States must continue to meet its international military obligations that were first undertaken during the Cold War, conduct its global "war on terror," as well as confront the growing strategic threats from Asia and the Middle East. The United States thus has maintained 1.13 million active-duty military personnel in the United States and has deployed over 500,000 troops overseas. A substantial percentage of these overseas troops are meeting Cold War military obligations, including 78,580 based in NATO countries, 34,385 in Japan, and 28,500 in South Korea (U.S. Department of Defense, 2010; U.S. Department of State, 2010). The United States must constantly maintain and modernize these forces, especially in light of the growing sophistication of foreign conventional and nuclear military forces and international terrorist groups.

The Obama administration continues to face the long-term threat from international terrorism; the administration is especially concerned that groups such as al Qaeda can gain access to weapons of mass destruction (WMD) such as chemical, biological, radiological, and nuclear weapons. Since October 2001, the United States has pursued its "war on terror," resulting in various types of military operations carried out in countries such as Afghanistan, Iraq, Yemen, the Philippines, Georgia, and Colombia (Perl, 2007). Of these operations, the most controversial was Operation Iraqi Freedom, which was launched on March 20, 2003, in order to prevent Saddam Hussein from using WMD and to establish a democratic government that would promote a more peaceful Middle East. After six years and the deaths of 4,415 U.S. troops and countless numbers of Iraqi civilians, the Bush administration negotiated a timely withdrawal of U.S. forces with the November 2008 U.S.-Iraq Status of Forces Agreement. The Obama administration subsequently announced in February 2009 the withdrawal of U.S. troops; renamed Operation New Dawn, approximately 50,000 troops will remain in Iraq as advisors until December 2011.

Concurrent with the Iraqi pullout, President Obama announced in his 2009 West Point speech to expand a Bush initiative to increase the number of combat troops in Afghanistan by 30,000 troops to total over 100,000 troops; Obama also announced his intention to begin withdrawing these troops in July 2011. Concurring with President Bush, President Obama stated that defeat of the al Qaeda in Afghanistan is a core interest of the United States. However Goodson and Johnson argue that the strategies implemented by Bush and adapted by Obama (i.e., to concentrate on the key Afghan population centers, to reconcile with the Taliban, and to replace NATO troops with Afghan troops) are similar to the failed Soviet strategies of the 1980s (Goodson and Johnson, 2011). As for closing the Guantanamo Bay detention center, President Obama initially issued an executive order on January 22, 2009, to suspend all legal proceedings at Guantanamo with the ultimate intention of closing the facility. However by March 2011, the president changed his mind and signed a second executive order allowing for indefinite detention for the remaining 172 terrorist detainees, who would now be tried by military commissions and not by the federal government (Finn and Kornblut, 2011).

Osama bin Laden would not join his fellow terrorists incarcerated in Guantanamo. After reportedly failing to capture bin Laden during the December 2001 battle of Tora Bora, U.S. military and intelligence agencies conducted a ten-year search, which culminated in a U.S. operation that killed bin Laden in Abbottabad, Pakistan on May 2, 2011. As the terrorist leader responsible for the bombings of the U.S. embassies in Tanzania and Kenya, the bombing of the USS Cole in 2000, and the September 11 attacks on the World Trade Center and the Pentagon, the death of the founder and leader of al Qaeda was a symbolic victory for the U.S. "war on terror." Secretary of State Hillary Clinton stated on May 2, 2011 that "History will record that bin Laden's death came at a time of great movements toward freedom and democracy, at a time when the people across the Middle East and North Africa are rejecting the extremist narratives and charting a path of peaceful progress based on universal rights and aspirations. There is no better rebuke to al Qaeda and its heinous ideology" (Clinton, 2011). However bin Laden's death most probably was not a major strategic loss for the global terrorist networks, which are fairly decentralized and located around the world.

While continuing to focus on the "war on terror" in Iraq and Afghanistan, the Obama administration also contended with the growing strategic threats from Asia and the Middle East. According to a 2009 Pew Global Attitude survey of twenty-five countries, thirteen countries believed that China has already or will replace the United States as the world's next superpower; two countries believed China was already the world's primary economic power (Pew, 2009, 43). Of the twenty-two countries surveyed in 2010, eight countries including the United States believed that China was the primary global economic power (Pew, 2010, 41). This public attitude is reflected in current popular commentary. Without a doubt, China's implementation of nearly thirty years of outwardly-oriented economic development enabled China to surpass Japan in 2010 to become the second largest country in the world in terms of GDP (IMF, 2011c). The Chinese technocratic leadership has used its $3 trillion in foreign currency reserves to finance domestic infrastructure projects such as high-speed trains and highways as well as securing raw materials in Africa, Australia, and Latin America necessary for China's continued industrial and export growth.

However, it is also important to remember that public opinion in the 1970s and 1980s exaggerated the military and economic strength of the Soviet Union and considered Japan to be the next "number one." Current public perception masks the reality of China, which remains a developing economy with low investment in education, low management skills, a poor competitive climate, a lack of technological innovation, and a growing gap of wealth inequality surpassing the United States. (Qu, 2011). Thus according to the United Nations Development Program (UNDP), China was ranked in 2010 as a "medium level" country and only reaching eighty-ninth in its human development index (UNDP, 2010). As for military power, the U.S. Department of Defense considers China's current ability to project its military power abroad for an extended period to be very limited (U.S. Department of Defense, 2010).

Despite these current problems, China has the desire and the financial capability to become a top military power. "China is developing and fielding large numbers of advanced medium-range ballistic and cruise missiles new attack submarines equipped with advanced weapons, increasingly capable long-range air defense systems, electronic warfare and computer network attack capabilities, advanced fighter aircraft, and counter-space systems." Once acquired, China will be able to attack "up to 1,000 nautical miles from the PRC coast." Thus in the future, China will be able to effectively engage military forces in Taiwan, the East and South China Seas, and portions of the Indian Ocean and the western Pacific (U.S. Department of Defense, 2010, I, 30-33).

China also continues to improve and modernize its medium and intercontinental missiles that can deliver a nuclear payload to most places around the world. China is developing advanced technologies, such as the J-20 stealth fighter, which made its first test flight during Secretary of Defense Robert Gates's visit to Beijing in January 2011. While the J-20 is an early prototype without any proven stealth capability, Chinese military authorities are using overt and covert means to obtain the technology necessary to defend China's "national interest." Perhaps realizing China's growing military potential, Robert Gates argued one month after his return that "any future defense secretary who advises the president to again send a big American land army into Asia or into the Middle East or Africa should 'have his head examined,' as General MacArthur so delicately put it" (Shanker, 2011).

In addition to the rising Chinese power, the United States must also contend in the long-term problem of nuclear proliferation and the missiles to deliver nuclear warheads, especially in regards to rising regional powers such as North Korea and Iran. In 1968, sixty-eight countries signed the Nuclear Non-Proliferation Treaty (NPT), which set forth the norms of non-proliferation, disarmament, and peaceful use of nuclear technology. Nearly a decade later in 1987, the Missile Technology Control Regime (MTCR) was established to restrict the transfer of missiles and related technology that could deliver a nuclear warhead 300 kilometers or more in distance. Currently 34 member nations are MTCR members, while another 131 members adhere to the Hague Code of Conduct against Ballistic Missile Proliferation established in 2002 (Hagûlh)na, Iran, and North Korea are not members of these proliferation regimes. Having withdrawn from the NPT in 2003, the North Koreans subsequently agreed to participate in six-party talks, which included the South Koreans, the United States, China, Russia, and Japan. In the middle of the fifth round of talks, the North Koreans exploded their first nuclear weapon on October 9, 2006; North Korea subsequently sold a nuclear plant to Syria, which was destroyed by the Israelis in 2007 (Lee, 2010). After 2007, they ended their participation in the six-party talks; by 2009, North Korea exploded a second nuclear weapon, test-fired their intercontinental ballistic missile, the Taepodong-2, expelled International Atomic Energy Agency (IAEA) nuclear inspectors, and announced their intention to resume building nuclear weapons. In order to inspect and disable the Yongbyon nuclear facilities and reenergize the six-party talks, the Bush administration in October 2008 delisted North Korea as a state sponsor of terrorism in the Department of State's annual global terrorism report to the U.S. Congress (Manyin, 2010, 4-10).

Following the North Korean sinking of the South Korean corvette Cheonan in March 2010, and the shelling of the South Korean island of Yeonpyeong in November, the Obama administration decided to tighten sanctions in a new executive order issued on April 18, 2011, that forbade "the importation into the United States, directly or indirectly, of any goods, services, or technology from North Korea," and obligating the U.S. Treasury secretary to "take such actions, including the promulgation of rules and regulations, and to employ all powers granted to the president by the International Emergency Economic Powers Act and the United Nations Participation Act of 1945 as may be necessary to carry out the purpose of this order" (Obama, 2011).

As for Iran, China sold technology to enrich Iranian stockpiles of uranium; these sales stopped after 1997. By 2011, "Beijing [sought] to convince U.S. leaders that China is a willing and responsible partner in maintaining the NPT regime, but it also helps Iran win the time, international space, and continuing economic wherewithal necessary for it to push its nuclear plans to a successful outcome" (Garver, 2011, 86). Despite the UN Security Council's 2006 call to suspend nuclear reprocessing, the Iranians continued to enrich uranium at several facilities, refused to provide a "substantive response" concerning the construction of ten new uranium enrichment facilities or suspend work on heavy water related projects, and engage in research and development (IAEA, 2011).

According to a Wikileaks release of a U.S. diplomatic cable dated February 24, 2010, the North Koreans sold nineteen BM-25 missiles to Iran, which have the capacity to deliver a nuclear warhead to Moscow and other European capitals (Broad, Glanz, and Sanger, 2010). Reporting on UN Security Council sanctions on North Korean imports and exports since 2009, a UN sanctions committee stated that North Korea has used various shell companies and barter arrangements to secretly transfer "nuclear-related and ballistic missile-related equipment, knowhow and technology" to Burma, Iran, Syria and other countries (McElroy, 2010). The IAEA is specifically concerned that Iran is developing a missile capable of delivering a nuclear payload (IAEA, 2011, 12). Such actions have convinced some U.S. policy makers that North Korea should reverse the Bush Administration's 2008 decision and reinstated North Korea on the U.S. list of terrorism-supporting countries (Manyin, 2010).

Long-Term Structural Problems:
International Economic Regime

To avoid the international economic conflicts and wars that had occurred during the inter-war period, forty-four global economic powers met at the Mount Washington Hotel in 1944 to establish a new set of rules and norms regarding international economic conduct that would eventually be known as the Bretton Woods System. Policy makers hoped that the newly established IMF and World Bank would guarantee a more transparent and stable international financial system that would allow member countries easy access to short-term loans to overcome balance of payments difficulties, access to long-term loans for post-war reconstruction and large-scale infrastructure projects, as well as access to advice and guidance necessary to maintain a healthy domestic and global economy. The International Trade Organization (ITO) would guarantee equal treatment of goods, greater transparency and a venue to resolve trade disputes.

Since its establishment, there have been two fundamental readjustments of the Bretton Woods system. Originally designed to rely on contributions from all member countries, the IMF and World Bank did not have sufficient capitalization in the early post-war era to resolve European balance of payments difficulties or finance its reconstruction. The U.S. Congress refused to ratify the Havana Charter, as it considered the ITO as a supranational organization that would regulate domestic economic affairs, such as those of the United States. As a result of these problems and the fear of communism in the late 1940s, the United States provided the world economy with liquidity by pumping the global economic system with U.S. dollars through the European Recovery Program (Marshall Program) and by incurring a balance of payments deficit; the ITO was replaced by the General Agreement on Tariffs and Trade (GATT), which was a far more decentralized organization that lowered trade barriers through a series of consensual trade rounds. The second fundamental readjustment occurred after the global markets determined that President Johnson's domestic war on poverty and international war on communism were creating increasingly larger balance of payment deficits and weakening U.S. long-term growth. With the depletion of U.S. gold reserves and growing U.S. inflation, President Nixon readjusted the Bretton Woods system in August 1971 by unilaterally revoking the convertibility of the U.S. dollar into gold, which had been the key source of global liquidity over the years.

With the introduction of a floating exchange system and the emergence of new global economic actors, the United States retained its hegemonic role as the global economic power. However, the United States sought to coordinate macroeconomic policy by meeting on a regular basis with the foreign and finance ministers of the other highly industrialized economies (Canada, France, Germany, Italy, Japan, the United Kingdom, and by 1998 Russia); their coordinated responses were reflected in the positions they took within the IMF and World Bank. Such coordination was critical in the 1980s as the U.S. dollar had appreciated by 50 percent against the British Pound, the German Mark, and the Japanese Yen. With the signing of the Plaza Accord that reduced the value of the U.S. dollar by 30 percent, the United States increased exports, reduced its deficit, and recovered from the recession of the early 1980s. The G7/8 subsequently coordinated policies to stabilize the international currency markets (Louvre Accord of 1987), the Mexican "bailout" of 1994, the cancellation of $40 billion of debt belonging to the world's poorest countries in 2004-5 as well as other transnational problems such as the environment, AIDS, and terrorism (Nelson, 2009, 3-4).

Such coordination could not prevent the Asian Financial Crisis of 1997, which had a devastating impact on Indonesia, South Korea, and Thailand. While providing various financial rescue packages to the affected economies, the IMF and its "Washington Consensus" approach to promoting the free market were blamed for the ensuing political and economic upheavals in the Asian region. As the World Bank's chief economist stated:

> The success of the Washington consensus as an intellectual doctrine rests on its simplicity: its policy recommendations could be administered by economists using little more than simple accounting frameworks. A few economic indicators—inflation, money supply growth, interest rates, budget and trade deficits—could serve as the basis for a set of policy recommendations. Indeed, in some cases economists would fly into a country, look at and attempt to verify these data, and make macroeconomic recommendations for policy reforms all in the space of a couple of weeks (Stiglitz, 1998, 3).

While the Asian crisis did not have as detrimental an impact on the U.S. and European economies, G7 leaders realized the need of more regularized meetings between the G7 and a small group of emerging economies who had become increasingly important players in the international economy. Leaders could better share more information, coordinate macroeconomic policies, and enforce agreed upon norms of behavior.

The G20 was subsequently established in 1999 as a loosely organized group of finance ministers and central bank governors of nineteen countries, including the G7, the BRIC countries (Brazil, Russia, India, and China), Indonesia, South Africa, and South Korea that make up two-thirds of the world's population and 90 percent of its GNP (www.g20.org). The G20 has had difficulty coordinating action, as it is without a centralized bureaucracy and its membership enjoys various different political and economic structures.

However as the global financial crisis became acute after 2007, the G20's power and influence has grown exponentially (Nelson, 2009, 4). President Sarkozy of France has even suggested that the G20 should take ultimate authority over the IMF. Thus the annual meetings of the G20 also include:

> The president of the World Bank, the managing director of the IMF and the chairs of the International Monetary and Financial Committee and the Development Committee in the G-20 meetings [,which] ensures that the G-20 process is well integrated with the activities of the Bretton Woods Institutions. The G-

20 also works with, and encourages, other international groups and organizations, such as the Financial Stability Board and the Basel Committee on Banking Supervision, in progressing international and domestic economic policy reforms. In addition, experts from private-sector institutions and non-government organizations are invited to G-20 meetings on an ad hoc basis in order to exploit synergies in analyzing selected topics and avoid overlap (www.g20.org).

Actions taken by the G20 have already prompted the IMF to increase regulatory reforms of "systemically important" financial institutions (Giles, 2011) and adopt the Seoul Development Consensus in 2010, which was designed to replace the Washington Consensus model by allowing a greater role for government intervention (Oxfam, 2010).

While continuing the Bush administration's strategy of cooperating with the G7/8 and G20, the Obama administration has not initiated any fundamental reforms of the international financial system. "The obsessive accumulation of dollars by emerging markets, led by China, exacerbates global current account imbalances. By shoveling vast amounts of cheap lending at the United States, such reserve accumulation also facilitates the credit bubble that led to the global financial crisis" (*Financial Times* Editorial, 2011). In light of U.S. economic difficulties, President Nicholas Sarkozy of France has suggested that the role of the U.S. dollar as the global reserve currency should be reevaluated, as its loss in value had a negative impact on commodity prices and international trade. This was especially true after the United States approved an economic stimulus package that pumped $600 billion into the U.S. economy in 2010.

The international trade regime originally established by the Bretton Woods agreements in 1944 has also encountered major long-term structural problems. The GATT successfully reduced international barriers to trade and investment by instituting a series of trade negotiation rounds. During the Uruguay Round that was concluded in 1994, member states agreed that the GATT would be superseded by the World Trade Organization (WTO), which had a greater capability to monitor the established norms of international trade, such as non-discrimination, reciprocity, and transparency. In comparison with the GATT, the most important change to the WTO was the empowering of the Dispute Settlement Body, which settles complaints against member states, and thus attempts to avoid "tit-for-tat" retaliation that led to the various international trade conflicts during the GATT period.

Unfortunately, the WTO failed to reach an agreement on a new round of negotiations. In November 2001, the WTO initiated a ninth round of multilateral trade negotiations, the Doha Development Round. The first major hurdle occurred in 2007, when President Bush lost congressional fast track trade authority, which had allowed the president to negotiate at Doha without fear that the U.S. Congress would amend or filibuster the finalized agreement. Subsequently, the United States, China, and India failed in 2008 to reach an agreement on the ability of developing countries to impose import tariffs on agricultural goods that had incurred a price decrease or a surge of imports of foreign goods. This failure has imperiled agreement on several contentious issues, such as international trade in agriculture, intellectual property rights, and special treatment accorded to developing countries.

As with the fundamental reforms of the global financial system, President Obama has yet to proffer any new initiative to break through the Doha impasse. To counter Chinese criticisms, the president did state that he did not want to start the negotiations from the beginning, but that significant changes were necessary before agreement could be reached (Corcoran, 2010). While the G20 has issued a statement of principles on international trade and an international code on trade, President Obama failed in his attempt for the G20 to provide a detailed code of behavior that would limit foreign reserves and trade surpluses (Schneider and Wilson, 2010).

As the Obama administration entered into the second half of the presidential term, the president negotiated with the House Republicans over a long-term strategy to reduce the deficit and the overall debt. While continuing to finance expensive Cold War military obligations, the Obama administration adapted Bush administration policies or searched for alternate strategies to deal with the global "war on terror," the current military operations in the Middle East, the nuclear proliferation and missile control regimes, and emerging powers in Asia and the Middle East. Economically, the Obama administration continued the Bush policy of multilateral management of international financial transactions, but failed to initiate any fundamental change in the Bretton Woods system, where the dollar continued to be the primary reserve currency and international trade negotiations remained at an impasse.

In sum, the Obama administration's adaptations of post-war security and economic arrangements have worked in certain areas, while becoming increasingly ineffectual in other areas, thus endangering the achievement of long-term strategic and economic goals of the United States.

Understanding Policy Adaptations: The Ideational Learning Model

To understand the Obama administration foreign policy initiatives, this study argues that the Obama administration has shared the long-term policy objectives with the previous Bush administration, which are to promote a strong and secure nation, a healthy economy, and the establishment of a peaceful, democratic, and market-oriented community of nations. However, the two administrations' policy elites held differing views on the strategies to achieve the state's long-term goals. By his midterm, President Obama continued to adapt previous Bush administration strategies as well as failed to undertake paradigmatic change in international strategic and economic structures originally established at the end of World War II.

One approach to analyzing the foreign policy process is the ideational learning model, which focuses on the individual, their Weltanschauung, and how their policy preferences influence policy formation over time. As the core actor that enjoys the most privileged position of leadership, policy elites form a relatively well-defined group, which can overcome the objections of other groups or individuals (Dahl, 1958, 466). For the purposes of this chapter, U.S. foreign policy elites include the president, vice president, heads of the fifteen executive departments, the director of national intelligence, cabinet-ranked officials such as the United States Trade Representative, the UN ambassador, as well as key officials within the National Security Council and the National Economic Council. According to rational choice institutionalism, these policy elites consciously pursue long-term goals at the lowest possible cost, and desire to build a secure and prosperous state that would ensure their political party's continued rule.

Policy elites "arrive at their theories by inductive processes, as they look to the past for information, understanding, and inspiration" (Adler, 1992, 17). Their choice of strategies is influenced by certain endogenous and exogenous variables: their Weltanschauung based on previous interactions with the international and domestic sectors; interactions with other actors pursuing their long-term goals; access to production inputs such as capital, land, and labor, etc. Opinion groups form around a collective consensus over the strategies to achieve long-term goals; over a period of time, each opinion group gains longitudinal learning, which they utilize in adapting strategies to make them more effective (Moltz, 1993, 24f).

Key foreign policy elites in the Bush Administration such as Vice President Cheney, Secretary of Defense Rumsfeld, Deputy Defense Secretary Paul Wolfowitz, and the Defense Policy Board Advisory Committee Chairman Richard Perle, developed their world view during the Cold War era while working in executive branch and the Department of Defense during the previous Republican administrations. As unilateral realists, these policy elites believed the United States was the unipolar power that must aggressively take action, even if it contravened international laws and norms, in order to achieve U.S. long-term goals (Bilgin and Morton, 2002). Thus in December 2001 the United States unilaterally withdrew from the 1972 Anti-Ballistic Missile Treaty. Following 9/11, President Bush argued in the National Security Strategy of the United States issued in September 2002 that the United States would destroy terrorist threats by:

> . . . defending the United States, the American people, and our interests at home and abroad by identifying and destroying the threat before it reaches our borders. While the United States will constantly strive to enlist the support of the international community, we will not hesitate to act alone, if necessary, to exercise our right of self-defense by acting preemptively against such terrorists, to prevent them from doing harm against our people and our country (Bush, 2002).

Such unilateral action resulted in the use of coercive force to establish a democratic Middle East, starting with the Iraq invasion of 2003. Instead of leading by example (Monten, 2005, 113), these elites embraced a proactive strategy of preemptive war to achieve the United States' long-term goals to promote a strong and secure nation, a healthy economy, and the establishment of a peaceful, democratic, and market-oriented community of nations.

During its first two years, the Obama administration was composed of cooperative realists such as Secretary of State Hillary Clinton and the UN representative Susan Rice, who gained foreign policy experience during the post-Soviet era, and believe the United States must strive to cooperate with its global partners to achieve U.S. long-term goals; only under extraordinary circumstances should the state act unilaterally. According to President Obama's National Security Strategy of the United States issued in May 2010:

> We will draw on diplomacy, development, and international norms and institutions to help resolve disagreements, prevent conflict, and maintain peace, mitigating where possible the need for the use of force. . . . When force is necessary, we will continue to do so in a way that reflects our values and strengthens our legitimacy, and we will seek broad international support, working with such institutions as NATO and the U.N. Security Council.
>
> The United States must reserve the right to act unilaterally if necessary to defend our nation and our interests, yet we will also seek to adhere to standards that govern the use of force. Doing so strengthens those who act in line with international standards, while isolating and weakening those who do not. We will also outline a clear mandate and specific objectives and thoroughly consider the consequences—intended and unintended—of our actions (Obama, 2010).

Instead of actively imposing its ideals by unilateral force (Monten, 2005, 113), these elites embraced a soft power strategy of leading through example to achieve the United States' long-term goal to promote a strong and secure nation, a healthy economy, and the establishment of a peaceful, democratic, and market-oriented community of nations. This focus on elite Weltanschauung and how it can change over time is the core idea of the ideational learning model.

The new institutionalist literature provides various useful concepts and measures, especially as many theories focus on the role of ideas in bringing about institutional order and change (Hall and Taylor, 1995). Peter A. Hall incorporates learning process dynamics in his work on paradigm shifts from Keynesian to monetarist regimes in Great Britain (Hall, 1993). Interestingly, Mark Blyth observes that such approaches primarily focus on institutional change, while ideas play a secondary role (Blyth, 2002). This study adopts Blyth's emphasis on ideas while incorporating concepts and measures from the new institutionalist literature.

Elites' views are not static, but change whenever elites undergo simple and complex learning. To determine the best strategies, elites employ a simple learning process, which "uses new information merely to adapt the means, without altering any deeper goals in the ends-mean chain. The actor simply uses a different instrument to attain the same goal" (Nye, 1987, 380). Simple learning occurs when elites review the effectiveness of existing policies either as a routine matter or as a result of implementation problems or crisis; simple learning also takes place when elites experiment with new policy strategies (Heilmann, 2008, 3-5). Simple learning can result in relatively minor or routine adaptations of policy (first order changes), or large-scale policy adaptations, which are not "radically altering the hierarchy of goals behind policy" (second order changes) (Hall, 1993, 281-282).

Thus ideational learning involves simple learning that results in a series of policy adaptations. Under rare evolutionary or revolutionary circumstances, these strategy adaptations can fail over time, which results in "anomalies" and paradigm shifts (Kuhn, 1962). Strategy adaptations are unable to overcome basic flaws or contradictions in the state's long-term goals; crisis created by such failures can act as a catalyst for complex thinking. Elites who have gained expertise over time in a particular policy field (longitudinal learning) and "new thinkers" who enjoy "highly complex cognitive schemata [and] are more sensitive to new information" recognize these anomalies as a paradigm failure and question the long-term goals of the state (Stein, 1994, 165). These elites can undergo a complex learning process, which "involves recognition of conflicts among means and goals in causally complicated situations, and lead to new priorities and trade-offs" (Nye, 1987, 380). Complex learning can result in a paradigm shift, which radically alters long-term goals and the strategies to achieve those goals (third order change) (Hall, 1993, 283-287).

Paradigm shifts can be either comprehensive or sectoral. Comprehensive paradigm shift occurs when revolutionary elites undergo complex learning initiated by the complete rejection of the policy adaptations adopted by the country's ruling elites. As when the Soviet and Chinese Communist revolutionaries assumed political leadership in 1917 and 1949 respectively, they become the new policy elites, who completely transform the state's political, economic, and social structures. Sectoral paradigm shift occurs when policy elites learn that adaptations of policy strategies have failed over time. Policy elites replace the existing sector's structure with one consistent with the state's long-term goals and strategies to achieve those goals. Sectoral paradigm shifts include many of the anti-authoritarian "color" revolutions in Eastern Europe and Central Asia since 2000 (political), China's transition from a revolutionary to techno-economic paradigm (economic), and the United States' adoption of the Civil Rights Act of 1964 (social).

Ideational Learning in Democratic Regimes

In comparison to elites in authoritarian states (Reardon, 2002), elites in democratic states such as the United States lack the autonomy to formulate policy and the capacity to implement specific strategies because of the existence of a vigorous civil society. While distributional coalitions and the electoral cycle influence the elites' ability to learn in a continuous fashion, previous lessons learned are often implemented at an incremental pace. Holding different Weltanschauung, policy elite opinion groups learn different lessons from similar events; they thus hold different opinions concerning strategy adaptations, but can only implement lessons they have learned when they are elected to power (Moltz, 1993, 305).

The perception of crisis acts as a catalyst to delegitimize the ruling opinion group and its preferred strategies to achieve long-term goals. After readjusting the previous strategy, the newly empowered policy elite opinion group introduces second order changes based on the results of strategy implementation of the past (simple learning/adaptation) or by experimenting with new strategies. If problems that occur during the implementation phase cannot be corrected by strategy adaptations, the crisis cycle is reinitiated (Reardon, 2002, 37-46). Policy cycling results in incremental learning. In relatively rare circumstances, this incremental learning process can create the conditions for complex learning, which brings about third order changes—or in Kuhnian terms, a paradigm shift.

The Perception of Crisis

The primary catalyst initiating the learning process in democratic and authoritarian regimes is crisis, which can be brought about by revolutionary political change, severe economic downturns and/or political upheavals, or the death of paramount leaders. Crises involve all the top policy elites, who are pressured to enact dramatic change to prevent total political or economic disorder (Grindle and Thomas 1991, chapter 4). States often reacted to impending crisis by changing political and/or economic policies. President Lyndon Johnson argued that the fundamental change in U.S. civil rights policy only came about because the country was shocked by the successful Russian launch of Sputnik, President Kennedy's assassination, and his vision of a new "Great Society" (Johnson, 1971, 70-71). Kent Calder argues that crisis was a major catalyst for change in highly bureaucratized, developed economies, "such as France, China, and Japan in the postwar period, [when] institutional conservatism often inhibit[ed] major innovation in the absence of crisis" (Calder, 1988, 40). Elites have used the perception of crisis as a policy tool to effect drastic policy changes within China, including the replacement and/or elimination of particular leading party elites (Reardon, 2002).

As initially argued in this chapter, the United States faced a crisis of confidence and legitimacy at the end of Bush's second term; in the month prior to the November 2008 election, only 25 percent of the people polled by Gallup approved of President Bush's performance in office, and 71 percent disapproved of his presidency, which was the highest disapproval rating since the poll was initiated in 1937 (Gallup, 2009). With 52.9 percent of the popular vote and 365 of the 538 electoral votes, Barack Obama was elected as the forty-fourth president of the United States. Democrats in the House of Representatives increased their majority to 257 to 178 Republican seats. In the Senate, Democrats also gained eight seats to fifty-seven, while the Republicans were reduced to forty-one seats.

Upon assuming office, the Obama administration initiated a foreign policy learning process that entailed five phases, which often overlapped and crossed over various policy areas: crisis; readjustment; adaptation and experimentation; review; and policy consensus.

The Policy Readjustment Phase

The perception of political and economic crisis at the end of the Bush administration marks the beginning of the policy readjustment phase of the foreign policy learning process. Having gained political legitimacy through its decisive electoral win in the 2008 presidential and congressional races, the Obama administration adopted various measures to reduce the most adverse effects of the Bush administration's strategies to counteract the political and economic crisis.

While it is arguable that the Obama administration failed to use the readjustment phase to build a strong consensus within the Democratic coalition and the country for future domestic policy change, the administration was successful in convincing its allies that the United States had changed the previous unilateral foreign policy strategies. In his inaugural address in January 2009, Obama clearly criticized the Bush administration's foreign policy by stating that he "reject[ed] as false the choice between our safety and our ideals" when deciding American defense strategy. Arguing that U.S. policy must change just as the world had changed, Obama praised past U.S. strategies of:

> earlier generations [who] faced down fascism and communism not just with missiles and tanks, but with the sturdy alliances and enduring convictions. They understood that our power alone cannot protect us, nor does it entitle us to do as we please. Instead they knew that our power grows through its prudent use; our security emanates from the justness of our cause, the force of our example, the tempering qualities of humility and restraint (Obama, 2009a).

In his speech in Cairo in June 2009, Obama argued that the "fear and anger" that Americans had felt following the 9/11 attack had "led us to act contrary to our traditions and our ideals." Unlike the 2001 invasion of Afghanistan, the Iraq invasion was a "war of choice" that had "caused substantial rifts between America and much of the world." The lesson that the United States had learned in Iraq was "the need to use diplomacy and build international consensus to resolve our problems whenever possible" (Obama, 2009b). In his Nobel acceptance speech, Obama would conclude that "Furthermore, America—in fact, no nation—can insist that others follow the rules of the road if we refuse to follow them ourselves. For when we don't, our actions appear arbitrary and undercut the legitimacy of future interventions, no matter how justified" (Obama, 2009c).

President Obama thus called for a new beginning in relations between the United States and Muslims around the world, which would be based on "mutual interest and mutual respect, and one based upon the truth that America and Islam are not exclusive and need not be in competition." The United States would partner with Muslim communities who are threatened by extremists, such as in Afghanistan. In Iraq, Obama agreed to carry out the November 2008 U.S.-Iraq Status of Forces Agreement, which set 2011 as the withdrawal date for all U.S. forces. In Afghanistan, the administration built up forces to defeat the Taliban insurgency, and planned to empower the Afghan military as it began U.S. troop withdrawal in 2011. As for Iran, Obama stated that the United States was willing to "move forward" in relations. As long as Iran complied with the Nuclear Non-Proliferation Treaty, a nuclear arms race in the Middle East could be avoided.

In sum, the Obama administration made clear its rejection of the unilateral strategy of the Bush administration and use of coercive force to bring about the establishment of a peaceful, democratic, and market-oriented community of nations, especially in the Middle East.

Policy Adaptation and Experiment Phase

Having begun the readjustment of the Bush administration foreign policy, the Obama foreign policy team entered the second phase policy cycle: policy innovation. During this second cycle phase, the administration rallied support for a new or revised foreign policy guided by a shared philosophy of "mutual interest and mutual respect." American foreign policy would now focus on multilateral diplomacy and uphold international norms of legal behavior.

In his "Address to the Nation on the Way Forward in Afghanistan and Pakistan" delivered at the U.S. Military Academy at West Point on December 1, 2009, President Obama declared his support for a consensus-building model to use force, such as that adopted by George W. Bush to invade Afghanistan just days after the 9/11 attack (Obama, 2009b). President Bush first had approached Congress for an authorization to attack those responsible for carrying out the 9/11 attacks, which passed with a nearly unanimous vote on September 14, 2001. Second, Article 5 of the North Atlantic Treaty Organization (NATO) was invoked, which stated that:

> an armed attack against one or more of them in Europe or North America shall be considered an attack against them all and consequently they agree that, if such an armed attack occurs, each of them, in exercise of the right of individual or collective self-defense recognized by Article 51 of the Charter of the United Nations. . . . Any such armed attack and all measures taken as a result thereof shall immediately be reported to the Security Council. Such measures shall be terminated when the Security Council has taken the measures necessary to restore and maintain international peace and security (North Atlantic Treaty Organization, 1949).

While never authorizing the U.S. Afghan Operation Enduring Freedom, the UN Security Council generally endorsed necessary steps to respond to 9/11, such as issuing a series of resolutions supporting the replacement of the Taliban government (UN Security Council, 2001a) and authorizing NATO's International

Security Assistance Force to maintain security in Kabul and surrounding areas (UN Security Council, 2001b). Comparing the Afghan operation to Vietnam in 1950-1960, President Obama praised President Bush's efforts to build "a broad coalition of 43 nations that recognize the legitimacy" of the operation.

This focus on a multilateral response and legal norms was also the focus of President Obama's initiatives to prevent nuclear proliferation. In his April 5, 2009, speech in the Czech Republic (Obama, 2009d), President Obama announced the signing of the New Strategic Arms Reduction Treaty (New START), which was ratified by the U.S. Senate in December 2010. New START reduced the number of strategic nuclear launchers and deployed nuclear warheads and guaranteed on-site inspections, and replaced the START I treaty, which had expired in 2009. President George H. W. Bush had never been successful in having the U.S. Senate ratify its replacement, START II; President Clinton never completed negotiations for a START III. President George W. Bush was never truly interested in negotiating a strong multilateral agreement on nuclear weapons such as START III, and unilaterally withdrew from the 1972 Anti-Ballistic Missile Treaty.

During his Czech speech, Obama further called for the U.S. ratification of the Comprehensive Test Ban Treaty, which had been first adopted by the two-thirds of the members of the UN General Assembly in 1996 and rejected by the U.S. Senate in 1999. He proposed new measures to promote civilian nuclear cooperation, to control vulnerable nuclear material, to detect illicit transit of nuclear materials such as the 2003 Proliferation Security Initiative and the 2006 global Initiative to Combat Nuclear Terrorism. He also called for a global summit on nuclear security, which was convened in April 2010 with the participation of forty-six governments and thirty-eight heads of state. While issues such as North Korean and Iranian nuclear proliferation remained on the table, the Obama administration believed that a collective response to increasing global nuclear security was the only credible solution.

The Obama administration experimented with this emphasis on multilateral response and legality when dealing with the 2011 Libyan civil war. Following the uprisings in Egypt and other areas of the Middle East, peaceful protests against Muammar Gaddafi and his forty-two years in power erupted throughout Libya. The conflict escalated into a full-fledged civil war in February 2011 with the establishment of the Transitional National Council located in the eastern coastal city of Benghazi.

Because of attacks on civilians, the United States closed its Tripoli embassy on February 25, froze billions of dollars of Libyan government and leadership assets, and called for the resignation of the Libyan leader. Subsequently, the UN Security Council imposed sanctions on and froze the assets of Colonel Gaddafi, his family, and his close advisors. The UN also referred the case to the International Criminal Court, and imposed an arms embargo on Libya. Pushed by the British, the French, the Lebanese, and the twenty-two-member Arab League, ten members of the Security Council invoked Chapter VII of the UN Charter on March 17, which allows UN members "to take all necessary measures . . . to protect civilians and civilian populated areas under threat of attack . . ." To enforce the no-fly zone, the United States subsequently launched 112 Tomahawk cruise missiles at twenty different military targets within Libya. NATO eventually assumed control of the no-fly zone and supervised the arms embargo operation; seventeen countries including France, Britain, Qatar, and the United States continued to manage ground unit attacks. Instead of taking the political and military lead and imposing its solution, the Obama administration has used the Libyan operation as a unique experiment in multilateral effort to enforce legal norms to protect Libyan lives.

The outcome of the experiment might depend on the willingness of the United States and other nations to bring about the end of the Gaddafi regime. The Obama administration no doubt will be reviewing the effort during the current policy implementation phase and attempt to overcome several implementation problems. If contending elites in the Republican or Democratic parties are successful in convincing the U.S. public the Obama cooperative strategy could lead to widespread chaos, the Obama strategy could lose legitimacy and the foreign policy learning process be renewed.

Conclusion

This chapter has argued that the Bush and Obama administrations shared similar long-term policy objectives, which were to promote a strong and secure nation, a healthy economy, and the establishment of a peaceful, democratic, and market-oriented community of nations. However, the two administrations differed in the realist strategies that they adopted: the Bush policy elites favored a unilateral approach, while the Obama administration has favored a cooperative approach.

In terms of strategic policy, the Obama administration continues to finance expensive military obligations initially undertaken during the Cold War era, which obligates the United States to maintain large numbers of military forces in Western Europe and East Asia. However, the Obama administration has reversed the Bush era of unilateral action and adopted a more cooperative, legalist approach to the use of power to achieve the state's long-term goals. By Obama's midterm, the United States experimented with going through the UN Security Council to implement the Libyan no-fly zone and the use of NATO to enforce UN resolutions. The administration continues to build upon cooperative arrangements such as the New START, the Comprehensive Test Ban Treaty, the Missile Technology Control Regime, the six-party talks in Korea, and UN sanctions against Iran to prevent the spread of nuclear weapons and begin discussions of disarmament.

The death of Osama bin Laden at the mid-point of President Obama's first term in office embodied the new Obama approach. The successful operation to eliminate bin Laden was an important symbol of American persistence and an important example of the new American approach to the use of force. As the world's unipolar power, the United States showed its willingness to defend its national security by unilaterally carrying out the Pakistan operation without the approval of the Pakistan government. Yet just as the United States carefully complied with international legal norms in carrying out the Libyan operation, the Secretary of State reiterated the importance of continued cooperation with the Pakistani government to "stop al Qaeda and its syndicate of terror" despite concerns that the Pakistani government, military, and intelligence agencies have collaborated with al Qaeda, the Taliban, and other terrorist groups.

However, President Obama continued to adapt previous Bush administration strategies as well as failed to undertake paradigmatic change in international economic structures originally established at the Bretton Woods conference of 1944. There had been two fundamental readjustments of these multilateral structures in the late 1940s and early 1970s reflecting the changes of the United States' hegemonic role as the global economic power. The need to coordinate macroeconomic policy and international trade policy has become increasingly acute following the Asian Financial Crisis of 1997 and the Global Financial Crisis starting in 2007. The Obama administration has continued the Bush administration's strategy of accepting a greater role for the G20 nations in macroeconomic policy. Yet the G20 remains a weak organization that has been ineffective in dealing with crucial economic problems, such as the excessive accumulation of the U.S. dollar and the obstacles preventing a successful conclusion of the WTO Doha round of international trade talks.

As it completes its first four years, the Obama administration has changed U.S. strategic strategies and engaged in more multilateral forums of cooperation. This approach more truly reflects the dreams of WWII leaders, who envisioned a cooperative, multilateral world where global problems would be resolved through multilateral venues such as the United Nations. While engaging in a vigorous internal discussion over reducing the domestic deficit and long-term debt, the Obama administration continues to adapt old strategies to maintain the international economic order. Such adaptations have become increasingly ineffectual in dealing with the emerging economies of the twenty-first century. During its remaining time, the Obama administration no doubt will confront more adaptation failures, which will only increase the pressure upon global leaders to consider more fundamental paradigmatic changes to forestall future economic disorder.

References

Adler, Emanuel. 1992. "The Emergence of Cooperation: National Epistemic Communities and the International Evolution of the Idea of Nuclear Arms Control." *International Organization* 46 (1): 101-145.

Belasco, Amy. 2010. "The Cost of Iraq, Afghanistan, and Other Global War on Terror Operations Since 9/11." September 2, Washington, DC: Congressional Research Service, No. RL 33110.

Bilgin, Pinar and Adam David Morton. 2002. "Historicising representations of 'failed states': beyond the cold-war annexation of the social sciences?" *Third World Quarterly* 23 (1): 55-80.

Blyth, Mark M. 2002. *Great Transformations: Economic Ideas and Institutional Change in the Twentieth Century.* Cambridge: Cambridge University Press.

Broad, William J., James Glanz, and David E. Sanger. 2010. "Iran Fortifies Its Arsenal with the Aid of North Korea." *New York Times*, November 28.

Bush, George W. 2002. *The National Security Strategy of the United States of America.* September 17. www.au.af.mil/au/awc/awcgate/nss/nss_sep2002.pdf

Calder, Kent. 1988. *Crisis and Compensation.* Princeton, NJ: Princeton University Press.

Cashell, Brian W. 2010. *The Economics of the Federal Budget Deficit.* February 2, Washington, DC: Congressional Research Service, No. RL31235.

Cassin, Jeffrey K. 2006. "United States' Moral Authority Undermined: The Foreign Affairs Costs of Abusive Detentions." *Cardozo Public Law, Policy & Ethics Journal* 4: 421-456.

Clinton, Hillary Rodham. 2011. "Remarks on the Killing of Osama bin Ladin." May 2. www.state.gov/secretary/rm/2011/05/162339.htm

Corcoran, Terence. 2010. "National sovereignty stands tall at the G20." *The Financial Post*, June 28.

Dahl, Robert A. 1958. "A Critique of the Ruling Elite Model." *The American Political Science Review* 52 (2): 463-469.

Delisle, Elizabeth Cove, Barbara Edwards, Daniel Hoople, David Rafferty, and Joshua Shakin. 2011. "Monthly Budget Review." April 7, Washington, DC: Congressional Budget Office.

Erlanger, Steven and Sheryl Gay Stolberg. 2009. "Surprise Nobel for Obama Stirs Praise and Doubts." *New York Times*, October 9.

Financial Times Editorial. 2011. "Bretton Woods II and the dollar; G20 seminar fails to agree on serious monetary reform." *Financial Times*, April 4.

Finn, Peter and Anne E. Kornblut. 2011. "Guantanamo Bay: Why Obama hasn't fulfilled his promise to close the facility." *Washington Post*, April 23.

Gallup Poll. 2009. "Presidential Approval Ratings—George W. Bush." www.gallup.com/poll/116500/Presidential-Approval-Ratings-George-Bush.aspx

Garver, John W. 2010. "Is China Playing a Dual Game in Iran?" *The Washington Quarterly* 34 (1): 75-88.

Giles, Chris. 2011. "G20 to agree criteria for countries set for IMF scrutiny." *Financial Times*, April 16.

Goodson, Larry and Thomas H. Johnson. 2011. "Parallels with the Past—How the Soviets Lost in Afghanistan, How the Americans Are Losing." April 25. Foreign Policy Research Institute E-Notes. www.fpri.org/enotes/201104.goodson_johnson.afghanistan.html

Grindle, Merilee and John Thomas. 1991. *Public Choices and Policy Change: The Political Economy of Reform in Developing Countries.* Baltimore: The Johns Hopkins University Press.

Hague Code of Conduct against Ballistic Missile Proliferation (HCoC). www.hcoc.at.

Hall, Peter A. 1993. "Policy Paradigms, Social Learning, and the State." *Comparative Politics* 25 (April): 275-296.

Hall, Peter A. and Rosemary C. R. Taylor. 1995. "Political Science and the Three New Institutionalisms." *Political Studies* 44 (5): 936-957.

Heilmann, Sebastian. 2008. "Policy Experimentation in China's Economic Rise." *Studies of Comparative and International Development* 43: 1-26.

International Atomic Energy Agency. Board of Governors. 2011. "Implementation of the NPT Safeguards Agreement and the relevant provisions of Security Council resolutions in the Islamic Republic of Iran." February 25. www.iaea.org/Publications/Documents/Board/2011/gov2011-7.pdf

International Monetary Fund. 2011a. "Global Financial Stability Report: Durable Financial Stability: Getting There from Here." April, Washington, DC.

———. 2011b. "Fiscal Monitor: Shifting Gears: Tackling Challenges on the Road to Fiscal Adjustment." April. Washington, DC.

———. 2011c. "World Economic Outlook Database, April 2011." April. Washington, DC.

Jervis, Robert. 2009. "Unipolarity: A Structural Perspective." *World Politics* 61 (1): 188-213.

Johnson, Lyndon B. 1971. *The Vantage Point; perspectives of the Presidency, 1963-1969.* New York: Holt, Rinehart and Winston.

Kuhn, Thomas S. 1962. *The Structure of Scientific Revolutions*, third edition. Chicago: The University of Chicago Press.

Lee, Sung-Yoon. 2010. "The Pyongyang Playbook." *Foreign Affairs*, August 26. www.foreignaffairs.com/articles/66581/sung-yoon-lee/the-pyongyang-playbook

Levit, Mindy R. 2010. *The FY2011 Federal Budget.* August 4, Washington, DC: Congressional Research Service, No. R 41097.

Manyin, Mark E. 2010. *North Korea: Back on the Terrorism List?* June 29, Washington, DC: Congressional Research Service, No. RL30613.

McElroy, Damien. 2010. "North Korea 'runs international nuclear smuggling network.'" *The Telegraph*, November 12.

Moltz, James Clay. 1993. "Divergent Learning and the Failed Politics of Soviet Economic Reform." *World Politics* 45 (2): 301-325.

Monten, Jonathan. 2005. "The Roots of the Bush Doctrine: Power, Nationalism, and Democracy Promotion in U.S. Strategy." *International Security* 29 (4): 112-156.

Nelson, Rebecca M. 2009. *The G-20 and International Economic Cooperation: Background and Implications for Congress.* December 9, Washington, DC: Congressional Research Service, No. R40977.

North Atlantic Treaty Organization. 1949. *The North Atlantic Treaty, April 4, 1949.* www.nato.int/cps/en/natolive/official_texts_17120.htm

Nye, Joseph. 1987. "Nuclear Learning and U.S.—Soviet Security Regimes." *International Organization* 41 (3): 371-402.

Obama, Barack. 2009a. "President Barack Obama's Inaugural Address." January 20. www.whitehouse.gov/blog/inaugural-address/

———. 2009b. "Remarks by the President on a New Beginning." June 4. www.whitehouse.gov/the-press-office/remarks-president-cairo-university-6-04-09

———. 2009c. "Remarks by the President at the Acceptance of the Nobel Peace Prize." December 10. www.whitehouse.gov/the-press-office/remarks-president-acceptance-nobel-peace-prize

———. 2009d. "Remarks by President Barack Obama." April 5. www.whitehouse.gov/the_press_office/Remarks-By-President-Barack-Obama-In-Prague-As-Delivered/

———. 2010. "National Security Strategy." May. www.whitehouse.gov/sites/default/files/rss_viewer/national_security_strategy.pdf

———. 2011. "Executive Order—Prohibiting Certain Transactions with Respect to North Korea." April 18. www.whitehouse.gov/the-press-office/2011/04/18/executive-order-prohibiting-certain-transactions-respect-north-korea

Oxfam. 2010. "The Making of a Seoul Development Consensus: The essential development agenda for the G20." Oxfam Briefing Note, October 11.

Perl, Raphael F. 2007. "International Terrorism: Threat, Policy, and Response." January
3, Washington, DC: Congressional Research Service, No. RL33600.

Pew Research Center's Global Attitudes Project. 2009. "Most Muslim Publics Not So
Easily Moved: Confidence in Obama Lifts U.S. Image Around the World." July 23.
pewglobal.org/2009/07/23/confidence-in-obama-lifts-us-image-around-the-world/

Pew Research Center's Global Attitudes Project. 2010. "Muslim Disappointment: Obama
More Popular Abroad Than At Home, Global Image of U.S. Continues to Benefit."
June 17. pewglobal.org/2010/06/17/obama-more-popular-abroad-than-at-home/

Qu Xing. 2011. "China's Real Responsibilities." *China Daily*, February 18.

Reardon, Lawrence C. 2002. *The Reluctant Dragon: Crisis Cycle in Chinese Foreign
Economic Policy*. Seattle: University of Washington Press.

Schneider, Howard and Scott Wilson. 2010. "Obama leaves summit as G020 countries
agree to set economic standards." *Washington Post*, November 12.

Shanker, Thom. 2011. "Warning Against Wars Like Iraq and Afghanistan." *New York
Times*, February 25.

Stein, Janice Gross. 1994. "Political Learning by Doing: Gorbachev as Uncommitted
Thinker and Motivated Learner." *International Organization* 48 (2): 155-183.

Stiglitz, Joseph. 1998. "More Instruments and Broader Goals: Moving Toward the Post-
Washington Consensus." January 7. The World Bank, News & Broadcast.

U.N. Security Council. 2001a. "Security Council Sets United Nations Course For Supporting New Governance in Afghanistan; Urges No Reprisals," Resolution 1378.
November 14. www.un.org/News/Press/docs/2001/sc7212.doc.htm

————. 2001b. "Security Council Authorizes International Security Force for Afghanistan; Welcomes United Kingdom's Offer to Be Initial Lead Nation," Resolution
1386. December 20. www.un.org/News/Press/docs/2001/sc7248.doc.htm

U.S. Department of Defense. 2010. "Annual Report to Congress: Military and Security
Developments Involving the People's Republic of China." www.g20.org

U.S. Department of State. 2010. "Background Notes: South Korea." December 10.
www.state.gov/r/pa/ei/bgn/2800.htm

Chapter 6

African-American Perspectives of the Obama Presidency

Shayla C. Nunnally

Introduction

On November 4, 2008, Senator Barack H. Obama made history, becoming the nation's forty-fourth president and first, African-American[1] president. That President Obama was elected is highly significant, given the United States' history on race and its centuries of mistreating black people. Ever since its inception and lasting through the mid-twentieth century, the U.S. government observed de jure and de facto racism, which precluded black Americans from humanity, citizenship, and ultimately, participating in the electoral process. Thus, in the fashion of the politics of both change and hope, many black Americans witnessed the election of an African-American president, an achievement that many thought would probably never happen in their lifetimes. It is also through President Obama's election that, for the first time, many blacks also were able to obtain what Pitkin (1967) referred to as both *descriptive representation* (based on congruent race between them and their elected public official) and *substantive representation* (based on congruent partisanship between them and their elected public official) at the highest level—the office of the presidency.

In view of the presidency in general, substantive representation also theoretically entails the ability of a president to promote policies that respond to constituents' interests. Scholars have debated how blacks can influence presidential politics, often forgoing the possibility that a black president could be elected to respond to blacks' interests through his political agenda. Instead of considering even the possibility of electing a black president, as Walters (1988, 2005) maintains, what seemed to be a more practical view of black presidential politics involved blacks making cross-racial appeals to leverage their interests with both major political parties and white presidents. Blacks' ultimate goal was to impress upon these major political actors and presidential administrations the value of blacks' votes and their group-specific interests.

Despite the importance of engaging the group-specific interests of African Americans, especially given the historic omission, downplay, and politicking over these interests in various presidential administrations (Shull, 2000), for President Obama (and even other presidents), normatively, presidential responsiveness also entails representing a constituency that expands beyond one's racial group and partisan interests. But, what does this mean for an *African-American* president to be able to maneuver his power in order to mollify a multiracial American public? What consideration, furthermore, must be made given whites' historic perceptions about black politicians' character and personal interests, which negativized them as incompetent and racially expedient in favor of black group interests? That is, to what extent must we consider the special circumstances of an African-American president, who by default of his race, possibly faces a precarious predicament as far as appearing to be responsive to both blacks and whites, especially when extant public opinion continues to indicate that these groups' interests and public policy attitudes often fissure along racial lines (Kinder and Winter, 2001; Kinder and Sanders, 1996)? These questions leave several additional inquiries open for debate and potential research as far as attitudes toward an African-American president and the implications of a president's race for Americans' perceptions of his political effectiveness.

For example, it follows that we should consider whether as an African-American president, President Obama can transcend racial attitudes to be able to appeal to the interests of a multi-racial American electorate. Put simply, do people feel that the president's race (as a black American) affects his effectiveness in promoting policies writ large, regardless if they are related to race or not? This question is the basis of the public opinion research in this analysis.

Using national public opinion data from the 2009 Pew Research Center "Racial Attitudes in America II Survey," this chapter investigates the factors explaining the perception that opposition to President Obama's policies is rooted in racism towards the president's race as a black American. It compares blacks' and whites' attitudes about this perception to determine whether there is a racial divide.

Given the weight of historic racial discrimination experiences for blacks, I anticipate that more blacks than whites will be attuned to race being a factor in Americans' opposition to the president's policies. Sensitivity to recurring discrimination against blacks as a group, however, should increase both blacks' and whites' perceptions that the president's race affects opposition to his policies. In addition to a racial divide in these perceptions, Republicans should be less receptive than Democrats to racial opposition against the president because they will perceive opposition as more principled in partisan differences between Republicans and a Democratic president.

To develop the theoretical basis for this research, I first discuss the significance of race and representation in American politics. Second, I examine how whites historically have perceived blacks negatively as candidates and politicians. Third, I discuss how race and (or) gender affected the 2008 presidential primaries and general election to illustrate the racialization of both Obama as a presidential candidate and as president. Further, I discuss how his mere racial presence in the office of the U.S. president introduces race by default into the analysis of perceptions about his presidency. Fourth, I provide an overview of blacks' and whites' perceptions of discrimination against blacks to preface how they may perceive opposition and implicit racial bias against a black president. Fifth, I review the influence of the media and media consumption in racial perceptions and prospective attitudes about the president to suggest how television versus print media consumption can enhance perceptions of the president being treated disparately because of his race. In sum, the literature review will combine these literatures to suggest how President Obama's race can racialize the politics and perceptions of his presidency's opposition.

Theoretical Background

The Racialization of Representation

Blacks did not acquire the full right to the franchise until the passage of the Voting Rights Act of 1965. Of special note is the extent to which, historically, race and politics have been intimately intertwined as far as representation, such that racial groups have leveraged their numerical majorities to influence electoral outcomes in their group's favor. Most often, however, this electoral power favored the political interests of whites to the detriment of blacks, who lacked responsiveness to their political interests because of racial discrimination. This made the perceived need to elect politicians supportive of blacks' interests a major aspect of blacks' political agenda (McAdam, 1982). Synonymous to this objective was the belief that perhaps blacks' representation was best entrusted in representation by black rather than white politicians.

Assumedly, black politicians could bear representation most akin to the interests of their fellow racial group members: shared racial group experiences would enhance politicians' empathy for blacks' plight. The mere presence of a black politician would render descriptive representation. However, for the most effective policy responsiveness, arguably, this representation should be counterbalanced with substantive representation, or congruent policy interests often appeased by shared partisanship between blacks and their representatives.

Extant literature on race and representation often debates whether descriptive or substantive representation will improve blacks' relationships with a political system that formerly excluded them (Swain, 1995; Guinier, 1995; Tate, 2003). This literature questions the role that black representatives have in enhancing blacks' connectedness to the American political system. This debate focuses on (1) systemic structures aiding in the election of black representatives and (2) psychological responses to the election of black representatives.

To overcome the historic disparity in whites' support of black candidates, systemic solutions involved developing redistricting plans to manipulate demographic concentrations of blacks to accommodate the group's ability to elect black representatives. Paradoxically, these plans often over-concentrated blacks (and Latinos) into districts that increased their descriptive representation at the expense of their substantive representation by isolating blacks' districts in a way that enhanced Republican wins in surrounding districts (Lublin, 1996; Canon, 1999). With as much as 90 percent of blacks identifying as Democrats, such redistricting plans further marginalized blacks' representation in Congress, as the legislature also became majority Republican. The effects of these systemic structures attest to the concern for blacks acquiring substantive representation through greater representation by Democratic representatives. Aside from structural changes to accommodate responsiveness to blacks, the election of black representatives can provide psychological satisfaction and perhaps greater political efficacy, as blacks have been historically very politically distrusting (Tate, 2003).

With descriptive representation, perhaps blacks could find better psychological resolve. Since the extension of the franchise to blacks, especially post-1965, and the ability of blacks to cast their votes freely for the candidates of their choice, the number of elected black representatives has increased (Keyssar, 2000; Walters, 1988, 2005). However, despite arguments about the power of descriptive representation for blacks' representation, public opinion about this representation offers contradictory results. For example, the presence of a black representative does not necessarily increase blacks' political trust, but it does increase the likelihood that blacks contact their representatives (Tate, 2003; Gay, 2002). Unlike blacks, whites represented by blacks become less engaged with the political system (Avery, 2009; Gay, 2002). This is to suggest that, despite the psychological gains blacks experience via descriptive representation, whites who are represented by blacks experience opposite effects: they become politically demobilized. Thus, despite gains in descriptive representation for blacks as a historically under-represented group, disparate white attitudes about this representation further complicate the relationship between race and representation. Indeed, it appears that when one racial group gains psychological benefits from representation, the other group—either real or perceived—experiences psychological losses.

Whites' Negative Perceptions of Black Politicians and the Politics of Racial Defaultism

Despite liberalization of white racial attitudes over time (Schuman et al., 1997), recent research still illuminates whites' prejudice toward black candidates, whether it is via racialized stereotyping (McDermott, 1998; McDermott, 1997), disparate views about them when compared to white candidates (Highton 2004; Reeves, 1997; Plutzer and Zipp, 1996), or resistance to such candidacies altogether (Voss and Lublin, 2001; Lublin and Voss, 2000). The Obama presidential candidacy faced similar racialized stereotyping, as I detail later, and who is to say that once elected, such views have subsided. This leaves room for us to explore such attitudes post-election of the nation's first African-American president, especially by using a black-white paradigmatic framework often used in public opinion research on racial attitudes.

Part of whites' fears in electing black politicians rests in their perceptions about the potential quality of these elected officials' service and the uncertainty of their racial expediency on behalf of black interests (Reeves, 1997). Undoubtedly, for both blacks and whites, fears about quality representation depend upon race and trust, and depending upon whether there is incongruency between the race of the politician and the constituent, distrust is more likely. Distrusting attitudes among whites about black politicians have even made black candidates' electoral bids more cumbersome than white candidates'.

For one, white voters are slightly more willing to vote for white candidates than black candidates (Voss and Lublin, 2001), especially when white voters have higher racial prejudice attitudes (Terkildsen, 1993). In the media, black candidates are often portrayed negatively, as their coverage focuses on their indiscretions, incompetence, immoral commitments to public office, and associations with extreme political views (Larson, 2006). Compared to white politicians, black candidates are also characterized more negatively (Williams, 1990). When black politicians are perceived more positively, it is often with respect to social welfare issues and issues affecting racial minorities (McDermott, 1998). In sum, these characterizations tend to be racialized respective to candidates' ascription as black, racial group members. For black politicians who seek cross-racial appeal (especially among whites) to win elections, these aforementioned attitudes lead many to assume de-racialized campaign strategies that de-emphasize race-related issues, policies, and actions that may be misconstrued as expedient for blacks (Orey and Ricks, 2007; McCormick and Jones, 1993; Bullock, 1984).

Black politicians who evoke de-racialization strategies may find them beneficial in the sense of attracting white voters, but in hand, they may prove distracting for black voters, who sense black candidates distancing themselves from policies that disproportionately affect their racial group (Henry, 2008). Increasingly, such de-racialization strategies have expanded to include styles of leadership, wherein post-civil rights, black politicians attempt to build universal political agendas that shy away from highlighting policies that address the disparate conditions of black communities (Gillespie, 2010).

As Gillespie (2010) claims, instead, such de-racialized leadership styles invite building a diverse electoral following that feeds such black politicians' political aspirations for re-election and higher office. For the aspirations of presidential candidate Obama, scholars like Frasure (2010) claim that assuaging both black and white interests simultaneously engaged Obama in "Jekyll and Hyde politics," wherein she states, "Clearly, then, Jekyll and Hyde politics rubs both ways, as Obama has simultaneously confronted the *inverse* (emphasis in original text) of the African-American racial identity cue among segments of the White electorate, whereas a perception of 'too Black' or having a policy agenda too closely aligned with African Americans is the 'bad' Obama, while putting forth a universalistic policy agenda which transcends race is the 'good' Obama."

This is to say that for candidate Obama, especially as President Obama, politicking race even by transcending it accrues different political payoffs. However, in view of mainstream politics, demobilizing race offers him the best benefit. But, in being an African-American politician, controlling when race enters the political context is a less controllable factor for a politician who by his mere presence as a black person and as a nuanced figure as a U.S. president introduces race by default. This *racial defaultism* is what must be considered as far as a potential limitation in the president's bargaining power, despite whites' liberalization about race and race-related policy issues. By reviewing the imposition of race in then Senator Obama's 2008 presidential bid, we see the extent to which racial defaultism has influenced his campaign responses.

Race on the Obama Campaign Trail: Presidential Election 2008

For presidential candidate Obama, despite attempts to avoid focusing on his race, the media continually mentioned his being black and conducting a historic candidacy as a "viable" presidential candidate (Kensky, Hardy, and Jamieson, 2010; McIlwan, 2007). Early in his campaign, some members of the black elite questioned whether Obama was "black enough" to represent blacks' interests (Henry, 2008; Cobb, 2008). Competing presidential candidate, then Senator Joe Biden, referred to Obama as "articulate and clean" and unlike any former black presidential candidate. In the media, Obama was implicitly branded as "racially extreme" because of his former church membership with the Trinity United Church in Chicago, where Reverend Jeremiah Wright served as his pastor. Wright also was depicted as possessing beliefs antithetical to American patriotism. Former Senator Hillary Clinton, Obama's leading competitor in the 2008 presidential primaries, branded Obama as "elitist" after his campaign gaffe that claimed some Americans in rural areas were "bitter" and "clinging to their guns" in contempt of people different from them. This gaffe led *Newsweek* (May 5,

2008 issue) to characterize this political misstep in terms of Obama's "Bubba Gap" (see also Thomas et al., 2008; Seelye, 2008).

Evocations of candidate Obama being Muslim further highlighted the politics of "difference" vis-à-vis mainstream, white and Christian America. Despite using de-racialization strategies during his campaign in order to build cross-racial appeal, candidate Obama was forced to address his connections with Reverend Wright via his speech, "A More Perfect Union" (2008), which described race in America and its perspectives from white and black racial backgrounds. Most importantly, the speech offered to posture Obama's stance on the status of race in America without offending either of these racial groups.

Repeatedly, Obama has had to declare his faith as a Christian to counter claims that he is Muslim. His candidacy also became embattled in pundits' debates about whether a *black* president should be elected before a *woman* president.[2] By default and beyond his control, candidate Obama's race introduced commentary, political mobilizing (positive and negative), and political strategies that drew attention to the significance of his race in his presidential candidacy (Henry, 2008). Other accounts of his campaign trail detail the egregiously extreme, violence-oriented, and life-threatening reactions to the black presidential candidate's race and successful campaign (Parks and Rachlinski, 2009).

Ultimately, while race influenced voting for Obama (Kensky, Hardy, and Jamieson, 2010), it did not lead to an electoral loss for his candidacy. Despite a highly contested primary election campaign against Senator Hillary Clinton, Senator Obama won the Democratic Party nomination and went on to win the presidency in the general election against Senator John McCain, the Republican Party contender. With a mandate from the American people (having garnered 53 percent of the electoral votes compared to McCain's 47 percent), November 4, 2008 proved momentous as a historic breakthrough in American politics.

By dint of the 2008 presidential election, we see recent and exemplary evidence of whites being less oppositional to black candidacies. Then Senator Barack Obama commanded as much as 43 percent of the white vote in his presidential win. Nevertheless, over a majority of whites (55 percent) voted for McCain in comparison to only 4 percent of blacks (McClain and Stewart, 2010). While this voting pattern follows precedent in candidate support based on partisanship among blacks, wherein blacks overwhelmingly identify with the Democratic Party and likely would not support a Republican candidate, most whites still supported the white, Republican candidate.

For whites, despite a racial mismatch in descriptive representation as far as support of Obama as a black candidate, support of his candidacy is consistent with their support of previous Democratic presidential candidates, Al Gore (2000, 42 percent) and John Kerry (2004, 41 percent) (McClain and Stewart, 2010). In fact, as research indicates, whites' votes have been mostly cast with a leaning toward the Republican Party ever since the latter 1960s (Walters, 1988), and researchers often attribute this to the major parties' realignment during this era over the issue of civil rights for African Americans (Carmines and Stimson, 1989). Thus, as the evidence suggests, whether it is a matter of electing black candidates or candidates representing certain major parties, race continues to influence representation in American politics.

The Inauguration of a New America? Post-Racial Politics or Politics as Usual?

After the election of the nation's first, African-American president, media pundits questioned whether America had become a "post-racial" society—a society that could overlook the race of a presidential candidate and vote for him to ascend to the highest elected office in the country. Within a few short months of President Obama's inauguration, however, the sentiments of post-racialism seemingly faded.

The president's proposal to reform health care was met with vehement opposition, and it precipitated the protest of the Tea Party wing of the Republican Party, which questioned overly-expansive government. Pundits questioned whether the Tea Party protests were rooted in anti-black animus and resistance to the power of an African-American president, in part, because several Tea Party demonstrators held signs that arguably portrayed the president in racially-stereotypical ways (Robinson, 2010).

Aside from the Tea Party, challenges to President Obama's persona questioned his nation of birth status. If it were disproven that Obama was born in the United States, then he would be disqualified from presidential office. Others continue to question whether he is Muslim, suggesting perhaps that he lacks grounding in American, Christian values. Still, others have questioned his patriotism, initially asking why he refused to wear an American flag on his lapel. Other charges imply that Obama is a communist provocateur, who usurps power to expand the power of federal government in ways that are antithetical to democracy and capitalistic values.

By September 9, 2009, the "words heard around the world" brought attention to non-collegial congressional behavior when Rep. Joe Wilson (R-SC) levied the words, "You lie!" in response to President Obama's address about the need for health care reform and its inapplicability to undocumented persons. The debates and protests about health care were point-blank vitriolic. One must ask, "Were these and other protests rooted in opposition to the policy or to the race of the president?"

Recent public opinion data show a racial divide in opinions about the President. Pew Research Center data from November 2009, for example, indicate that 95 percent of blacks view President Obama positively, compared to 56 percent of whites. Overall, at the time of this survey, 65 percent of Americans said they have either a very (33 percent) or mostly (32 percent) positive view of the president. Although whites mostly viewed the president favorably, still 38 percent viewed him *un*favorably. These unfavorable attitudes are more pronounced when we account for the partisanship and gender of white respondents.

Only 31 percent of white Republicans viewed President Obama favorably, compared to 89 percent of white Democrats. White independents also showed less favorable attitudes toward the president, as only 55 percent viewed him favorably. As far as gender, white women viewed the president more favorably than white men—62 percent of white women compared to 49 percent of white men, indicating a 13 percentage-point difference. Such racially- and gender-distinctive attitudes toward the president provide evidence for the likelihood of racialized perceptions about President Obama's treatment.

Perceptions of Discrimination Toward the President

Newer scholarship on the Obama presidential candidacy finds evidence that racialized campaigning suppressed the vote for Obama's candidacy (Kensky, Hardy, and Jamieson, 2010). If race suppressed the vote for Obama, then can race suppress support for his policies? Moreover, to what extent does the American public perceive that the president's ability to influence, set, and act on a policy agenda is affected by his race? Much of the debate about reactions to the president's race relates to the historic racial divide between blacks and whites. For the sake of this analysis, I am interested in the opinions of blacks and whites about whether they feel the president's race is an impediment to his policy effectiveness. In order to assess these perceptions, it is important to review blacks' and whites' attitudes about race and racial discrimination.

Extant research shows that, despite the dissolution of Jim Crow and an era of blatant inequality, black Americans continue to experience racial discrimination (Laudrine and Klonoff, 1996; Sanders Thompson, 1992 and 1996; Sigelman and Welch, 1991). Although the effects of racial consciousness can be cued differently based on explicit or implicit cueing among African Americans about issues that are universally applicable to the racial group versus marginally applicable to subgroups of the black population (such as the black poor; see White, 2007), it is believed here that a specific political issue does not have to be present for Americans to perceive explicit or implicit racial cueing, as other scholars have suggested (Mendelberg, 2001). Rather, the mere presence of a black president cues racial attitudes among blacks and other Americans in a way that the issues the president discusses do not, themselves, have to be symbolically racialized or triggered as race-related through the use of code-words.[3]

Simply put, the president's race itself serves as a racial cue because it can be interpreted as a schema for which people perceive the conglomeration of power, interests, and (in)sincerity that a president bears on his presidency. Thus, racial attitudes (negative or positive) are projected on the president's actions based on the racial group of the evaluator, his/her sense of group position relative to the president's race, and the perceived relationships between the evaluator's racial group and the president's racial group.

For blacks, given the linking effects of black identity and racial group consciousness which evoke collective memory about the group's racial discrimination (Dawson, 1994; Allen, Dawson, and Brown, 1989), they should be more sensitive than whites to the perception that opposition to President Obama's policies is rooted in attitudes about his race. For whites, however, race is often observed and acted upon differently, as extant research continues to indicate a racial divide in public opinion between blacks and whites (Kinder and Winter, 2001; Kinder and Sanders, 1996) and whites and other racial and ethnic minority groups (Lopez and Pantoja, 2004). Racial policies exacerbate the black-white opinion divide (Kinder and Winder, 2001).

In the public opinion literature about white racial attitudes, scholars debate whites' attitudinal orientations, and several theories attempt to explain whites' predominantly negative attitudes toward race-related policies and even implicitly race-related policies (Sears, Sidanius, and Bobo, 2001). Group competition theories suggest that whites see themselves as a racial group that competes for resources with other groups in a zero-sum game, wherein whites lose resources at the expense of non-white groups' winning them (Bobo and Hutchings, 1996; Bobo and Kluegel, 1993). Through the framework of modern racism or racial resentment, scholars suggest that whites express negative attitudes about racial policies because they associate such policies with rewarding blacks with benefits that they perhaps do not deserve because of blacks' stereotyped behaviors, which perceivably violate core American values like the Protestant work ethic (Kinder and Sanders, 1996; Kinder and Sears, 1981).

Other scholars suggest that racial attitudes are not integral for whites' opposition toward race-related policies. Instead, whites' opposition lies in their ideological perspectives about the role of government in people's lives, to which whites oppose the government becoming excessively involved in issues like poverty and discrimination, which disproportionately affect blacks (Sniderman and Piazza, 1993; Sniderman and Tetlock, 1986). Given these theories about white public opinion on race, the expectation is that whites' views will be distinctly different from blacks'.

Residual attitudes stemming from the racial-gendered context of the 2008 presidential primaries may also have import in determining whites' attitudes about the president's treatment. Although Hughes and Tuch (2003) find that white women are more supportive of electing a black president than white men, their research predates the race-gender controversy that emerged during the 2008 presidential primaries. Heightened exposure about the dynamic of electing the first black male president versus the first female president (although, she was also white) may have evoked racial and gender consciousness among Americans that can be mapped on the president's presidency. For black women especially, such discussions equally may have highlighted their desire to seek representation by a president that could either share their race or their gender, thus heightening their intersectional consciousness across race and gender for two underrepresented groups in the occupation of the American presidency.

Unfortunately, Hughes and Tuch's research does not inquire about whether whites are more willing to support a black (male) or a (white) female president over the other. This is to say that an important aspect of determining race-related attitudes in this study will comprise accounting for the intersection of race and gender in perceiving attitudes about the president's treatment. Although one controversy during the 2008 presidential primaries focused on whether a black male president should be elected before a (white) female president, it is believed that white women will express attitudes that are more sensitive than white men to President Obama's treatment because they will be more attuned to the politics of a historically under-represented group member navigating his powers in an office that formally had been occupied by only white males. Nevertheless, both black men and women will be more perceptive of race-related opposition to the president's policies.

Additionally, whites (and even blacks) who perceive blacks' conditions as more equitable to whites will be less receptive to the notion that general opposition to President Obama's policies is an outgrowth of racism. To be more specific, people who feel that African Americans continue to experience much discrimination in our society also should sense more than those who do not that the president experiences disparate treatment because of his race. However, people who feel that blacks have accomplished equal rights with whites should perceive that racial discrimination is not an explanation for opposition to the president's policy proposals.

Racial attitudes about the president's morality can be couched in beliefs about whether the president shares values with people personally. People with a detached moral connection with the president should be less receptive to racial opposition toward him. They should liken opposition to Obama's policies as emblematic of dissatisfaction with qualities that make the president less attractive for people to work with him, and thus support his policies.

As mentioned previously, exposure to media can elicit implicit or explicit racial appeals, especially among whites (Kinder and Winter, 2001; Mendelberg, 2001) but also among blacks (White, 2007), and these appeals can detract support of explicitly or implicitly race-related policies. Theories about racial cueing also suggest that elites play a role in activating race in people's cognition.

For example, Nelson, Sansbonmatsu, and McKlerking (2007), find that elite cueing of implicitly racist issues (e.g., the criminal justice system) depends upon in-group (same-race between elites and evaluators) versus out-group (different-race between elites and evaluators) cueing. They also find that whites are more receptive to race-based arguments from their in-group member-elites who racialize non-racial issues than blacks are. In their study, for blacks, race and partisanship combined to influence blacks' attitudes, although unexpectedly, with black Republicans, followed by white Democrat elites influencing their perceptions of implicitly racial cues.

This study illustrates how the race of a political elite can influence opinions about the content of a message. This, however, does not provide evidence for how people view allegations of reactions to a political actor's public policies based on the political actor's race, itself. Here, I suggest that racial cueing is an artifact of the president's race—race by default. Although it cannot be accurately measured in this study how much people are exposed to messages that may be disparaging in racially explicit or implicit ways, in this study we can control for the exposure one has to print and television media to determine its effects on perceptions about President Obama's policy opposition.

Media Consumption, Political Behavior, and Race

Scholars of the influence of media on political behavior debate whether the consumption of media has deleterious ("media malaise") or politically-engaging (politically mobilizing) effects on people's political behavior (Newton, 1999). Part of this debate also questions the extent to which the form (print or television) or the content (educational or entertainment) of media decreases people's political engagement.

Television media can have heightened sensory effects on viewers consuming information because of the evocation of visual imagery combined with auditory intonations that print media cannot capture (Graber, 2006). As it goes for race, both television media (Entman and Rojecki, 2000) and print media (Gilens, 1999) disproportionately characterize blacks in negative ways, and this extends further to political coverage of black politicians, who are often characterized in disparaging ways with respect to their being incompetent, corrupt, or novel as political competitors (Larson, 2006; Niven, 2004).

Television viewers are likely exposed to messages, multiple images, emotive expressions, and scenarios that may be processed as more distinctly biased or not toward the president. Therefore, despite being unable to control for specific television programming content, selective exposure, and positive or negative slants in coverage, television-viewing media consumers should be more sensitive to the president's treatment, as they can form opinions possibly based on information gathered from hyper-sensory content of news about him. Reading the news, comparatively, should have a negligible effect on these perceptions because there are likely fewer iterative and multiple-sensory stimuli than television imagery to influence readers' perceptions about the president. In sum, I suggest that television news viewing should elicit a different effect on its consumers than print media.

Specialized media also target specific audiences, providing them with relevant information that affects them as a member of a social or even ideological group. Historically, black media have served as outlets for black Americans to gather political information about the circumstances of their racial group, even when broader media outlets excluded issues and stories related to them (Dawson, 1994). Consumers of black media do not have to be exclusively black Americans. However, it is expected that the content of such media will likely discuss race-related issues about the circumstances of black Americans that will enhance viewers' racial consciousness and perhaps even exposure to race-related issues affecting the president. Thus, for black media consumers in general, their sensitivities should be heightened and sensitive to racial opposition toward President Obama.

Data and Methods

2009 Pew Research Center Social and Demographic Trends Project

The data for this analysis come from the 2009 Pew Research Center's "Racial Attitudes in America II Survey," which was sponsored by the Pew Research Center for the People & the Press and Pew Social & Demographic trends project and conducted by the Princeton Survey Research International from October 28 through November 30, 2009. The sample consists of a nationally representative sample of N = 2,884 adults living in the continental United States, including an oversample of African-American and Hispanic respondents. The analysis here focuses on the opinions of blacks (n = 875) and whites (n = 1631) only (see Appendix).

It is expected that Republicans will be less receptive than Democrats to race affecting President Obama's policy proposals, as they associate opposition more with fundamental differences in principles rather than race. Independents, as interlopers between Republican and Democratic perspectives, also should display greater odds than Democrats of perceiving race not being a reason for opposition to President Obama's policies.

Results

According to univariate results, 57 percent (n = 468) of black respondents in the Pew survey feel that race is a major reason for opposition to President Obama's policies. This compares to only 19 percent of whites (n = 152) who think race is a major reason. In fact, most whites (44 percent, n = 663) report that race is not a reason for opposition to President Obama's policies, although 38 percent (n = 573) believe that race is a minor explanation. Comparatively, only 19 percent of blacks (n = 152) feel that race is not a reason for opposition to Obama's policies, leaving only 24 percent (n = 199) who believe that it is a minor reason.

Turning to table 6.1, we see a partisan breakdown of opinions about opposition to Obama's policies. Clearly, across all partisan identifications, blacks are more likely than whites with similar partisanship to report that race is a major reason for opposition to President Obama's policies. However, a closer inspection of partisanship elucidates the divergence in black Democrats', versus black Republicans', views—whereas black Democrats are most likely to report race being a major reason, black Republicans are most likely to report that race is not a reason. Unlike black Democrats, white Democrats are most likely to report that race is a minor reason for opposition to President Obama's proposals as opposed to his race. Both white Republicans and Independents are most likely to report that race is not a reason explaining his opposition.

Table 6.1. Black and White Respondents' Perceptions of Race as the Reason for Opposition to President Obama's Policies (By Race and Partisanship)

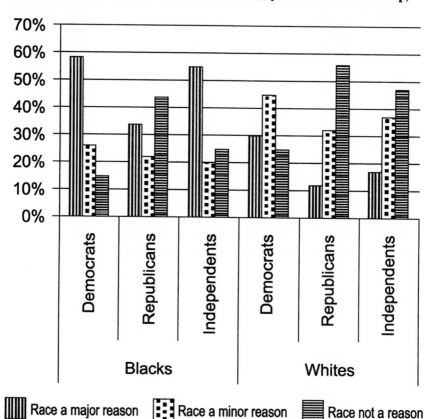

Source: 2009 Pew Research Center Social Trends, Racial Attitudes II Survey

Note: The question was "Thinking about opposition to Barack Obama's policies, do you think that his race is a major reason, a minor reason, or not a reason people oppose Barack Obama's policies?" Responses are coded 1 = a major reason; 2 = a minor reason; and 3 = not a reason.

The multinomial logit regressions in table 6.2 illustrate racial-gender differences between blacks' and whites' opinions about race being a major reason for opposition to President Obama's policies. However, the statistically significant relationships are contrary to those hypothesized. Whereas black women have greater odds than white women of expressing race being a major reason for opposition to President Obama, black men, instead, have greater odds than white women of expressing that race is not a reason for opposition toward him. Older and more affluent Americans also have greater odds of believing that race is not a reason for opposition toward Obama, when compared to the odds of race being a major reason. Being Republican and independent of partisan affiliation also increases the odds that one sees race as no reason for Obama's opposition, when compared to race being a major reason.

As expected, people who express that President Obama shares their values have greater odds of believing that race is a major reason for the opposition he encounters than believing that race is not a reason whatsoever. Additionally, contrary to expectation yet with modest effects, regular consumption of print media actually increases the odds that Americans perceive racial discrimination in the president's opposition as opposed to race not being a reason. Visual media consumption also increases the odds that people see race as not being a reason for opposition toward the president, when compared to race being a minor reason. Believing that blacks still face much racial discrimination in today's society has the dual effect of increasing the odds that people feel race is a major reason and a minor reason in explaining President Obama's opposition, when compared to race not being a reason at all.

In the analysis of the model of blacks, there are no socio-demographic effects on this group's perceptions of race being a factor in President Obama's treatment. Yet, having a higher level of education increases the odds that blacks perceive race being a minor explanation for the president's treatment compared to race having no import whatsoever. However, for blacks, believing they share values with the president increases the odds that they see race as a major reason for his political opposition, although with modest effects. Only black Republicans have greater odds than black Democrats to report race not being a factor in the president's opposition. Perceiving blacks still face much racial discrimination increases the belief that race undergirds opposition to the president.

As for whites, having a greater income increases the odds that they believe race is not a reason for the president's opposition, when compared to race being a major reason. Shared values with the president increases the odds (compared to race not being a reason) that whites perceive race as either a major or a minor reason for President Obama's opposition. Print media consumption among whites modestly increases the odds that they will be sensitive to racial opposition toward the president (as opposed to race having no reason), whereas visual media consumption increases the odds that whites view race as having no import in the president's political bargaining (compared to race having no reason). White Republicans and Independents have greater odds of perceiving race as having no import in opposition to the president's policies, with respect to race

Table 6.2. Multinomial Logit Models of Race Being a Reason for Opposition to President Obama's Policies

	All Groups (Compared to White Females)		Blacks		Whites	
	Race a Major Reason for Opposition	Race a Minor Reason for Opposition	Race a Major Reason for Opposition	Race a Minor Reason for Opposition	Race a Major Reason for Opposition	Race a Minor Reason for Opposition
Black (Women)	1.120**** (.3115)	-.2074 (.3207)	--	--	--	--
Women	--	--	.4954 (.3451)	.0795 (.3999)	-.3657 (.2591)	-.3294 (.2078)
(White) Male	.3222 (.2516)	.3230 (.2056)	--	--	--	--
Black* Male	-.8580** (.3992)	-.5491 (.4107)	--	--	--	--
Age	-.0117* (.0060)	-.0012 (.0057)	-.0086 (.0107)	-.0075 (.0121)	-.0109 (.0081)	.0029 (.0067)
Income	-.0837* (.0489)	-.0448 (.0454)	.1016 (.0903)	.0341 (.1024)	-.1902*** (.0634)	-.0658 (.0522)
Education	.0010 (.0680)	.0618 (.0628)	.1644 (.1286)	.2622* (.1463)	-.0826 (.0885)	.0011 (.0723)
South	.0381 (.1996)	-.1751 (.1879)	-.2318 (.3494)	-.2672 (.3990)	.3205 (.2689)	-.1495 (.2222)
Country Needs Changes for Blacks' Equality	.1221 (.2252)	.1019 (.2017)	.4290 (.4739)	.1598 (.5569)	.0223 (.2746)	.0635 (.2231)
Obama Shares Values with Respondent	.5264**** (.1204)	.4742**** (.1023)	.4015* (.2432)	.4214 (.2896)	.5908**** (.1492)	.4964**** (.1120)
Print Media Consumption	.3406* (.1959)	.0429 (.1815)	.0787 (.3822)	-.3463 (.4351)	.4471* (.2635)	.1073 (.2103)
Visual Media Consumption	-.1755 (.2244)	-.4146** (.2031)	-.2635 (.4268)	-.3975 (.4868)	-.1812 (.2965)	-.5652** (.2326)
Black Media Consumption	--	--	.0289 (.1501)	.2407 (.1714)	--	--
Republican	-1.030**** (.3073)	-.6826*** (.2592)	-2.499** (1.198)	-.8902 (.9836)	-.8042** (.3445)	-.6017 (.2802)
Independent	-.7037*** (.2415)	-.4121* (.2235)	-.7415 (.4518)	-1.231** (.5883)	-.6653** (.3094)	-.2900 (.2554)
Blacks Still Face Discrimination	.6849**** (.1350)	.3337*** (.1220)	.4720** (.2244)	.1951 (-2.582)	.8873**** (.1937)	.3466** (.1455)
Constant	-2.889**** (.7263)	-1.824*** (.6485)	-2.736** (1.336)	-2.582* (1.55)	-2.571*** (.9353)	-1.364* (.7220)
Pseudo R²	0.14		0.08		0.11	
N =	887		296		566	

Source: 2009 Pew Research Center Social Trends and Racial Attitudes II Survey
Note: Standard errors are indicated in the parentheses; *p≤.10; **p≤.05; ***p≤.01; ****p≤.001; the baseline category is "race is not a reason in opposition to the president's policies."

being a major reason. However, believing that blacks still face recognizable discrimination in today's society has a liberalizing effect on whites' perspectives about race being a major reason for President Obama's political opposition.

Conclusion

The results of this study elucidate how perceptions of President Obama's treatment are, indeed, racially divided. Whereas most blacks perceive that the president experiences political opposition rooted in racism, most whites perceive that race is not a reason for this political disdain. Among both blacks and whites, believing that President Obama shares values and interests with one personally increases the perception that race does have some effect on his role in the policymaking process. Being Republican increases the odds that neither blacks nor whites will perceive race as not being a factor in his political opposition, and only among whites does being independent of party allegiances increase the odds of not seeing race as a reason in comparison to the odds of race being a major reason.

Socioeconomic factors also affect blacks and whites differently. While education enhances the odds of blacks perceiving a minor effect of race on the opposition toward the president's policy bargaining in comparison to race not being a factor, for whites, income has the effect of increasing the odds that they will not see race as a factor whatsoever, when compared to race being a major reason. Most often, believing that blacks still face discrimination has a sensitizing effect among blacks and whites to perceiving that race affects the opposition to the president.

The broader implications of this research suggest that, despite making history and breaking racial barriers in electoral gains as a black candidate, black Americans perceive that a major obstacle the president faces is overcoming discrimination based on his race. In view of this perception, we must reflect on what this means for blacks feeling as if the election of a black president really has political, substantive effects.

With the election of an African American to the highest office in the United States, the group for which many scholars have theorized that descriptive and substantive representations by a black representative will have psychological resolve clearly still worries about the effects of race on the bargaining power of black politicians. This perception stands to affect blacks' political efficacy and their faith in the political system's ability to deliver justice and equality without racial discrimination. Even more, these results imply that the leverage politics that presidential scholar Ronald Walters suggests blacks engage in may be even more limited by the groups' political bargaining power. In addition the black representatives in attempting to influence policy outcomes may face discriminatory treatment that undermines their effectiveness. Clearly blacks see no exception in the presidency. Obama's election contributed to a more positive psychological effect in relation to descriptive representation. As to the actual exercise of power, Obama in office may be perceived by African Americans to be less able to execute his responsibilities and realize his objectives due to a continuing race-based opposition.

Appendix

Dependent Variable. Respondents were asked, "Thinking about opposition to Barack Obama's policies, do you think that his race is a major reason, a minor reason, or not a reason people oppose Barack Obama's policies?" Responses are coded 1 = a major reason; 2 = a minor reason; and 3 = not a reason. Because the dependent variable is an unordered nominal variable, I use multinomial logit regression to determine factors that predict whether one finds the president's race is either 1, "a major reason," or 2, "a minor reason," in comparison to the baseline category for this analysis, which is 3, "not a reason."

Negative coefficients in this analysis indicate that the statistically significant covariates lead to increased odds that race is "not a reason," whereas positive coefficients, depending upon the comparative category, indicate either increased odds that race is a "major reason" or a "minor reason" in explaining opposition to the president's policies. I model three separate models for (1) both black and white public opinions for a comparative analysis, (2) white public opinion only, and (3) black public opinion only.

Independent Variables. Standard sociodemographic variables control for *race* (1 = black, 0 = white); *gender* (1 = female, 0 = male); *black*men* (interaction for attitudes of black men); *income* (1 = less than $10,000 through 9 = $150,000 or more); *education* (1 = none, or grade 1-8 through 7 = post-graduate training or professional); *south* (1 = South, 0 = non-South); *age* (18 through 97 or more). Again, blacks (male and female) should be more receptive than whites (male and female) to the effect of race on opposition to President Obama's policies. Because of the significance of gender in the presidential primary race between Obama and Hillary Clinton, I include interaction terms between race and gender to control for disparate attitudes between white women and all other racial-gender groups.

Changes for Blacks' Equal Rights with Whites. Respondents were asked, "Which of these two statements comes closer to your own views—even if neither is exactly right: 1 = "Our country needs to continue making changes to give blacks equal rights with whites," or 0 = "Our country has made the changes needed to give blacks equal rights with whites." Because perceptions of need to correct racial injustice imply that racial discrimination still exists, people who feel that the nation needs to continue making changes to give blacks equal rights with whites should have a greater odds of feeling that race is a major reason for opposition to President Obama's policies.

Shared Values with President Obama. Respondents were asked, "How much would you say Barack Obama shares the values and interests of people like you?" Responses are coded 1 = Not at all to 4 = A lot. Because values can be racialized in a way that people detract morality and humanity from blacks, this measure captures attitudes about the morality the president shares with them personally. Assuming that people will see themselves as being moral, if they detect a difference in their morality and the president's, then, they should see him in immoral terms. That is, people who feel President Obama shares their values and interests will be more receptive to racial discrimination in opposition to his policy proposals.

Contemporary Discrimination Against Blacks. Respondents were asked, "Please tell me how much discrimination there is against each of these groups in our society today. How about [blacks]? Would you say there is a lot, some, only a little, or none at all?" Responses are coded 1 = Not at all to 4 = A lot. In perceiving that blacks perceive much discrimination today, people should be sensitized to the plight of the president as a black person who also potentially faces racial discrimination. Therefore, they should have greater odds of perceiving race to be a major reason for opposition to the president's policies.

Consumption of Media. *(1) Reads the Newspaper.* Respondents were asked whether they read the newspaper either "regularly" (code = 1) or "not regularly" (code = 0). Reading the newspaper should have a negligible effect on respondents' perceptions of President Obama's treatment. However, *(2) Viewing National Television News* (1 = regularly, 0 = not regularly), opens respondents to being exposed to rhetoric that may be perceived as politically damaging to the president's agenda. Thus, "regularly" consuming national television news should sensitize people to the influence of race on the president's agenda setting.

Consumption of Black Media. This measure is included in a model of public opinion specific to blacks only. It comprises an additive scale of black respondents' consumption of black radio shows, black magazines, black newspapers, and black web pages. Each of these measures is scaled 1 = "regularly" and 0 = "not regularly," leading to a scale from 0 through 4, with higher numbers on the scale indicating greater consumption of black media (α = .63). Through exposure to black media, respondents should be introduced to information about the president that highlights racial consciousness-raising issues, especially as they relate to African-American politics. Such exposure should also include any critiques that question the relevance of race in the president's execution of his powers.

Partisanship. To control for the effects of partisanship and general support of the president due to partisan congruency, the models account for dummy variables for being a *Republican* (1 = Republican, 0 = else) and an *Independent* (1 = Independent, 0 = else), which leaves being a *Democrat* as the comparative category. I incorporate dummy variables for the aforementioned categories to control for the relevance of the "American center" in supporting the Obama presidential candidacy.

Notes

1. I use "black," "black American," and "African American" interchangeably to reference people of African descent in the context of the United States.

2. Former vice-presidential candidate for the Democratic Party in the 1988 presidential election, Geraldine Ferraro alluded to gender hindering Clinton's candidacy more than race hindering Obama's candidacy. Renowned feminist Gloria Steinem (2008) also wrote an op-ed in the *New York Times* citing the urgency of electing a woman president before a black president.

3. Scholars like Mendelberg (2001), Hurwitz and Peffley (1997), and Gilens (1996) argue that certain words and issues have become racialized over time because they have become increasingly associated with racial and ethnic minorities. For example, welfare

and crime have become intimately associated with blacks in ways that people do not have to be told explicitly that these issues related to the conditions of this group. Instead, the mere mention of words like "welfare," "crime," or even "urban" can be used in political discourse and elicit underlying (perceivably negative) racial attitudes without mentioning explicitly a specific racial group or that the issue relates to "race." Much of this work on explicit and implicit cueing of race has focused on public opinion effects elicited among whites. However, White (2007) appends this research by examining and confirming the extent to which racial consciousness can be implicitly cued and changed among blacks in a way that either enhances or decreases their support of (social welfare) programs that traditionally have been cued as implicitly racialized among whites.

References

Avery, James M. 2009. "Political Mistrust among African Americans and Support for the Political System." *Political Research Quarterly* 62:132-145.
Bobo, Lawrence and James R. Kluegel. 1993. Opposition to Race-Targeting: Self-Interest, Stratification Ideology, or Racial Attitudes? *American Sociological Review* 58(4): 443-464.
Bobo, Lawrence and Vincent L. Hutchings. 1996. Perceptions of Racial Group Competition: Extending Blumer's Theory of Group Position to a Multiracial Social Context. *American Sociological Review* 61 (December): 951-972.
Bullock, Charles S., III. 1984. "Racial Crossover Voting and the Election of Black Officials." *Journal of Politics* 46(1): 238-251.
Canon, David. 1999. *Race, Redistricting, and Representation: The Unintended Consequences of Black Majority Districts.* Chicago: The University of Chicago Press.
Carmines, Edward G. and James A. Stimson. 1989. *Issue Evolution: Race and the Transformation of American politics.* Princeton, NJ: Princeton University Press.
Cobb, William Jelani. 2008. "As Obama Rises, Old Guard Civil Rights Leaders Scowl." *Washington Post.* January 13. www.washingtonpost.com/wp- dyn/content/article/20 08/01/11AR2008011102000_p.
Entman, Robert M. and Andrew Rojecki. 2000. *The Black Image in the White Mind: Media and Race in America.* Chicago: The University of Chicago Press.
Frasure, Lorrie. 2010. "Jekyll and Hyde: Barack Obama, Racial Identity, and Black Political Behavior." In *Whose Black Politics? Cases in Post-Racial Black Leadership.* ed. Andra Gillespie. New York: Routledge, 133-154.
Gay, Claudine. 2002. Spirals of Trust? The Effect of Descriptive Representation on the Relationship between Citizens and Their Government. *American Journal of Political Science* 46(4): 717-732.
Gilens, Martin. 1999. *Why Americans Hate Welfare: Race, Media, and the Politics of Antipoverty Policy.* Chicago: The University of Chicago Press.
Gillespie, Andra. 2010. "Meet the New Class: Theorizing Young Black Leadership in a 'Postracial' Era." In *Whose Black Politics? Cases in Post-Racial Black Leadership.* ed. Andra Gillespie. New York: Routledge, 9-42.
Graber, Doris A. 2006. *Mass Media and American Politics.* Washington, DC: CQ Press.
Griffin, John D. and Patrick Flavin. 2007. "Racial Differences in Information, Expectations, and Accountability." *Journal of Politics* 69(1): 220-236.
Henry, Charles P. 2008. "Obama '08—Articulate and Clean." *The Black Scholar* 38(1): 3-16.

Highton, Benjamin. 2004. "White Voters and Black Candidates for Congress." *Political Behavior* 26(1): 1-25.

Hughes, Michael and Steven A. Tuch. 2003. Gender Differences in Whites' Racial Attitudes: Are Women's Attitudes Really More Favorable? *Social Psychology Quarterly* 66(4): 384-401.

Kensky, Kate, Bruce W. Hardy, and Kathleen Hall Jamieson. 2010. *The Obama Victory: How Media, Money, and Message Shaped the 2008 Election.* Oxford: Oxford University Press.

Keyssar, Alexander. 2000. *The Right to Vote: The Contested History of Democracy in the United States.* New York: Basic Books.

Kinder, Donald R. and David O. Sears. 1981. "Prejudice and Politics: Symbolic Racism versus Racial Threats to the Good Life." *Journal of Personality and Social Psychology* 40(3): 414-431.

Kinder, Donald R. and Lynn Sanders. 1996. *Divided by Color: Racial Politics and Democratic Ideals.* Chicago: The University of Chicago Press.

Kinder, Donald R. and Nicholas Winter. 2001. "Exploring the Racial Divide: Blacks, Whites, and Opinion on National Policy." *American Journal of Political Science* 45(2): 439-456.

Larson, Stephanie Greco. 2006. *Media and Minorities: The Politics of Race in Entertainment.* Lanham, MD: Rowman and Littlefield Publishers, Inc.

Lopez, Linda and Adrian D. Pantoja. 2004. Beyond Black and White: General Support for Race-Conscious Policies among African Americans, Latinos, Asian Americans, and Whites. *Political Research Quarterly* 57(4): 633-642.

Lublin, David. 1996. *The Paradox of Representation: Racial Gerrymandering and Minority Interests in Congress.* Princeton, NJ: Princeton University Press.

Lublin, David and Stephen Voss. 2000. Racial Redistricting and Realignment in Southern State Legislatures. *American Journal of Political Science* 44: 792-810.

McAdam, Doug. 1982. *Political Process and the Development of Black Insurgency, 1930-1970.* Chicago: The University of Chicago Press.

McClain, Paula D. and Joseph M. Stewart. 2006. "Can We All Get Along?" *Racial and Ethnic Minorities in American Politics.* Boulder, CO: Westview Press.

McCormick, Joseph P. and Charles E. Jones. 1993. "The Conceptualization of De-Racialization." In *Dilemmas of Black Politics.* Georgia Persons, ed. New York: HarperCollins College Publishers, 66-84.

McDermott, Monika. 1997. "Voting Cues in Low Information Elections: Candidate Gender as a Social Information Variable in Contemporary United States Elections." *American Journal of Political Science* 41(1): 270-283.

———. 1998. "Race and Gender Cues in Low-Information Elections." *Political Research Quarterly* 51: 895-918.

McIlwan, Charles. 2007. "Perceptions of Leadership and the Challenge of Obama's Blackness." *Journal of Black Studies* 38(1): 64-74.

Nelson, Thomas E., Kira Sanbonmatsu, and Harwood K. McClerking. 2007. "Playing a Different Race Card: Examining the Limits of Elite Influence on Perceptions of Racism." *Journal of Politics* 69(2): 416-429.

Newton, Kenneth. 1999. "Mass Media Effects: Mobilization or Media Malaise?" *British Journal of Political Science* 29(4): 577-599.

Niven, David. 2004. "A Fair Test of Media Bias: Party, Race, and Gender in Coverage of the 1992 House Banking Scandal." *Polity* 36(4): 637-649.

Obama, Barack. 2008. "A More Perfect Union." March 18. Text of Speech: www.huffingtonpost.com/2008/03/18/obama-race-speech-read-th_n_92077.html

Orey, Byron D. and Boris E. Ricks. 2007. "A Systematic Analysis of the Deracialization Concept." *National Political Science Review* 11: 325-334.

Parks, Gregory S. and Jeffrey J. Rachlinski. 2009. "Barack Obama's Candidacy and the Collateral Consequences of the 'Politics of Fear.'" eds. Manning Marable and Kristen Clarke. *In Barack Obama and African American Empowerment: The Rise of Black America's New Leadership.* New York: Palgrave MacMillan, 225-239.

Pitkin, Hannah. 1967. *The Concept of Representation.* Berkeley: University of California Press.

Plutzer, Eric and John F. Zipp. "Identity Politics, Partisanship, and Voting for Women Candidates." *Public Opinion Quarterly* 60(1): 30-57.

Reeves, Keith. 1997. *Voting Hopes or Fears?: White Voters, Black Candidates and Racial Politics in America.* New York: Oxford University Press.

Robinson, Eugene. 2010. "Racism and the Tea Party Movement." November 2. www.realclearpolitics.com/articles/2010/11/02/race_and_the_tea_partys_ire_10780 5.html (accessed April 9, 2011).

Sanders Thompson, Vetta L. 1992. A Multi-faceted Approach to the Conceptualization of African American Identification. *Journal of Black Studies* 23 (September): 75-85.

Sanders Thompson, Vetta L. 1996. Perceived Experiences of Racism as Stressful Life Events. In *Community Mental Health Journal* 32: 223-233.

Schuman, Howard, Charlotte Steeh, Lawrence Bobo, Maria Krysan. 1997. *Racial Attitudes in America: Trends and Interpretations.* Cambridge, MA: Harvard University Press.

Sears, David O., Jim Sidanius, and Lawrence Bobo. 2000. *Racialized Politics: The Debate about Racism in America.* Chicago: The University of Chicago Press.

Seelye, Katharine. Q. 2008. "The Race Factor in Pa. Primary." *New York Times,* April 23. thecaucus.blogs.nytimes.com/2008/04/23/the-race-factor-in-pa-primary/

Shull, Steven A. 1999. *American Civil Rights Policy from Truman to Clinton: The Role of Presidential Leadership.* Armonk, NY: M.E. Sharpe.

Steinem, Gloria. 2008. "Women Are Never Front-Runners." *New York Times,* January 8. www.nytimes.com/2008/01/08/opinion/08steinem.html. (accessed April 7, 2011).

Swain, Carol. 1995. *Black Faces, Black Interests: The Representation of African Americans in Congress.* Cambridge, MA: Harvard University Press.

Tate, Katherine. 2003. *Black Faces in the Mirror: African Americans and Their Representatives in the U.S. Congress.* Princeton, NJ: Princeton University Press.

Terkildsen, Nayda. 1993. "When White Voters Evaluate Black Candidates: The Processing Implications of Candidate Skin Color, Prejudice, and Self-Monitoring." *American Journal of Political Science* 37(4): 1032-1053.

Thomas, Evan, Holly Bailey, and Richard Wolffe. 2008. "Only in America." May 5, 2008. *Newsweek,* 28-33.

Voss, Stephen and David Lublin. 2001. "Black Incumbents, White Districts: An Appraisal of the 1996 Congressional Elections." *American Political Research* 29: 141-182.

Walters, Ronald. 1988. *Black Presidential Politics in America: A Strategic Approach.* New York: State University of New York Press.

Walters, Ronald. 2005. *Freedom Is Not Enough: Black Voters, Black Candidates, and American Presidential Politics.* Lanham, MD: Rowman and Littlefield Publishers, Inc.

White, Ismail K. 2007. "When Race Matters and When It Doesn't: Racial Group Differences in Response to Racial Cues." *American Political Science Review* 101(2): 339-354.

Williams, Linda. 1990. "White/Black Perceptions of the Electability of Black Political Candidates." In *Black Electoral Politics*, ed. Lucius J. Barker. New Brunswick, NJ: Transaction Publishers.

Chapter 7

Minority Party Strategies and Political Successes in Opposition to the Obama Policy Agenda

R. Lawrence Butler

Introduction

As Barack Obama rose to take the oath of office as President of the United States, he stood on the verge of a once-in-a-generation opportunity. After two consecutive landslide victories in congressional elections, his Democrats controlled 59 percent of the seats in the House of Representatives and fifty-eight seats in the Senate, which still had one contest undecided. Democrats were very close to being able to engage in responsible party governance to enact Obama's ambitious agenda.

For over a century, a number of political scientists (for example, Wilson, 1885; Hasbrouck, 1927; Schattschneider, 1942; Ranney, 1962; and Chambers and Burnham, 1975) had praised the virtues of the Responsible Party Government model. In this model, patterned after parliamentary systems, candidates for national office run on a unified party platform and vote together as a group to pass the majority's agenda into law. The advantages of such a system are that it clarifies voter choices, leads to the adoption of coherent policy, and provides accountability. However, the Responsible Party Government model has never translated well into the American system of separated powers, checks and balances, and supermajority Senate rules.

On April 28, 2009, those barriers were cleared. Republican Senator Arlen Specter (PA) announced that he was switching to the Democratic Party. In Minnesota, it had become apparent that Democrat Al Franken would ultimately win the last remaining undecided Senate election. (On June 30, the Minnesota Supreme Court declared him the victor.) For the first time in thirty years, one party controlled the White House, the House of Representatives, and a filibuster-proof majority in the Senate.

By the time of the 2010 midterm elections, President Obama and the Democrats had enacted a stimulus package, an overhaul of the healthcare system, and major revisions to the system of regulations for the financial services industry. However, after Republicans picked up sixty-three House seats to win control of that chamber and six Senate seats, Democrats were scrambling to enact other parts of the president's agenda. Cap and Trade had been passed by the House but never came to a vote in the Senate. Comprehensive immigration reform had not been brought to the floor of either chamber. Don't Ask Don't Tell was still the law of the land, the START II treaty remained unratified, and the U.S. prison facility at Guantanamo Bay remained open. In 2010, neither the House nor the Senate passed any appropriations bills. During the post-election lame duck session, Congress repealed Don't Ask Don't Tell and ratified START II, but it also renewed the Bush era tax rates for all income levels (Democrats wanted them to rise for those making over $250,000 per year) and passed a short continuing resolution giving Republicans the opportunity to cut spending in the new Congress.

Strategizing Party Positioning in Congress

The goal of this paper is to examine the strategic choices made by the two parties during the 111th Congress and by moderate senators of both parties. Was the Obama agenda crippled by a brilliant and well-executed Republican strategy of obstruction? Or did Democrats make strategic errors that slowed themselves down? The analysis will draw heavily on a spatial voting model of Congress to assess those choices and determine who blocked much of the Obama agenda. It will also examine the electoral incentives of Senate moderates and the importance of the partisan public relations battle in determining the outcome. Finally, it examines the Democrats' management of the legislative process to assess whether their strategy unnecessarily slowed the enactment of the president's initiatives.

Polarization and Majority Party Strategy

In addition to the size of the majority, an important factor in determining party legislative strategies is the level of polarization in Congress. If there is a large ideological overlap between the two parties, then a partisan strategy becomes less attractive. Democrats could count on some liberal Republicans to support their legislative initiatives. However, when ideological polarization supplements the partisan divide, bipartisanship becomes less likely (see Appendix).

Figure 7.1. Polarization in the House and Senate, 1961-2010

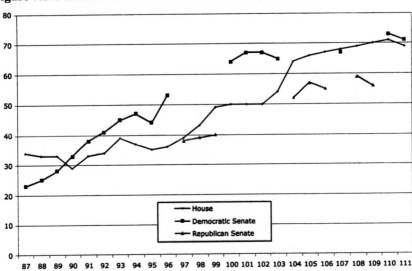

Source: Compiled by author.

Over the past fifty years, ideological polarization of the Congress has soared. Figure 7.1 shows the increase in polarization in the Congress since the Kennedy administration. In the House of Representatives, polarization fluctuated with no clear trend during the 1960s and 1970s. After that, it rose steadily with sharp increases in the first six years of the Reagan administration and in President Clinton's first term. The Senate polarization data require greater explanation. Since the beginning of the Nixon administration, Senate Republicans have been consistently more ideologically diffuse than have Senate Democrats. Thus, σ_m increases whenever the Republicans take charge and decreases when the Democrats regain control. Thus, we have split the Senate time series in two, separating Congresses with Democratic control of the Senate from those with Republican control.[1] The data show that both Democratic and Republican Senates have grown much more polarized in the past fifty years.

Entering the 111th Congress, there could be no doubt about the strong ideological polarization in both the House and Senate. Indeed, in the 111th Congress there was no ideological overlap between the parties at all in either chamber. No Democrat was more conservative than any of his Republican colleagues. Moreover, this was not a new phenomenon. Perfect polarization had existed in the Senate since conservative Democrat Zell Miller (GA) retired in 2004, and in the House since January 2004, when Ralph Hall (TX) switched to the Republican Party. The Specter defection did not change the degree of polarization as he was, at the time, the most liberal Republican in the Senate. Moreover, research on party switchers demonstrates that their voting habits more closely resemble those of their adopted party once they defect (Nokken, 2000; McCarty, Poole and Rosenthal, 2001; Nokken and Poole, 2004).

Utilizing this spatial voting model under the conditions that existed in 2009 makes the strategic choice of Democratic legislative leaders an obvious one. Strictly from a policy perspective, responsible party governance was the only logical strategy. Democrats did not need Republican votes in either chamber, and any effort to attract them could only push the policy outcome to the right—farther away from Democratic preferences and the Obama proposals. Such a partisan strategy would be easy in the House, where Democrats held a 9 percent cushion and could afford to have numerous members cast negative votes. In the Senate, however, responsible party governance would require unanimity among Democrats.

Minority Party Strategy

Little scholarly research has been conducted on minority party strategy. The seminal work on this subject, Charles O. Jones's *The Minority Party in Congress* (1970), catalogs the internal and external political conditions facing congressional minorities and describes the strategies available to them. Jones argues that a minority party's potential influence is determined by a variety of political conditions. The external conditions include the extent of party unity, the strength of the President, the partisan balance of the electorate, and the presence of unified or divided government. Internal conditions include the size of the majority, the strength of party leadership, and the duration of minority status.

These conditions facing the minority party determine the range of potential strategies available to them. Jones describes eight potential options.

1) Support—The minority supports the majority-building efforts of the majority party.
2) Inconsequential Opposition—The minority party opposes majority initiatives without offering alternatives.
3) Withdrawal—The minority party takes no position on majority initiatives.

4) Cooperation—The minority party contributes to the crafting of majority initiatives.

5) Innovation—The minority party seeks to build majorities to enact its own initiatives.

6) Consequential Partisan Opposition—The minority party opposes majority initiatives without offering alternatives.[2]

7) Consequential Constructive Opposition—The minority party opposes majority initiatives but offers alternative solutions.

8) Participation—The minority party is able to participate in policy making because it controls the White House.

The political conditions described above limit the range of strategies available to the minority party but do not necessarily determine which will be used. Minority parties are concerned both with winning elections and influencing public policy. The balance of these priorities also contributes to the strategic selection.

The ubiquity of filibusters in the contemporary Senate has increased the influence of the minority party since Jones's book was published. Most significant legislation is subject to filibuster. With forty-one seats, the minority party has the potential to shape policy outcomes. Thus, the threshold over which the majority party in the Senate renders the minority powerless has risen to sixty seats, a level seldom achieved.

The size of the Democratic majority, unified government, and the ideological polarization of the parties make the conditions for Republicans in the 111th Congress most resemble Jones's Restricted Minority category. In such circumstances, Jones sees three viable strategies: Support, Inconsequential Opposition, or Withdrawal. In the 111th Congress, the Republicans' strategic choice was obvious. With Democrats having a dominant strategy of party governance, and having the numbers to carry it out, Republicans had no reason to believe that they could affect policy outcomes. Even if they worked constructively with the majority, there was no incentive for Democrats to make any policy concessions. Being irrelevant with respect to policy, Republicans were freed to adopt a strategy of minimizing policy losses and maximizing political gains. With an energized activist base and the hope of making substantial gains in the 2010 elections, withdrawal would have been foolish. Thus, a strategy of unified opposition to Democratic initiatives was the only sensible option for Republicans.

The Republicans' plan to maximize the effectiveness of this political strategy had three elements. First, change the political dynamic to increase the incentive for moderate Democrats to oppose their party leadership. Second, slow down the process so that Democrats would achieve less in the current Congress. Third, position themselves to make large gains in the midterm elections so that Democrats would no longer be able to exclude Republicans. The best strategy to achieve these goals was to forget about policy making and instead adopt a "position taking" strategy. Oppose the Democrats' initiatives and lay out political arguments that would lead the public to do likewise. Such an obstructionist approach was not new. In fact, Nancy Pelosi had used it to great effect as Minority

Leader and Speaker during the second term of President George W. Bush (Butler, 2010). The result was consecutive landslide victories for Democrats in 2006 and 2008.

The Political Calculus for Senate Moderates

Pure spatial voting models like those of Krehbiel (1998) and Brady and Volden (2005) leave little room for political effects. In these stylized models, the preferences of the sixtieth senator from the left in the 111th Congress determine policy outcomes. However, legislators' preferences change as the political environment evolves. Fenno (1973) first established that legislators have three goals: policymaking, re-election, and gaining institutional influence. Since congressional rules and norms give the majority party a great deal more power than the minority, legislators of all ideologies want their party to succeed. This creates an incentive for them to support their party leaders to the maximum extent possible. However, this can be offset by the threat of losing their own re-election contest if the mood of their electorate turns against them.

Over the course of 2009, it became clear that Republicans were winning the political battle. President Obama's approval rating inevitably fell from its 65 percent level on the day of inauguration, but by the beginning of 2010, it had dropped all the way to 48 percent. By July 2009, more people said they opposed the President's healthcare plan than supported it—a gap that grew to 10 points by the end of the year. Democrats fell from a 4-point advantage on the generic congressional ballot question to a 1-point deficit. The percentage of adults identifying themselves as Democrats fell by 5 points during 2009 to 32, while the percentage identifying themselves as Republicans fell by only 1 point to 24.[3] By all measures, public support for the Democrats and their initiatives fell significantly during President Obama's first year in office.

This decline in their party's fortunes increased the incentive for moderate Democrats to vote against their party's positions, thus making responsible party governance more difficult. This effect was of little importance in the House because of its majority rules. Democrats controlled 9 percent more seats than they needed for a majority, so they could afford to have as many as thirty-nine of their members vote with Republicans on any given issue. In the Senate, however, Democrats had no margin for error. With Republicans adopting a strategy of Inconsequential Opposition, every Democrat was needed to break a filibuster.

Electoral pressures, however, come from more than the macro-political environment. This is particularly true in the Senate, in which only one-third of its members are up for re-election each cycle. Let us look, therefore, at the electoral circumstances of the most moderate senators from both parties who served during 2009.[4]

Table 7.1. DW-NOMINATE Scores for Five Most Moderate Senators in Each Party

Democrats		Republicans	
Nelson (NE)	-0.027	Snowe (ME)	0.085
Lincoln (AR)	-0.183	Collins (ME)	0.098
Bayh (IN)	-0.185	Murkowski (AK)	0.246
Carper (DE)	-0.189	Voinovich (OH)	0.261
Nelson (FL)	-0.195	Cochran (MS)	0.292

Source: Data drawn from DW-NOMINATE scores for the 111th Congress, available at Voteview.com.

Of the five Republican Senators listed in table 7.1, only Lisa Murkowski and George Voinovich held seats whose terms expired in 2010. Voinovich announced in January 2009 that he would not seek re-election. Murkowski's Alaska gave President Obama only 38 percent of its vote in 2008. Moreover, Murkowski faced a potential primary challenge from the right, so she had no electoral incentive to vote with the Democrats.[5] Similarly, Thad Cochran represented the state of Mississippi, which John McCain carried by a 56-43 margin in 2008, so he also had no political incentive to support the Obama agenda.

Only Olympia Snowe and Susan Collins of Maine could reasonably have been persuaded to break from their party and side with Democrats. President Obama carried their home state 58-40 and neither faced an immediate threat of a primary challenge. In a different political climate, they might have decided to support significant portions of the Democratic agenda. However, as Democrats were losing the battle for public opinion, Snowe and Collins had little incentive to bail them out. Thus, they adhered to the Republican Party strategy throughout the 111th Congress and worked to block the Obama agenda.

Among moderate Democrats, only the seats of Blanche Lincoln and Evan Bayh were on the ballot in 2010. In February 2010, Bayh announced that he would not seek re-election, removing any electoral incentive for him to break from his party. Sen. Lincoln faced the most daunting electoral challenge of any incumbent up for re-election in 2010. Her home state of Arkansas had given President Obama only 39 percent of its vote. However, she also faced the prospect of a primary challenge from Arkansas' more liberal Lieutenant Governor Bill Halter. The primary challenge increased her incentive to vote with her party, but even if she cleared that hurdle she would have to win over her conservative state in the general election.[6]

The potential impact of the sour political climate varied among the three remaining moderate Senate Democrats. Tom Carper's Delaware had supported

President Obama 62-37 and was the home state of Vice President Joe Biden, so Carper had little incentive to buck his party. Bill Nelson represented the swing state of Florida, which theoretically could have caused him problems. However, President Obama carried this increasingly conservative state 51-48, offsetting the macro-political pressure Nelson might have felt.

While not facing the voters until 2012, Sen. Ben Nelson of Nebraska always had to worry about his re-election prospects. Although President Obama had earned one of Nebraska's electoral votes by narrowly winning the Omaha-based second district, John McCain had carried the state by a 57-42 margin. Moreover, his own ideology was well to the right of his Democratic Senate colleagues. As table 7.1 shows, on a unidimensional ideological scale, Nelson was closer to Republican Sen. Snowe than he was to Sen. Lincoln, the second most conservative Democrat. Thus, even though he was not up for re-election in 2010, the political wind blowing against the Democrats was a powerful force dragging him to oppose his party's legislative agenda.

This analysis of the electoral conditions of Senate moderates demonstrates the great cost to the Democrats of losing the public opinion war. If Democrats and their signature legislation had remained popular, it would have been much easier for them to keep their moderates on board—and Republican Senators Snowe and Collins might have hopped on the train as well. Instead, the macro-political climate made the votes of Snowe and Collins unwinnable for Democrats and increased the difficulty of holding their party together. The Democrats' loss of popular support made responsible party governance much more difficult to accomplish.

Democrats' Legislative Strategy

In a parliamentary system, the process by which responsible party governance occurs is a straightforward one. During the campaign, the party lays out an agenda and its candidates run on that platform. Parliamentary leaders, therefore, need only draft the legislative language in conjunction with their members, bring the bill to the floor, and pass it. In the American system, such a process would be much more complex even if one party controlled the White House, the House of Representatives, and sixty Senate seats. First, individual candidates do not run on a unified platform, so the legislative agenda and bill language would need to be crafted after the elections. Second, legislation needs to be passed by both the House and the Senate, then signed into law by the president. Thus, the agenda and the bill language would need to be acceptable to all three institutional actors.

How could this work in practice? One method would be for the president, as leader of his party, to call a summit of the leaders of both chambers. At that summit, the leaders, in consultation with their members, would craft an agenda and develop legislation acceptable to at least 60 senators and 218 House members. That legislation would then be put into formal legislative language, offered on the floor of both chambers, and passed without amendment. A second approach would be for the White House staff, as agents of the leader of the party, to draft the legislation with both chambers agreeing to pass whatever is submitted. Of these two options, the first method likely would be more effective because the process would identify the areas in which careful compromise is necessary to assure broad acceptance from all players.

Under this process, the minority party would still be able to use the Senate's tradition of unlimited debate to slow things down. However, with sixty members, the majority party would be able to muscle the legislation through with only limited delays. An example of this occurred during the debate over President Obama's healthcare reform initiative. On December 18, 2009, Senate Democrats finalized a bill that they all agreed to support. Republicans used every delaying technique available, but the bill passed six days later.

During the 111th Congress, neither the president nor congressional Democrats followed this process. President Obama called no summit, preferring to let Congress take the lead in drafting his major initiatives. Perhaps he had overlearned the lessons of the Clinton administration's failed attempt at healthcare reform. Then, a White House task force led by the first lady crafted an intricate, detailed plan and presented it to Congress. Congress balked and passed nothing. However, Jonathan Alter (2010) argues that the Obama approach reflected his legislative leadership philosophy, not just his interpretation of the Clinton effort:

> By letting Congress take the lead, he gave lawmakers the ownership necessary for genuine action . . . Obama showed a few cards early, but he liked to stay flexible on his bottom line until the House and Senate were resolving their differences at the end of the process.

Instead of empowering Congress by allowing their leaders to participate in the development of the bill in private, Obama let the messy and lengthy legislative process take its course, stepping in to bless compromises when needed to advance the bill.

Senate Democrats were very slow to take advantage of the opportunity provided by their filibuster-proof majority. The Finance Committee spent months trying to negotiate an agreement that could win the support of Sen. Olympia Snowe (ME), the least conservative member of her caucus. Ultimately, she did support the committee bill, but the negotiations lasted until mid-October 2009. The Senate Committee on Health, Education, Labor and Pensions had also passed a bill in July 2009 on a straight party-line vote that did not include the compromises that became part of the Finance Committee bill. Until December, Senate Majority Leader Harry Reid (NV) continued to search for a bill that would blend the two committee approaches while still winning Senator Snowe's vote. Ultimately, he gave up on winning any Republican support and crafted a Democrats-only coalition. Once that deal was finalized, Democrats passed the bill through the Senate quickly despite several Republican filibusters.

In the House, Speaker Nancy Pelosi (CA) had no such hesitation about party governance. With her large majority, she had frequently passed legislation with little or no Republican support. In November, with the vote of only one Republican representative, the House passed its version of healthcare reform. While this clearly represented an exercise in unicameral party governance, Pelosi intentionally crafted a bill that was too liberal for moderate Democratic Senators to support. Her strategy was to position the House so that she would have the maximum possible leverage to drag the Senate to the left during conference negotiations (Butler, 2010). This transformed party governance from a one-stage game to a two-stage game. By shifting the creation of a bicameral agreement from the beginning of the process to the end, she forced an extra round of negotiations. As if the Senate bill and the House bill had not taken long enough to work out, now another round of talks had to be launched, which delayed final passage for an additional three months.

The Republicans' choice of an obstructionist strategy was an obvious one. Since Democrats did not need their help to pass legislation, delay and position-taking with an eye toward the next election were their only options. It took the White House and Senate Democrats a full year to recognize that Republicans were executing their strategy to perfection, so party governance was their only option. During that time, Democrats managed to enact a stimulus package and set up healthcare reform for final passage—two important parts of the Obama agenda—but much remained to be done. By the time the Democrats found their footing, the rug was pulled out from under them.

Senator Scott Brown Ends Party Governance

On January 19, 2010, Republican Scott Brown won a special election to finish the term of the recently deceased Senator Edward M. Kennedy (D-MA). Brown had effectively capitalized on the populist angst in the state and the utter ineptitude of his Democratic opponent's campaign. This left Senate Democrats one seat shy of a filibuster-proof majority. Now they would have to convince at least one Republican to support their initiatives to enact the Obama agenda. Brown himself was an attractive target for such Democratic wooing. He proved to be the third most liberal Republican behind only Maine Senators Snowe and Collins. Moreover, he would be facing re-election in three years in navy blue Massachusetts, with President Obama on the ballot, and likely against a more competent opponent. Nonetheless, Republican unity held.

Over the course of Obama's first year in office, two things had occurred that raised the cost of defection for moderate Senate Republicans. One was the development of a sense of collective grievance. Senate Republicans were angered by what they saw as heavy-handed tactics during the healthcare reform endgame, such as late-night and weekend sessions running all the way to Christmas Eve. Such perceived slights can be a powerful unifier of even the most downtrodden minority. Connelly and Pitney (1994) chronicle the transformation of House Republicans from quiescence to confrontation in the late

1980s, despite having been in the minority for thirty years and having little immediate hope for majority status. Procedural and administrative strong-arming, particularly by Speaker Wright (D-TX), and the controversy over a razor-close election in Indiana encouraged even the most accommodating moderates to mount the battlements with their fiery younger colleagues.

Additionally, the mood of the voters had changed. The president's popularity had declined, as had support for many parts of his agenda. The Republican base had been activated and a new populist conservative movement—the Tea Party—had arisen and mobilized. Polls showed that Republicans would make major gains in the 2010 midterm elections, perhaps even retaking one or both chambers. Knowing that they would have much greater influence in the next Congress, Republicans had every incentive to continue to delay the Obama agenda.

Thus, the newly empowered Senate Republican minority opted for a strategy of Consequential Partisan Opposition. They could have opted to be a constructive policy making force, but the political climate led them to continue their obstructionism. The extent to which Senate Republicans were wedded to their strategy can be seen in the actions of Senators Snowe and Collins during the lame-duck session of December 2010. Both had pledged, along with all other Republicans, to block consideration of any measure until the Senate had passed a continuing resolution and dealt with the extension of Bush-era tax rates. When Senator Reid called up legislation to repeal the military's Don't Ask, Don't Tell policy—a bill both had long supported—they joined a filibuster against its consideration until later in the session.[7] Given the mood of the Republican caucus and the impending elections, few significant pieces of the Obama agenda had any hope of enactment after Sen. Brown's election.

Conclusion

As President Barack Obama stood at the dais of the House of Representatives to deliver his 2011 State of the Union address, he looked out upon a new political environment. Seated behind him was a Republican Speaker of the House, John Boehner of Ohio. Among the crowd sat a Republican Senate caucus that was six members larger, including a handful of populist conservatives who had been swept into office with the backing of the Tea Party movement. The message of his speech was quite different from that of his inaugural address. Gone was the lofty language of endless hope, replaced by calls for bipartisan effort to address the country's immediate problems. His unfinished agenda now had to get past a Republican House, and thus had to be scaled back dramatically.

In the 111th Congress, Republicans effectively executed their strategy of delay and confrontation, but that by itself was not enough to stop the Obama agenda. Democrats' large majorities combined with the ideological polarization of the Congress enabled them to engage in party governance for the first time in decades. They had the ability to ignore Republicans and sidestep any obstacles laid in their path. In losing the battle for public opinion, Democrats made it easier for Republicans to remain united, and made it harder to keep their own moderates from straying. Moreover, they made a series of errors in legislative strategy that slowed their pace dramatically. President Obama needed to take a much more active role in creating policy consensus among Democratic lawmakers. Senate Majority Leader Reid and his committee chairs were too slow in recognizing the need for party governance. And Speaker Pelosi needed to cut a deal with the Senate before bringing bills to the House floor instead of forcing a conference. As a result, Democrats simply ran out of time.

Appendix

We examine the ideological positions of House and Senate members over the period using DW-NOMINATE score.[8] DW-NOMINATE is an algorithm that establishes a multi-dimensional ideological position for each member of Congress based on every floor vote they have cast in the chamber (Poole and Rosenthal, 2007). A statistical analysis of the changes in the ideological clusters for each of the parties in each of the chambers since the 87th Congress (1961-62) reveals the emergence of stark polarization of the Congress.

We measure polarization using a technique first proposed by Aldrich, Berger and Rohde (2002) that compares the ideological dispersion of the majority party to that of the chamber as a whole.[9] This index calculates the level of polarization in either chamber for each Congress using the formula

$$(1) \qquad\qquad 100(1 - \sigma_m/\sigma_a)$$

where σ_m is the standard error of the first dimension DW-NOMINATE scores for the members of the majority party and σ_a is the standard error of the first dimension DW-NOMINATE scores for all members of the chamber. This statistic takes on a value of 100 if all members of the majority party are ideologically identical and a value of 0 if their ideological dispersion equals that of the entire chamber.

Notes

1. For the 107th Congress, partisan control of the Senate switched hands several times. We treat Democrats as the majority party because they held the advantage for the vast majority of the Congress.

2. The difference between Inconsequential and Consequential Opposition involves the ability of the minority party to influence the policy outcome. With Inconsequential Opposition, the minority has no influence so it chooses to oppose. With Consequential Opposition, the minority has the ability to affect the policy outcome, but it chooses to obstruct rather than exercise that influence.

3. Polling data retrieved from Pollster.com, which derives its estimates from all publicly-available surveys.

4. For the purposes of this analysis, we will dismiss Pennsylvania Senator Arlen Specter's time as a Republican. Interestingly, as Nokken, 2000; McCarty, Poole and Rosenthal, 2001; and Nokken and Poole, 2004 would have predicted, Specter's voting record as a Democrat placed him near the ideological center of his new party.

5. Murkowski lost her Republican primary to a Tea-Party-backed candidate, Joe Miller, but won the general election as a write-in candidate.

6. Sen. Lincoln survived the primary challenge after narrowly winning a run-off contest, but lost the general election decisively, 58-37, to Republican Congressman John Boozman.

7. The bill ultimately passed the Senate with the votes of both Snowe and Collins, and was signed into law.

8. DW-NOMINATE scores for every Congress since 1789 are available online at www.voteview.com.

9. For the purpose of this analysis, third-party members are included in the party with which they caucus.

References

Aldrich, John H., Mark M. Berger, and David W. Rohde. 2002. "The Historical Variability in Conditional Party Government, 1877-1994." In *Party, Process, and Political Change in Congress: New Perspectives on the History of Congress*, ed. David W. Brady and Mathew D. McCubbins. Stanford, CA: Stanford University Press.

Alter, Jonathan. 2010. *The Promise: President Obama, Year One*. New York: Simon & Schuster.

Brady, David W. and Craig Volden. 2005. *Revolving Gridlock: Politics and Policy from Jimmy Carter to George W. Bush, 2nd ed.* Boulder, CO: Westview Press.

Butler, R. Lawrence. 2010. "Party Governance Under Speaker Nancy Pelosi." In *The State of the Parties 6th ed.*, ed. John C. Green. Lanham, MD: Rowman and Littlefield.

Chambers, William Nisbet and Walter Dean Burnham, eds. 1975. *The American Party Systems: Stages of Development, 2nd ed.* London: Oxford University Press.

Connelly, William F., Jr. and John J. Pitney, Jr. 1994. *Congress' Permanent Minority?: Republicans in the U.S. House*. Lanham, MD: Rowman and Littlefield.

Fenno, Richard F., Jr. 1973. *Congressmen in Committees*. Boston: Little, Brown and Company.

Hasbrouck, Paul DeWitt. 1927. *Party Government in the House of Representatives*. New York: The MacMillan Company.

Jones, Charles O. 1970. *The Minority Party in Congress*. Boston: Little, Brown and Company.

Krehbiel, Keith. 1998. *Pivotal Politics: A Theory of U.S. Lawmaking*. Chicago: The University of Chicago Press.

McCarty, Nolan, Keith T. Poole, and Howard Rosenthal. 2001. "The Hunt for Party Discipline in Congress." *American Political Science Review*, 95: 673-687.

Nokken, Timothy P. 2000. "Dynamics of Congressional Loyalty: Party Defection and Roll-Call Behavior, 1947-97." *Legislative Studies Quarterly*, XXV: 417-444.

Nokken, Timothy P. and Keith T. Poole. 2004. "Congressional Party Defection in American History." *Legislative Studies Quarterly*, XXIX: 545-568.

Poole, Keith T. and Howard Rosenthal. 2007. *Ideology and Congress.* New Brunswick, NJ: Transaction Publishers.

Ranney, Austin. 1962. *Responsible Party Government: Its Origins and Present State.* Urbana: The University of Illinois Press.

Schattschneider, E. E. 1942. *Party Government.* New York: Farrar and Rinehart.

Wilson, Woodrow. 1885. *Congressional Government.* Boston: Houghton-Mifflin.

Chapter 8

Coalitional Divisions and Realignment Dynamics in the Obama Era

Arthur C. Paulson

Introduction

When Barack Obama was running for president, he often stated his intention to change how things work in Washington. Above all, he seemed to represent the hope that extreme partisan divisions could be bridged and replaced by bipartisan cooperation in policy making.

This hope has hardly been fulfilled. The health care reform proposed by the Obama administration generated ideologically polarized debate, fears of socialism among opponents, and almost entirely partisan voting in both houses of Congress. The Republicans gained control of the House of Representatives in the 2010 Congressional elections after a campaign in which the most fundamental aspects of the role of government were questioned. The Tea Party motivated Republican voters, moved their party to the right, and sharpened public debate even further. There is nothing unhealthy about public debate shaped by clear ideological differences, but the discourse is often bitter and personal with charges flying across the partisan divide in both directions. Rep. Joe Wilson (R-South Carolina) shouted, "You lie!" at the president as he was delivering his State of the Union Address in 2010. Most notable among the personal attacks are charges by more extreme opponents of President Obama questioning his Americanism, his patriotism, his religion, and even his citizenship.

When Rep. Gabrielle Giffords (D-Arizona) was wounded in shootings in Tucson that took the lives of six people and injured fourteen others, some liberals proclaimed their belief that the rhetoric of extreme conservatives created an atmosphere in which such a senseless event was likely to occur.

As President Barack Obama prepared to deliver his 2011 State of the Union address, Senator Mark Udall (D-Colorado) suggested that the regular partisan seating on opposite sides of the aisle for the speech be replaced by seating in bipartisan pairs. Numerous pairs of Senators and Representatives from opposite parties announced that they would sit together, and indeed, the atmosphere at the State of the Union was a good deal more temperate, perhaps even placid, than it had been in recent years.

But the harshness of public discourse cannot be explained by personal behavior alone, or cured by seating at a speech, even if that may be a beginning. Indeed, at this writing, we face the possibility of government shutdown over the budget. Rather, we are living with a party system that has developed over the past half century that is ideologically polarized by the standards of the American experience. This is the party system that is likely to shape the elections of 2012, and elections thereafter into the foreseeable future.

This essay will apply a discussion of today's party system to consider the outlook for the elections of 2012. I will conclude with comments on the prospect for a more civil public discourse.

Parties, Factions and Ideology in American Politics

There is nothing new about ideological extremes in American politics. The Know Nothings, the Wobblies, and the Ku Klux Klan all have had their role to play. Even the abolitionists were considered extremists in antebellum America. What is historically new is the ideological polarization of the party system. Even that did not just happen recently.

The Umbrella Parties

Historically, American political parties are understood better as factional systems than as rational acting organizations. Until critical system change that took place between 1948 and 1972, the major parties were umbrella parties, loose coalitions among interests and factions, each spanning the ideological spectrum of American life (Aldrich, 1995; Paulson, 2007).

The Democratic umbrella has covered a multi-factional system: The party regulars, including labor, the big city organizations, and a working class electoral base; the more middle class reformers; and the more rural, southern, and generally conservative faction (Mayer, 1996a; Paulson, 2007; Rae, 1994). The first two factions are relatively liberal, and there was little to choose between them until they held the Presidency and emerged as a majority within the Democratic Party during the New Deal. Since then, party regulars usually have prioritized economic issues, while the reformers have focused more on the causes of emerging social movements.

The South was once, of course, the factional home of white supremacy in American politics. Southern conservatives held their power within the Democratic Party through seniority in Congress that landed them committee chairs when the Democrats were in the majority, and the two-thirds rule that gave the South an effective veto power over nominations at Democratic National Conventions. As late as 1924, the Democrats narrowly defeated a proposed platform plank condemning the Ku Klux Klan.

The Republican umbrella has covered a more bi-factional system: The relatively moderate-to-liberal Wall Street faction, with its cosmopolitan, internationalist big business interests, and the Main Street faction (Polsby, 1978), with its more conservative, small business, nationalist or isolationist interests. A more complex understanding is offered by Nicol Rae (1989, 1998) who has analyzed the Republicans as a multi-factional system, Wall Street composed of the progressives and moderates, and Main Street composed of the stalwarts and fundamentalists. While a majority of Republicans in Congress came from Main Street, the Wall Street faction delivered presidential nominations for a generation after 1940 to Wendell L. Willkie, Thomas E. Dewey and Dwight D. Eisenhower, defeating Mr. Republican, Senator Robert A. Taft of Ohio, three times. The Republican Party was the party of Lincoln, until the Goldwater revolt of 1964.

From Umbrella Parties to Polarized Parties

An ideologically polarized party system in American politics has emerged since liberal Democrats and conservative Republicans have become the dominant factions in their national parties. The process was more gradual in the Democratic Party and more sudden in the Republican Party. But what made the impact of party change so systemic was that for the first time, factional struggles within both parties reached critical points almost simultaneously, between 1964 and 1972 (Paulson, 2000, 2007, 2009).

For the Democrats, the key moments of party change came in 1936, when the Democratic National Convention replaced the two-thirds rule with majority rule; 1948 when the Democratic National Convention effectively reversed its 1924 roll call be adapting an aggressively pro-civil rights plank into its platform; 1968 when a convention divided over the Vietnam War sought to build party unity by committing to party reform; and 1972, when Senator George McGovern of South Dakota won the Democratic Presidential nomination. The Democrats have ever since been the more liberal of the two major parties.

For the Republicans, the critical turning point is more singularly identifiable: The nomination of Senator Barry Goldwater for the Presidency in 1964. The Goldwater nomination was the result of a self-conscious and well organized ideological revolt from the ground up, in which conservative Republicans seized control of the party at the grass roots, a control they never have relinquished (Novak, 1965; White, 1965; Perlstein, 2009). Since 1964, the Republicans have become the conservative party in American politics.

These decisive factional struggles between 1964 and 1972 were accompanied by electoral realignment in Presidential elections. This realignment did not look like the previous ones, and David Mayhew (2002) has artfully stated his doubt that periodic realignment is a reality in American politics. While I vigorously defend realignment to be a historic reality and a useful concept for electoral analysis (Paulson, 2007), we can concede the point for the sake of argument. If we were to stipulate that periodic electoral realignment is a figment of our imagination, we find one compelling realignment in the 1964-1972 period. Rather than the "surge" realignment (Burnham, 1970; Key, 1955; Pomper with Lederman, 1980; Sundquist, 1983), in which a general shift creates a new majority party, the 1964-1972 sea change was an "interactive" realignment, in which decisive minorities within each party coalition engage in a cross-cutting shift toward the opposing party (Clubb, Flanigan and Zingale, 1990). The decisive shift was among white southerners, who moved from their historic home in the Democratic coalition toward the Republicans (Black and Black, 1992). Since 1968, the Republicans have won seven out of eleven Presidential elections, carrying the South in all seven.

At the same time, there has been a widely overlooked shift in the northeast, once the base of the Republican coalition, toward the Democrats (Speel, 1998; Reiter and Stonecash, 2010). The result is a reversal of American political geography. Figure 8.1 compares the electoral map of the states from the realignment of 1896 through 1944, when the South remained solidly Democratic, with the electoral map since 1964.

The 1964-1972 realignment in presidential elections was followed by a period of frequently divided government, until realignment in Congressional elections reached critical proportions in the 1990's. Democrats retained their majorities in Congress for more than two decades after 1972, prompting many observers to note party decay and dealignment (Broder, 1978; DeVries and Terrance, 1972; Jacobson, 1990; Ladd, 1981, 1991; Mayhew, 2002; Silbey, 1991; Wattenberg, 1990). But divided government turned out to be more the result of split tickets cast disproportionately in the South, where Republicans were carrying states and districts for president, and conservative Democrats were winning reelection to the House and Senate, in what James Q. Wilson (1985) called "realignment at the top, dealignment at the bottom." Over time, however, as southern conservative Democrats retired, switched parties, or lost primaries to more liberal Democrats, many of their states and districts became as Republican in congressional elections as they had already become in presidential elections (Paulson, 2007). In 1994, Republicans won control of the House and Senate, including majorities across the South, and national electoral coalitions of states and voters looked very similar in Presidential and Congressional elections (Burnham, 1996; Wilcox, 1995). These electoral coalitions have remained relatively stable ever since. In a play on Wilson's language, I have called this

Figure 8.1. Coalitions of States in Presidential Elections, 1896-2008

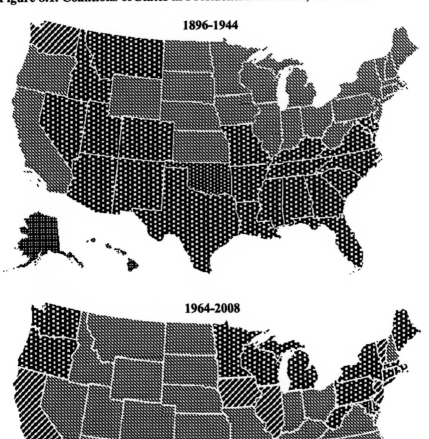

   States voting Democratic in most elections.

States voting Republican in most elections.

No partisan advantage across the era.

States not participating in elections.

Source: David Leip, *Dave Leip's Atlas of U.S. Presidential Elections*, www.uselectionsatlas.org, Accessed June 19, 2009. Reprinted by permission.

process "critical realignment at the top, secular realignment at the bottom" (Key, 1959; Paulson, 2007). More efficiently, James Campbell (2006) has called electoral change in the two-tier party system "staggered realignment."

Ideological polarization between the parties in Congress increased slowly after 1980, and became pronounced after the 1994 election. Since the New Deal, the voting records of southern conservative Democrats had been clearly distinguishable from northern Democrats, particularly when civil rights was at the top of the congressional and public agenda. Scattered Republicans in Congress tended to vote on the liberal side of issues. But after 1994, party line voting became the rule.[1]

Staggered realignment has also resulted in a new swing vote in the electorate. For about a generation the realignment of 1964-1972, the swing voters were mostly conservative Democrats who usually voted Republican for president and Democratic for Congress, and occasionally for a southern Democrat for President. Now, with these voters mostly Republican, the swing voter is more genuinely independent and moderate, with more ideological electorates in the primaries of both parties.

Obama and His Opposition
in the Polarized Party System

This is the political environment encountered by Barack Obama as he assumed office as the forty-fourth President of the United States: An ideologically polarized party system which had taken a half century to become entrenched and a Congress which had been as polarized across party lines for about fifteen years. In expressing his hope to change the ways things worked in Washington, President Obama was not merely encountering personalities and personal behavior. He was running into an altered party system which had changed the rules of governing.

Ideological polarization between the parties has promoted ideological homogenization within the parties, at least in terms of the partisan sorting of liberals and conservatives. This increases the necessity for party leaders and candidates to secure their partisan base while appealing to the independent voter in the middle of the road. Factions within each party, divided more by very particular interests and issue differences, offer differing strategies as to how face the electorate in 2012. While the Democrats have an incumbent president to support, their factionalism faces him with difficult political challenges and has made governance a difficult proposition, even when they were in the majority. And while the GOP has increasingly become a uniformly conservative party, the growth of the Tea Party is only the latest illustration of its internal factionalism, and of the prospects for a spirited contest for the Republican presidential nomination in 2012.

The Democrats

At first glance, the Democrats would appear to be the more divided of the two major parties. Certainly the Democrats are not as monolithically liberal as the Republicans are conservative, as evidenced by voting behavior in presidential primaries and voting records on Congress.

The Nomination of Barack Obama

Since 1972, liberal Democrats have generally retained their advantage in national nominating contests. Contested presidential nominations have been won by moderate Democrats under two conditions: When the liberal Democrats failed to unite on a candidate (1976 and 1992), or when a moderate Democrat was an incumbent president (Jimmy Carter in 1980) or an heir apparent (Al Gore in 2000). According to exit poll data, all of the Democratic nominees for president since 1976 secured at least a plurality among liberal Democrats in the primaries, excepting only Walter Mondale in his close contest against Gary Hart in 1984. See table 8.1.

While southern Democrats like have been instrumental in moving their party back toward the ideological center in recent years, their emergence has nonetheless played a critical role in the ideological polarization between the parties. They attracted the support of a growing African-American electorate in the south, whose numbers were exponentially expanded by the Twenty-fourth Amendment to the Constitution and the Voting Rights Act. Jimmy Carter's victory over George Wallace in the 1976 primaries effectively eliminated the old "white supremacy" faction of the Democratic Party. Even in the South today, the Democrats are the more liberal of the two major parties, and voters who would once have supported candidates like Wallace are practicing Republicans, no longer a factor in Democratic primaries, opening the door to candidates like Bill Clinton, Albert Gore, Jesse Jackson and Barack Obama. The nomination of Barack Obama in 2008 was made possible by the absence of the old Wallace vote plus the increased presence of the African-American vote in southern Democratic primaries, while Obama was generally securing the support of more liberal Democrats against Hillary Rodham Clinton across the North and West. It is of historic importance, and telling to our analysis of the party system, that the party that nominated the first African-American president had once been the electoral home of "white supremacy" in American politics.

Arthur C. Paulson

Table 8.1. Exit Polls in Democratic Presidential Primaries, 1976-2008

	Liberal	Moderate	Conservative	National
1976				
Carter	29	41	41	38
Brown	17	16	10	15
Wallace	6	12	22	12
Udall	19	9	6	11
Henry Jackson	8	8	10	8
Church	8	5	3	5
National	29	55	16	100
1980				
Carter	40	53	58	51
Kennedy	45	36	29	37
National	23	58	19	100
1984				
Mondale	34	41	37	38
Hart	36	37	35	36
Jesse Jackson	26	15	15	18
National	28	50	22	100
1988				
Dukakis	37	41	32	37
Jesse Jackson	37	25	23	28
Gore	9	17	25	17
Gephardt	5	8	10	8
Simon	5	5	5	5
National	27	49	24	100
1992				
Clinton	42	53	49	48
Tsongas	29	26	26	27
Brown	21	14	14	16
Kerrey	2	2	3	2
National	34	44	22	100
2000				
Gore	67	75	69	72
Bradley	29	22	27	26
National	51	40	9	100

Table 8.1. continued:

	Liberal	Moderate	Conservative	National
2004				
Kerry	**58**	**54**	**43**	**54**
Edwards	22	28	31	25
Dean	6	5	6	6
Clark	3	4	4	4
National	47	38	15	100
2008				
Clinton	47	**50**	**47**	**48**
Obama	**49**	42	44	47
National	47	39	14	100

Figures represent percentages of the vote in Presidential primaries. Data derived from exit polls weighted to state results and proportioned to national outcomes. Sources: For exit polls, 1976-2004, International Consortium for Political and Social Research (ICPSR). For 2008 exit polls: www.msnbc.com. Results of Presidential primaries drawn or derived from *Presidential Elections 1789-1996* (Washington, DC: Congressional Quarterly, 1997), pp. 186-227, for 1976-1996. For Presidential primaries since 2000: www.thegreenpapers.com., and *The New York Times*. Only primaries held in the "competitive phase" are included. For explanation of "competitive phase," see Appendix.

The battle for the Democratic presidential nomination between Senator Barack Obama of Illinois and Senator Hillary Rodham Clinton of New York in 2008 was spirited as it could be, but less divisive than it appeared.

All of the Democratic candidates in the original field were liberals of one sort or another. All were for national health insurance in some form. All of them supported government action to intervene in an economy that gave evidence of slipping toward recession in the midst of a crisis in the housing market. Whatever small differences there were among the candidates, there were no wedge issues dividing Democrats, as civil rights or the Vietnam War once did.

Issues did make a difference, but only as a matter of salience and degree. Democrats who prioritized opposition to the Iraq War favored Obama, while those who prioritized economic issues and health care leaned to Clinton. While both of the leading candidates were liberal Democrats, their imagery and appeal was not unlike the contest in the 1984 primaries. Clinton was cast as the candidate of the party establishment, not unlike Walter Mondale, while Obama was the reformer, not unlike Gary Hart.

In the absence of ideological factionalism between Obama and Clinton, demographic divides led to an almost even split in the vote (Conway, 2009; Paulson, 2009; Simien, 2009). Obama won among African Americans. Beyond that, his support was younger and more middle class, inheriting much of the coalition that supported McGovern in 1972 and Hart in 1984. Clinton won among white voters in general and white women in particular. She carried Hispanics, working class voters, and union members, inheriting much of the coalition that supported Humphrey in 1972 and Mondale in 1984.

Without deep ideological divides, once the Democratic presidential nomination was settled, there was a common interest in uniting the party to win the general election. The credentials controversies concerning Michigan and Florida were settled dramatically, but without threatening party unity. All the Democrats needed, all along, was a nominee on whom to unite. When Obama had secured a majority of the delegates at the close of the primary season, Clinton withdrew and endorsed her opponent vigorously.

Such a close race for the nomination could not have been settled without convention floor fights in the Democratic Party of 1924, 1948, 1968, or 1972.

The Obama Presidency

Certainly, expectations were high, perhaps unrealistically so, when Obama took office. He was a romantic figure, the first African-American president of the United States who reminded many of his supporters of John F. Kennedy and the heady days of the New Frontier. There remained left over public expectations of a governmental system centered on an active presidency, going back to the early days of the New Deal and Franklin D. Roosevelt, carrying through Kennedy, Lyndon B. Johnson and the Great Society, on to Ronald Reagan and "Reaganomics." If there were difficult issues on the public agenda, the president was expected to lead and deal with them. And there were difficult issues for the new president to say the least: financial crisis, recession and war.

Presidents have been effective in their dealings with Congress under one of two conditions: Either when they had a working partisan majority; or when they could build bipartisan majorities; or both. Franklin D. Roosevelt had overwhelming Democratic majorities for his New Deal. There was near unanimous support for the Federal Highway Act proposed by President Dwight D. Eisenhower, and President Johnson was able to assemble a bipartisan majority for Civil Rights in 1964. The following year after his landslide, Johnson enjoyed a working Democratic majority in both houses of Congress, but assembled bipartisan majorities for most of his Great Society programs, anyway. And President Reagan could not have had his tax cuts without bipartisan majorities in both houses of Congress. Among these presidents, only Roosevelt changed the way things worked in Washington in his time; the others worked the system effectively.

Despite the electoral "shellacking" his party took at the polls in the midterm elections, President Obama has to be scored as highly effective with Congress, given his success in passing two economic stimulus packages and health insurance reform. His way of accomplishing that, however, had to be through partisan majorities in Congress, rather than the bipartisan approach he indicated he would have preferred. The votes on the economic and health care bills were almost entirely along party lines, and both the debate in Congress and the surrounding public discourse reflected the ideological polarization of the party system.

To the extent that there were breaks in party line voting, they were found more frequently among Democrats than Republicans, particularly on health care reform. When the Obama health care legislation finally passed three Democrats in the Senate and thirty-three in the House opposed it, while the Republicans were unanimous in opposition in both houses (Congressional Quarterly, 2010a, 2010b). The Democrats who opposed the health care overhaul were overwhelmingly moderate Democrats from "red" states, many of whom have also criticized the president on what they consider to be his unimpressive leadership on the federal budget deficit.

Although liberal Democrats supported the health care package almost unanimously, many (particularly in the House) objected to the disappearance of the public option from the bill. President Obama has also encountered criticism from liberal Democrats on his military decisions in the Middle East, and his maintenance of Guantanamo and the Military Tribunals.

In spite of (or because of) Obama's success with legislation, the Democrats suffered a major defeat in the Congressional elections of 2010. They lost sixty-five seats and control of the House, and six seats in the Senate to narrowly retain a majority there. Much of the public apparently remains frustrated over lingering unemployment and budget deficits, even as economic growth is appearing to recover. Only time will tell whether, in terms of re-election, President Obama has lost a battle (the mid-term elections) but won the war (re-election), or won the battle (legislation: stimulus, health care, etc.) but lost the war.

Looking to 2012, there is little chance that any displeasure with President Obama from within the Democratic Party will manifest itself as serious opposition to his renomination. Certainly there will be no challenge on the scale of the Reagan challenge to Ford in the 1976 Republican primaries, or the Kennedy challenge to Carter in the 1980 Democratic primaries. President Obama has about the same standing among Democrats today as President Nixon did among Republicans in 1972. Like Nixon, Obama has conducted a presidency that places him near the center of his party. Like Nixon, he may face a challenge in the primaries, but it is unlikely to be more than symbolic.[2]

Moreover, when Democrats disagree with their president, the divide is not deeply ideological, as it was on civil rights, or when President Johnson was challenged over the Vietnam War, or when Kennedy challenged Carter. Democrats who disagree on the details of public policy have little motive to oppose him, and no alternative but to support him. An effective challenge to his renomination is almost impossible, and party unity behind his bid for re-election almost certain.

The Republicans

Even more than the Democrats are "liberal," the Republicans are America's conservative party. Since 1964, conservative Republicans have dominated presidential nominations, except in 1976, when President Gerald Ford, an incumbent only by way of the Watergate scandal, narrowly held off the challenge of Ronald Reagan. The last real ideological showdown in the Republican primaries came in 1980, when Ronald Reagan was nominated and elected. Since then, Republican presidential primaries have been contests between moderate conservatives and ultraconservatives. See table 8.2.

Nevertheless, evidence of current factionalism with the Republican Party is found in two observations: First, Senator John McCain of Arizona won the Presidential nomination in 2008 with the base of his support in the primaries found among moderate-to-liberal Republicans. Second, the Tea Party challenged the party establishment effectively in the primaries before the mid-term election of 2010, and appears to be poised to play an important factional role in the 2012 contest for the Republican presidential nomination. However, John McCain is more conservative than his conflicts with the party establishment would make it seem, and there is less new about the Tea Party than its dramatic emergence over the past two years would make it appear.

The multi-factional analysis of the Republican Party offered by Nicol Rae (1989, 1998) is useful in explaining these points. Despite ideological change, the historic roots traced by Rae provide a lineage for today's Republicans. Table 8.3 illustrates the following discussion by collapsing Rae's analysis of Republican factions into Nelson Polsby's, and by sorting candidates for the Republican presidential nomination over several decades.

Rae divides Polsby's moderate-to-liberal Republicans of "Wall Street" and conservative Republicans of "Main Street" each into two camps. "Wall Street" includes the "moderates" and the "progressives." Moderates have generally been fiscal conservatives who are more moderate or liberal on social issues (civil rights, abortion) and have been focused on a Downsian appeal to the median voter to win elections, while progressives have been more willing to present the party establishment with ideological challenges on issues of the day. Thomas E. Dewey, Dwight D. Eisenhower, Gerald Ford, and George H. W. Bush are examples of moderates, while Wendell L. Willkie and Nelson Rockefeller are examples of progressives.

Meanwhile, "stalwarts" and "fundamentalists" reside on "Main Street." Stalwarts are conservatives who are products of the party establishment and play the inside game. They have usually provided Republicans with their congressional leadership, from Robert Taft and Everett Dirksen, to Robert Dole and Dennis Hastert, to Mitch McConnell and John Boehner. They are conservatives, even conservative Republicans to a degree McCain was not in 2008. But they are at least in theory willing to compromise on policy, most of them place fiscal conservatism ahead of social issues, and party ahead of ideology. They recog-

Table 8.2. Exit Polls in Republican Presidential Primaries, 1976-2008

	Liberal	Moderate	Conservative	National
1976				
Ford	**64**	**60**	41	**53**
Reagan	36	39	**56**	46
National	10	53	37	100
1980				
Reagan	34	**45**	**66**	**51**
Bush	31	33	27	31
Anderson	**35**	15	7	14
National	10	58	32	100
1988				
Bush	**55**	**57**	**54**	**55**
Dole	31	31	22	26
Robertson	6	6	16	12
National	7	38	55	100
1992				
Bush	**68**	**71**	**65**	**68**
Buchanan	27	25	31	29
	9	34	57	100
1996				
Dole	**48**	**51**	**49**	**50**
Buchanan	15	14	27	22
Forbes	22	22	16	18
	8	30	62	100
2000				
Bush	37	41	**64**	**53**
McCain	**58**	**56**	29	42
	12	34	54	100
2008				
McCain	**55**	**52**	32	**40**
Romney	18	22	**35**	29
Huckabee	13	13	25	21
	10	28	62	100

Sources: For exit polls, 1976-2004, International Consortium for Political and Social Research (ICPSR). For 2008 exit polls: www.msnbc.com. Results of presidential primaries drawn or derived from *Presidential Elections 1789-1996* (Washington, DC: Congressional Quarterly, 1997), pp. 186-227, for 1976-1996 and www.thegreenpapers.com., and the *New York Times*. Figures represent percentages of the vote in Presidential primaries. Data derived from exit polls weighted to state results and proportioned to national outcomes. Only primaries held in the "competitive phase" are included. See Appendix for explanation of "competitive phase."

nize that to win on the issues, they have to govern; and to govern, they must win elections.

The fundamentalists are more ideological purists who proclaim the importance of standing on principle, even at electoral cost. When Barry Goldwater won the Republican presidential nomination, for example, he hardly expected to win the 1964 election; he merely expected the GOP to become the conservative party. Today's Tea Party activists similarly seem to expect Republicans in Congress to stand on conservative principle, even if doing so paralyzes governance and loses elections. However much they are conservative ideologues, the fundamentalists are not all the same. Some are Christian fundamentalists, some are libertarians, some are unbending fiscal conservatives, and even the Tea Party has a mixture of all of them in its bag.

Table 8.3. Candidates for Contested Republican Presidential Nominations, 1940-2008, Sorted by Faction According to Nicol Rae Model

Year	Progressive	Moderate	Stalwart	Fundamentalist
1940	**Willkie**	Dewey	Vandenburg	Taft
1944	Willkie	**Dewey**	Bricker----------	
1948	Stassen	**Dewey**	Taft--------------	
1952	----------**Eisenhower**		Taft--------------	
1964	Rockefeller	Scranton	---------**Goldwater**	
1968	Rockefeller	---------**Nixon**--------		Reagan
1972	McCloskey	-----------**Nixon**----------------		Ashbrook
1976		**Ford**-------------	----------Reagan	
1980	Anderson	George Bush	---**Reagan**---	
1988		**George Bush**	Dole	Robertson
1992		**George Bush**		Buchanan
1996		Forbes	**Dole**	Buchanan
2000		McCain	**George W. Bush**	
2008		**McCain**	Romney	Huckabee
2012		Huntsman	Romney	Huckabee
			Gingrich	Palin
			Pawlenty	Bachmann
			Barbour	Paul
			Daniels	Santorum

Sorting done by author using classifications of Republican factions by Nicol Rae (1989).

The conservatism of today's Republican Party is illustrated by the following observations: First, there are few moderates and no liberals remaining in the national Republican leadership. Increasingly, liberal Republicans, such as Lowell Weicker, Jim Jeffords, Arlen Specter and Lincoln Chafee, have left the GOP altogether. In 2010, Chafee was elected Governor of Rhode Island as an independent. Remaining moderate Republicans in Congress, such as Senators Olympia Snowe and Susan Collins of Maine, are under increasing pressure to vote the party line, such as on the health care legislation. Even conservatives find themselves in danger of not being conservative enough for the Republican primary electorate. The experience of John McCain is a case in point.

The McCain Campaigns

Senator John McCain of Arizona sought the Republican presidential nomination in 2000 and 2008, the first time unsuccessfully, winning the second time. The main difference in the two campaigns is that in 2000, conservative Republicans united early, while in 2008 they never united on an alternative to McCain.

Governor George W. Bush of Texas, son of the former president, was the early front runner and almost consensus choice of party leaders in 2000. Bush may have been expecting to find his main opposition to his ideological right, with Steve Forbes presenting himself this time as a movement conservative. But McCain scored an upset victory over Bush in the New Hampshire primary while Forbes finished behind Bush, out of the running. McCain added victories in Arizona and Michigan, while Bush won crucial primaries in South Carolina and Virginia. When Bush won New York, Ohio, and California on Super Tuesday and established a strong lead across the country, McCain withdrew. While McCain polled 57 percent of the vote among moderate-to-liberal Republicans, conservatives made up 54 percent of the Republican primary electorate, and Bush carried them by well over 2-1.

Eight years later, Senator McCain tried again. When former Governor Mike Huckabee of Arkansas won the Iowa caucuses, he virtually guaranteed that he would be splitting the conservative vote with former Governor Mitt Romney of Massachusetts. A few days later, McCain won the New Hampshire primary with Romney placing second and Huckabee third. McCain then won primaries in South Carolina and Florida, assembling pluralities because conservatives were divided. On Super Tuesday, McCain clearly established his position as the front runner, with victories across the country including New York, New Jersey, Illinois, and California. In most states, McCain won with pluralities because of the split to his right, while Romney placed second. Huckabee scored victories in the south and hung on. Romney, who had won during the primary season only in states where he made a home state claim (native of Michigan, former Governor of Massachusetts, Mormon in Utah), withdrew a few days after Super Tuesday, removing McCain's serious opposition. When McCain beat Huckabee in Texas a month later and clinched a national majority of the delegates, Huckabee also withdrew.

In 2008, McCain won the nomination despite the fact that his support in the Republican primaries, both its total percentage and ideological distribution, was almost identical to what it had been in 2000. He polled 54 percent among moderates and liberals, beating Romney by almost 3-1. But moderates and liberals amounted to only 38 percent of the Republican primary electorate, while conservatives represented 62 percent, an eight point increase over their presence in 2000. Altogether, McCain polled 40 percent of the vote in the contested primaries, actually down two points from 2000. McCain won in 2008 because he held his own among conservative Republicans, losing to Romney by only three percentage points, largely because Huckabee was taking a quarter of their votes. The margin that Bush had enjoyed over McCain among conservatives eight years before had been nearly erased. Had conservative Republicans united on an alternative to McCain, he almost certainly would have been denied the nomination.

There was general speculation in 2008 that Mitt Romney failed to unite conservatives because many of them did not trust him. He had emerged in national politics as the moderate Republican governor of Massachusetts, pushing state-level health care reform through the state legislature and supporting abortion rights. Moreover, he was a Mormon, a point of some concern for many of the most conservative voters in Republican primaries. But to limit Romney's problems to his personal record misses the point. Here is where it seems instructive to apply Rae's analysis. The supporters of Mike Huckabee were mainly "fundamentalists" as Rae would put it, voters of the Christian right and conservative ideologues. Those conservatives more concerned with party affairs, winning elections, and the historic fiscal conservatism of the Republican Party, were more likely to vote for Romney in the primaries. The Romney voters, then, were disproportionately Rae's "stalwarts."

Moreover, although his base of support was among moderates and liberals, John McCain is no Nelson Rockefeller. In 2008, Americans for Democratic Action scored McCain's Senate voting record at 5, while the American Conservative Union gave him a score of 63 (Barone and Cohen, 2009). McCain may not be a conservative Republican, but he is a conservative and a Republican. If this were not the case, he could not have become the presidential nominee of America's conservative party.

The Tea Party

Even as the titular leader of his party, Senator McCain turned out not to be safe when it came to defense of his Senate seat, and the real threat came from his own party. In 2010, he was opposed in the Republican primary by former Rep. J. D. Hayworth, an ultraconservative. McCain shifted to his right, particularly on the illegal immigration issue, and won renomination. He went on to win re-election to a fifth term handily.

Other party establishment candidates in the 2010 Republican primaries were not so fortunate. Senator McCain was probably aided by the endorsement of his 2008 running mate, Sarah Palin, who generally campaigned for Tea Party candidates in primaries across the country.

The Tea Party has generally been treated as a populist group of right wing fundamentalists. This image is probably more true than false, but overly simple. Certainly, the Tea Party is a new organization, and it is populist in the sense that its organization to date seems structurally flat; grassroots in that it represents a groundswell of popular demand, but national in that its support is spread across the country and linked through the internet.

On the other hand, the Tea Party is not purely "fundamentalist" if by that term we are referring to Christian fundamentalism, and it is not purely populist, in that the 18 percent of Americans who call themselves Tea Party supporters are generally relatively wealthy, white, and male (Zernike and Thee-Brenan, 2010). Tea Party voters also call themselves "very conservative," and "Republican," with more conservative views than most Republicans. The Tea Party movement has roots in the history of the Republican Party, reminding us of the Goldwater movement before 1964. The Tea Party is clearly very conservative, but it assembles very conservative supporters of various brands, including fiscal conservatives, libertarians, and strict constructionists on the Constitution. If they are not all Christian fundamentalists, Tea Party voters are among the conservative ideological fundamentalists that have always been present in the Republican Party according to Nicol Rae. Like the Goldwater activists who organized at the grassroots prior to 1964, they are ideologues who are willing to stand on principle, even at the cost of losing elections, and expect the Republican Party to do the same.

The Tea Party has been credited with carrying the Republicans to victory in the 2010 mid-term elections. Certainly, the Tea Party provided person power, money and motive to Republican campaigns. Whether the Tea Party won the election for Republicans however, or cost them the Senate is unclear. Tea Party candidates probably accounted for about forty House seats won by Republicans. They may have cost the Republicans Senate seats in Delaware, Colorado, and Nevada, where Tea Party candidates defeated GOP moderates in the primaries. At the same time, Tea Party Republicans won Senate seats in Pennsylvania, Florida, Wisconsin, and Utah. Then, there was Alaska, where Senator Lisa Murkowski lost the Republican primary to Tea Party candidate Joe Miller, and rebounded to win re-election on a write-in.

The important impact of the Tea Party was not so much in general elections. Rather, the Tea Party and its presence was an important factor in Republican primaries across the country. In Florida and Pennsylvania, Tea Party-supported conservative challenges drove Governor Charlie Christ and Senator Arlen Specter respectively out of the Republican Party without a vote being cast. In Utah, the Republican State Convention endorsed Tea Partier Mike Lee, and Senator

Robert Bennett failed to qualify for the primary, despite his long-standing conservative voting record. In the short term at least, the Tea Party was moving the Republicans even further to their ideological right. The current impact of the Tea Party on the American party system is to accentuate its ideological polarization.

The Republicans in 2012

The Republicans have a habit of nominating their "next in line" for the presidency. In the "post-reform" period, Ronald Reagan, George H. W. Bush, Robert Dole, and John McCain all made reasonably strong runner-up bids for the nomination before finally winning it. If this pattern holds, Mitt Romney should be considered the early front runner for the Republican presidential nomination in 2012. He was the runner-up to McCain in the 2008 primaries among the candidates that Barbara Norrander (2000) would have called the "office-seekers." Mike Huckabee did not withdraw in 2008 until McCain had clinched a majority of the delegates because he was more of an "agenda-seeker" focusing on issues rather than to actually winning the nomination or the Presidency itself.

We are now at the opening stages of the "invisible primary," when candidates are organizing, raising money, securing endorsements, and trying to establish public support in the public opinion polls (Buell, 1996; Cohen, Karol, Noel, and Zaller, 2008a, 2008b; Hadley, 1976; Mayer, 1996b, 2003). The invisible primary is not nearly as developed as it was at this time four years ago. Only former Governor Tim Pawlenty of Minnesota has formed an exploratory committee, and former House Speaker Newt Gingrich has announced his intention to do so. Romney and Huckabee are the early leaders in the public opinion polls, followed most closely by Palin, Gingrich, and Rep. Ron Paul of Texas. If Romney is the front runner, it is that "next-in-line" pattern, not the polls, that makes it so. Indeed, if the polls indicate anything now it would be the possibility of a vigorous contest. Neither Romney nor any of his rivals surpass 25 percent in the polls, and the current standing has more to say about name recognition or the lack of it than about the progress of 2012 contest. Nevertheless, using Rae's model of Republican factions, we can engage in some informed speculation about 2012. See table 8.3 for a sorting of potential Republican candidates by faction.[3]

We can probably assume that Romney will run for president again, and that if he does, he is the only candidate with the potential of clinching the Republican presidential nomination early enough to foreclose a real contest. To have a chance to do that, Romney would have to unify the stalwarts who supported him in 2008, and add to that most of the moderates and progressives who voted for McCain in the primaries. His leading challenger for the McCain vote might be former Governor Jon B. Huntsman of Utah, a moderate Republican who endorsed McCain in 2008. Huntsman accepted appointment as ambassador to China from President Obama, and is now resigning and reportedly preparing to set up an exploratory committee for the Republican presidential nomination. To become a factor, Huntsman would probably have to score well in the New Hampshire primary. Then, his real challenge to survive would be his home state Utah primary, where Romney polled 90 percent of the vote in 2008. The question is whether Huntsman, particularly with his association with the Obama administration, is too moderate for a Republican primary electorate anywhere, or whether, running in a field of conservatives, he can replicate McCain's 2008 performance, even without McCain's name recognition.

Meanwhile, conservative Republicans are unlikely to unite across the board on Mitt Romney or any other candidate during the invisible primary. If they run, Pawlenty, Gingrich, Governor Mitch Daniels of Indiana, and Governor Haley Barbour of Mississippi are potential challengers for the support of the stalwarts. Daniels mixes fiscal conservatism with a call to downplay hardcore social issues. Barbour is a former Republican National Chairman and lobbyist who proclaims his ties to the party establishment as a virtue.

Moreover, fundamentalists will present at least one candidate. Their problem, if they want to secure the nomination for one of their own, is to unite on a candidate. As noted above, they are not a homogeneous faction. Early on, the Tea Party might promote Palin or Rep. Michelle Bachmann of Minnesota. Libertarians and Tea Partiers might support Rep. Ron Paul of Texas, who appears poised to run again. The Christian right might push Mike Huckabee or ex-Senator Rick Santorum of Pennsylvania. Huckabee has something of a "next in line" claim on fundamentalists if he enters the race. At this writing he is running about even with Romney in the polls. In any case, the fundamentalists will be a factor, and the Tea Party performance in the 2010 Republican primaries indicates that they have at least the potential to win in 2012, if they unite early on a single candidate.

Whoever the winner is, the Republican nominee for president in 2012 will be a conservative of one brand or another, and an ideological challenge to President Obama, with civil discourse or not, will follow.

Conclusion

Ideological extremism in American political life is nothing new. What is new is that rather than the umbrella party system we once had, in which there were extremes within each party along with moderate bipartisan coalitions between the presidency and Congress, we now have a polarized party system that accentuates the extremes.

A polarized party system is not necessarily all bad. We face extreme choices on compelling issues and civil partisan debate could even facilitate that process. Indeed, the party system between the internally divided Whigs and Democrats, along with the constitutional separation and division of powers, operated to maintain the status quo before the War Between the States, making the extreme choices then on the table all the more difficult to face. The question is whether an ideologically polarized party system can facilitate civil debate on difficult issues.

One of the barriers to such debate is found in an attitude of "American exceptionalism" in our political culture. Alexis DeTocqueville built his theory of American democracy around the classless consciousness he called "equality of condition" and faith in individualism and individual liberty among Americans, to argue that the majority in America exercised a tyranny on thought. Much more recently, following the same tradition, Louis Hartz (1955) argued that Classic Liberalism was not just an ideology in America, but a public religion which has "refused to pay its critics the compliment of an argument." In our own time, this cultural tendency feeds the habit, particularly but not exclusively on the ideological right, of attempting to label political adversaries, even within the mainstream, as disloyal or un-American. A most extreme example is the effort among some on the right to question whether Barack Obama is an American.

Another barrier to civil debate, as well as good cause to work hard to achieve it, is the changing nature of the economic issues we face. As the onset of postindustrial society was being recognized in the sixties, affluence was considered to render economic issues relatively easy to resolve, while cultural issues such as race, the Vietnam War and abortion were considered inherently divisive. As Walter Dean Burnham (1970, 141) put it:

> So long as these cultural struggles are intense "world-view" conflicts, there is one thing that cannot be done with them. They cannot be treated in a "more-or-less" fashion . . . as if they were equivalent to conflicts over taxes, tariffs, or minimum wages. The inherently involve questions not of more-or-less, but either-or.

Not long after Burnham wrote that, starting with the oil shocks of the 1970s, we began to move into an economy in which that political distinction no longer held. Recessions and energy crises in the 1970s began to create the image of a "zero-sum" economy in which anybody's gain must be somebody's loss. It now seems apparent that economic growth over the past thirty years has been based disproportionately on debt, both public and private, corporate and individual.

We live today in a postindustrial society within a global economy. Budget deficits and public debt, a less secure middle class, and a collection of pressing issues (war and peace, recession, education reform, health care reform, infrastructure development, climate change, energy, trade imbalances, manufacturing decline, etc.) all reflect a structurally low growth economy (Paulson, 1998). Economic issues today are "either-or" issues treated like "world-view conflicts." The economic challenges we face are not merely cyclical. They are structural, and extreme. Extreme ideological choices offered through our parties in civil debate may do more good than harm.

An ironic problem we appear to have is that we seem to have developed a parliamentary party system without having developed a parliamentary party government. The question now is whether this new polarized party system can enhance our capacity to face the future, in 2012 and beyond.

Appendix
The "Competitive Phase" of Presidential Primaries

Since 1988, Presidential nominations have been decided well in advance of the end of the primary season, with the exception of the Democratic presidential nomination in 2008. This has required that analysis of voting in the primaries take notice of when the nomination is effectively decided, since the meaning of primary election results before and after that point are very different. William G. Mayer (2008) offered excellent definitions of the "competitive phase" of primaries in his excellent essay on "Voting in Presidential Primaries." The concept is the same for this paper, but the actual point at which the "competitive phase" ends is different is some cases.

I use the standard set by Barbara Norrander (2000) as a guide: When the front runner takes a lead equaling 25 percent of a majority, the runner-up usually withdraws. I stretch the "competitive phase" to include primaries won by opponents of the front runner, and later decisive primaries won by the front runner. Below are the points treated as the end of the "competitive phase" of the primaries since 1976:

- *1976 Republicans*: End of the primary season.
- *1976 Democrats*: End of the primary season.
- *1980 Democrats*: End of the primary season.
- *1980 Republicans*: George H. W. Bush withdraws after winning Michigan primary and losing Oregon to Ronald Reagan on the same day. Reagan is near a national majority of the delegates, and only has to win the California primary, a foregone conclusion, to go over the top.
- *1984 Democrats*: End of the primary season.
- *1988 Republicans*: George H. W. Bush soundly defeats Robert Dole in the Illinois primary. Dole withdraws before the Connecticut primary two weeks later.
- *1988 Democrats*: Michael Dukakis sweeps the Ohio and Indiana primaries. Jesse Jackson wins the D.C. primary the same day, but Dukakis has achieved a lead in the delegate count above 25 percent of a national majority.
- *1992 Republicans*: President George H. W. Bush sweeps the primaries on Super Tuesday. Pat Buchanan announces that he will campaign thereafter only in California, acknowledging that Bush has won renomination.

- *1992 Democrats:* Bill Clinton bounces back from a narrow defeat in the Connecticut primary at the hands of Jerry Brown to sweep primaries in New York, Wisconsin, Minnesota, and Kansas.
- *1996 Republicans*: Robert Dole sweeps primaries across the country on Super Tuesday and his lead in the delegate count surpasses 25 percent of a national majority.
- *2000 Democrats*: Al Gore sweeps primaries across the country on Super Tuesday, and his lead in the delegate count surpasses 25 percent of a national majority. Bill Bradley withdraws.
- *2000 Republicans*: George W. Bush wins most of the Super Tuesday primaries against John McCain, including New York, Ohio, and California, and assumes a lead in the delegate count above 25 percent of a national majority. McCain withdraws.
- *2004 Democrats*: John Kerry sweeps the Super Tuesday primaries and takes a lead of more than 25 percent of a national majority. John Edwards withdraws.
- *2008 Republicans*: John McCain wins most of the primaries on Super Tuesday, and Mitt Romney withdraws. But Mike Huckabee survives by winning southern primaries that day and Louisiana a few days later. When McCain beats Huckabee in Texas and Ohio a month later, Huckabee withdraws.
- *2008 Democrats*: Entire primary season.

Notes

1. In 1999, *Congressional Quarterly* stopped publishing its scoring of the "conservative coalition" in Congress, roll calls where majorities of Republicans and southern Democrats voted on the same side, opposing northern Democrats, because that sort of vote no longer occurred often enough to be statistically useful. See "Influential Since the 1940s, the Conservative Coalition Limps Into History," *CQ Almanac 1998* (Washington, DC: Congressional Quarterly, 1999), pp. B9-B11.

2. Nixon was challenged by Rep. Paul McCloskey of California, an anti-war liberal Republican, and Rep. John Ashbrook of Ohio, an ultraconservative Republican, in 1972. In the New Hampshire primary, Nixon polled 69 percent of the vote, and he faced little opposition thereafter.

3. Who knows whether Donald Trump is serious about running for President? If he does, he certainly has the money to mount a campaign in the Republican primaries. There is not a sufficient record to place him among the factions of the Republican Party.

References

Aldrich, John H. 1995. *Why Parties? The Origin and Transformation of Party Politics in America*. Chicago: The University of Chicago Press.

Barone, Michael and Grant Ujifusa. 2009. The Almanac of American Politics 2010. Washington, DC: *National Journal.* Seymour Martin Lipset, ed. *Emerging Coalitions in American Politics.* San Francisco: Institute for Contemporary Studies.

Buell, Emmett. 1996. "The Invisible Primary." [book auth.] William G. Mayer. *In Pursuit of the White House: How We Choose Our Presidential Nominees.* Chatham, NJ: Chatham House.

Burnham, Walter Dean. 1970. *Critical Elections and the Mainsprings of American Politics.* New York: Norton.

———. 1996. "Realignment Lives: The 1994 Earthquake and its Implications." Colin Campbell and Bert A. Rockman, eds. *The Clinton Presidency: First Appraisals.* Chatham, NJ: Chatham House.

Campbell, James E. 2006. "Party Systems and Realignments in the United States." *Social Science History* 30: 359-386.

Clubb, Jerome M., William H. Flanigan, and Nancy H. Zingale. 1990. *Partisan Realignment: Voters, Parties and Government in American History.* Boulder, CO: Westview Press.

Cohen, Marty, David Karol, Hans Noel and John Zaller. 2008a. "The Invisible Primary in Presidential Nominations, 1980-2004." William G. Mayer, ed. *The Making of the Presidential Candidates 2008.* Lanham, MD: Rowman and Littlefield.

———2008b. *The Party Decides: Presidential Nominations Before and After Reform.* Chicago: The University of Chicago Press.

Congressional Quarterly. 1997. Presidential Elections 1789-1996. Washington, DC: Congressional Quarterly.

Congressional Quarterly. 1999. "Influential Since the 1940s, the Conservative Coalition Limps Into History," CQ Almanac 1998. Washington, DC: Congressional Quarterly.

Congressional Quarterly. 2010a. "Health Care Reconciliation—Passage." CQ Weekly (March 21, 2010). Cqpress.com/floorvote 111-222973000.

Congressional Quarterly. 2010b. "Health Care Reconciliation—Passage." CQ Weekly (March 25, 2010). Cqpress.com/floorvote 111-223056000.

Conway, M. Margaret. 2009. "The Scope of Participation in the 2008 Presidential Race: Voter Mobilization and Electoral Success." William J. Crotty, ed. *Winning the Presidency* 2008. Boulder, CO: Paradigm Publishers.

DeVries, Walter and V. Lance Terrance. 1972. *The Ticket Splitter: A New Force in American Politics.* Grand Rapids, MI: W.B. Ferdmans.

Hadley, Arthur T. 1976. *The Invisible Primary.* Englewood Cliffs, NJ: Prentice-Hall.

Hartz, Louis. 1955. *The Liberal Tradition in America.* Harcourt, Brace and World.

Jacobson, Gary C. 1990. *The Electoral Origins of Divided Government: Competition in U.S. House Elections,* 1946-1988. Boulder, CO: Westview Press.

Key, V.O. 1955. "A Theory of Critical Elections." *Journal of Politics* 17, pp. 3-18.

———. 1959. "Secular Realignment and the Party System." *Journal of Politics* 23: 198-210.

Ladd, Everett Carll. 1981. "The Brittle Mandate: Electoral Dealignment and the Presidential Election of 1980." *Political Science Quarterly.* 96: 1-25.

———. 1991. "Like Waiting for Godot: The Uselessness of 'Realignment' for Understanding Change in Contemporary American Politics." Byron E. Shafer, ed. *The End of Realignment? Interpreting American Electoral Eras.* Madison: University of Wisconsin Press.

Leip, David. 2009. Dave Leip's Atlas of U.S. Presidential Elections. www.uselections.org (accessed June 19, 2009).

Lipset, Seymour Martin ed. *Emerging Coalitions in American Politics*. San Francisco: Institute for Contemporary Studies.

Mayer, William G. 1996a. *The Divided Democrats: Ideological Unity, Party Reform, and Presidential Elections*. Boulder, CO: Westview Press.

———. 1996b. "Forecasting Presidential Nominations." Mayer, ed. *In Pursuit of the White House: How We Choose Our Presidential Nominees*. Chatham, NJ: Chatham House.

———. 2003. "Forecasting Presidential Nominations, or My Model Worked Just Fine, Thank You." *PS: Political Science and Politics* 36: 153-157.

———. 2008. "Voting in Presidential Primaries." Mayer, ed. *The Making of the Presidential Candidates 2008*. Lanham, MD: Rowman and Littlefield.

Mayhew, David. 2002. *Electoral Realignments: A Critique of an American Genre*. New Haven, CT: Yale University Press.

Norrander, Barbara. 2000. "The End Game in Post-Reform Presidential Nominations." *Journal of Politics* 62: 999-1013.

Novak, Robert. 1965. *The Agony of the GOP 1964*. New York: Macmillan.

Paulson, Arthur. 1998. "The Political Economy of Postindustrial America." Kul B. Rai, David F. Walsh and Paul Best, eds., *America in the Twenty-First Century: Challenges and Opportunities in Domestic Politics*. Upper Saddle River, NJ: Prentice-Hall.

———. 2000. *Realignment and Party Revival: Understanding American Electoral Politics at the Turn of the Twenty-First Century*. Westport, CT: Praeger.

———. 2007. Electoral Realignment and the Outlook for American Democracy. Boston: Northeastern University Press.

———. 2009. "The Invisible Primary Becomes Visible: The Importance of the 2008 Presidential Nominations, Start to Finish." William J. Crotty, ed. *Winning the Presidency* 2008. Boulder, CO: Paradigm Publishers.

Perlstein, Rick. 2009. *Before the Storm: Barry Goldwater and the Unmaking of the American Consensus*. New York: Perseus.

Polsby, Nelson W. 1978. "Coalition and Faction in American Politics: An Institutional View".

Pomper, Gerald with Susan Lederman. 1980. *Elections in America: Control and Influence in Democratic Politics*. New York: Longman.

Rae, Nicol. 1989. *The Decline and Fall of the Liberal Republicans*. New York: Oxford University Press.

———. 1994. *Southern Democrats*. New York: Oxford University Press.

———. 1998. "Party Factionalism, 1946-1996." Byron E. Shafer, ed. *Partisan Approaches to Postwar American Politics*. New York: Chatham House.

Reiter, Howard L. and Jeffrey M. Stonecash. 2010. *Counter-Realignment: Political Change in the Northeast*. Cambridge: Cambridge University Press.

Silbey, Joel H. 1991. "Beyond Realignment and Realignment Theory." Byron E. Shafer, ed. *The End of Realignment? Interpreting American Electoral Eras*. Madison: University of Wisconsin Press.

Simien, Evelyn M. 2009. "Clinton and Obama: The Impact of Race and Sex on the 2008 Democratic Presidential Primaries." William J. Crotty, ed. *Winning the Presidency* 2008. Boulder, CO: Paradigm Publishers.

Speel, Robert W. 1998. *Changing Patterns of Voting in the Northern United States: Electoral Realignment, 1952-1996*. University Park: Pennsylvania State University Press.

Sundquist, James L. 1983. *The Dynamics of the American Party System: Alignment and Realignment of Political Parties in the United States*. Washington, DC: Brookings.

Wattenberg, Martin P. 1990. *The Decline of American Political Parties: 1952-1988*. Cambridge, MA: Harvard University Press.

White, Theodore H. 1973. *The Making of the President 1972*. New York: Atheneum.

Wilcox, Clyde. 1995. *The Latest American Revolution? The 1994 Elections and Their Implications for Governance*. New York: St. Martin's Press.

Wilson, James Q. 1985. "Realignment at the Top, Dealignment at the Bottom." Austin Ranney, ed. *The American Elections of 1984*. Durham, NC: American Enterprise Institute/Duke University Press.

Zernike, Kate and Megan Thee-Brenan. 2010. "Poll Finds Tea Party Backers Wealthier and More Educated," *The New York Times*, April 14, 2010, www.nytimes.com. (accessed February 1, 2010).

Chapter 9

Recalibrating the Obama Presidency: The Off-Year Elections and Their Consequences

Maureen F. Moakley

Introduction

The 2010 midterm elections appeared to be a stunning setback for the Obama administration. We expect that the party that wins the White House usually loses congressional seats in the next election. Historically, there have been only a few notable exceptions related to exceptional patterns of electoral realignment. But while loss is the norm, the Democrats' defeat was stunning. They lost a total of sixty-three seats in the House, the most significant defeat since both 1946 when they gave up fifty-five seats and 1994, when they lost fifty-two seats. More importantly, their unified party control of the Congress and the presidency—which allowed them to pass some historic legislation—was shattered by losing the majority in the House. They also lost seven U.S. Senate seats and suffered extensive partisan defeats at the state level. The GOP elected seven new governors and achieved partisan control of twenty-nine state legislatures.[1] It was, by most accounts, a true "shellacking."

While the pattern of midterm elections remains fairly constant, the contemporary context of these elections is more unpredictable. Beyond the partisan results in this election, it is noteworthy that fifty-four House incumbents lost their bids for reelection, the highest number in at least thirty years.[2] This is highly unusual in that members of Congress not only have an advantage as an incumbent but also generally have a good sense of the political environment, understand their chances of reelection, and know when to withdraw or move on.

That seems to have changed. The "new normal" is a volatile political dynamic structured by forces linked to the economy and presidential popularity in an intensely expanded and erratic media environment. The result is a political milieu subject to domestic and global uncertainty and a political debate influenced by the extreme partisan polarization in the Congress where the GOP now controls the House.

In this chapter we consider the context of the 2010 election, review the extent of the losses especially in the U.S. House, and then consider the prospects for the Obama administration in the post-election environment. While news accounts stressed the dramatic nature of Democrats' loss, the leitmotif of most of the election coverage was volatility. Most of the analysis was framed in terms of "waves," and "swings," underscoring the unpredictable and dramatic nature of the election. Implicit in that framing is the notion that waves recede and pendulums swing back, an acknowledgment that electoral conditions remain extremely variable and unpredictable.

The administration was, after all, in a turbulent period. We were in the midst of the steepest economic downturn since the Great Depression, and operating in completely uncharted waters with recovery a distant prospect and the national debt escalating. We were also engaged in two foreign wars with no end in sight. In this uncertain political environment, the administration had to confront the most polarized Congress in recent history. Simultaneously, the administration attempted to pass unprecedented legislation dealing with the recovery stimulus, bailouts of the financial sector, and initiated a domestic initiative of historic proportions on health care reform.

After discussing why and how the Democrats sustained such a loss, we then consider the aftermath of the election and explore the possibility that the results present an opportunity for the president to create a platform on which he can take advantage of the singular office of the presidency with a divided government and forge a successful electoral strategy for a second term.

The Midterm Dynamic

The midterm represents something like the first national referenda on the new administration. Beyond the particulars related to individual districts and candidates, analysts agree that there are three main factors that influence the outcomes of these elections. One is the candidate exposure, particularly of the most recently elected congresspersons of the president's party after the previous presidential election. The second is the general economic conditions of the country at the time of the election and the third is support for the president's policy agenda as it is linked to overall presidential approval ratings (Busch, 2010). All three certainly played a role in 2010.

Exposure of the president's party refers to the sweep of a presidential election in bringing in some additional congressional seats, either from competitive or opposition districts in the opposite party's base, particularly in the House, as a sort of coattails effect. As Abramowitz notes, Democrat exposure was particularly high in 2010 in that 47 of the 256 House seats held by Democrats were in House districts that were carried by Republican presidential candidates in both 2004 and 2008, making these Democrats particularly vulnerable to swings back to the GOP in the midterm. Hence the loss of some seats was certainly expected although the extent of the losses surprised most observers (Abramowitz, 2010).

Clearly, the economy was critical, in terms of the actual dollar numbers related to the bailout and stimulus packages and the voters' perceptions of the current state of the economy. The country was experiencing a prolonged economic downturn that suggested we were in an economic free fall with no measureable solution. In the early negotiations over the bailout of the financial sector, there was a palpable hint of panic as members of the administration and leaders in the financial sector scrambled to deal with collapsing markets and institutions. In tandem with this, the administration passed a massive stimulus package. While the states and other constituents were haltingly accepting of federal largesse, particularly for programs that provided extensive unemployment benefits and funded various infrastructure projects in the states, there was a clear sense of unease on both sides of the partisan divide about the eventual cost of these programs. With all this and the huge deficits it began to generate, the status of the economy and recovery around the election time was sluggish, at best. Moreover, despite signs that the economy was beginning to pick up slowly, unemployment remained high at around 10 percent.

Election day exit polls demonstrated that the voters understood this and were sharply critical of the state of the nation, the current administration, and the Congress. These midterm voters were in a snarly mood. 74 percent of them were either dissatisfied or angry about how the federal government was working and a full 90 percent thought the state of the economy was not good or poor. 63 percent named the economy as the most important issue facing the country and 87 percent of these voters claimed to be worried about the "nation's economy in the next year."[3] The administration's response to the fiscal crisis, including the massive bailouts, had put us in uncharted territory economically and politically. This gave broad opportunities for opposition backlash, of which the GOP took full advantage. By the time of the election a full 66 percent of the voters felt the stimulus package had either *hurt* the economy or made no difference. Indeed, only 31 percent of the voters thought the stimulus had helped the economy at all!

As far as the voters were concerned, there was plenty of blame to go around. 73 percent of the voters disapproved of the way Congress was handling its job and their lack of support was bipartisan in that 53 percent had an unfavorable opinion of both the Democratic party as well as the GOP. The president did not fare much better. Fifty-one percent disapproved of the way Obama was handling his job (46 percent approved) and 36 percent claimed that one reason they voted was to express opposition to the president and 51 percent felt that Obama's policies would hurt the country.

The third factor is linked more closely to presidential approval. Although the president is not on the ballot, approval of the administration's policies is increasingly regarded as having an impact on midterm electoral contests for the Congress and in the states. This variable is generally translated into the job approval ratings of the president. Indeed, the general consensus among scholars is that this factor is becoming more significant in midterm elections (Sabato, 2011, 5).

Despite the fact that a full 73 percent of the voters disapproved of the way the Congress was doing its job, the political fallout came down on the president and his administration. Not only had the administration agreed to a massive and unprecedented bailouts and stimulus programs with what were heretofore fantastic levels of government money, but Obama had also pushed through an entirely new dimension of the welfare state—a national health initiative. Voters' concerns about the economy and the health care debate polarized opinion and caused considerable dissonance among voters. Nationally, 47 percent of the midterm voters wanted it repealed and only 32 percent wanted health care expanded. The Republicans did a masterful job of raising concerns, creating uncertainty, and encouraging opposition to a policy that in other iterations, a lot of the public generally supported. They seized momentum and framed the issue as "Obamacare"—or "Obamascare"—a socialized, expensive and unworkable plan that would undercut our existing health care system.

As the chapter by R. Lawrence Butler notes, the congressional Republicans adapted a strategy of party government wherein they concluded that their minority status compelled them to pursue an obstructionist strategy of unified opposition to Democratic initiatives. In terms of the administration's policies, their goal was to create enough fear and concern about the economy and health care to swing the midterm elections in their favor. While the GOP was destined to pick up some seats, the extent of their win was clearly related to the success of this strategy. The Republicans played a brilliant game of parliamentary politics—insofar as the object of participation is to win party control, not promote legislation. Just saying "no" proved effective and that—added to the president's failure to effectively communicate to the public the administration's position in these debates—certainly contributed to his party's loss.

Midterm Voters

We know that the portrait of the midterm voter is different than that of voters in general elections. Midterm voters as a group tend to be older, more affluent and more conservative. But in 2010 voters were even more affluent, older and more conservative than in 2006. As table 9.1 indicates, Republicans made notable gains among men, whites, and older voters. In addition, the voters of 2010 were considerably more conservative than the voters of 2006. As the Pew Center re-

Table 9.1. Primary Voters 2006 and 2010

	2006			2010			
	% of Voters %	Vote Rep %	Vote Dem %	% of Voters %	Vote Rep %	Vote Dem %	Rep Gains
Men	49	47	50	47	55	42	+8
Women	51	43	55	53	48	49	+5
White	79	51	47	78	60	38	+9
African American	10	10	89	10	9	90	-1
Latino	8	30	69	8	33	65	+3
Asian/Other	4	40	59	4	41	55	+1
White Men	39	53	44	37	62	35	+9
White Women	40	50	49	41	57	40	+7
18-29	12	38	60	11	40	56	+2
30-44	24	45	53	22	50	47	+5
45-64	44	45	53	44	52	46	+7
65 and Older	19	49	49	23	58	40	+9
Less than $50,000	40	38	60	37	43	54	+5
$50K-$100,000	38	48	50	37	53	44	+5
$100,000 or more	22	52	47	26	58	40	+6
Post-graduate	18	41	58	20	46	52	+5
College Graduate	27	49	49	28	55	42	+7
Some College	31	47	51	30	53	44	+6
High School Graduate	21	44	55	18	53	45	+9
Republican	36	91	8	36	95	4	+4
Democrat	38	7	93	36	7	92	0
Independent	26	39	57	28	55	39	+16
Conservative	32	78	20	41	84	14	+6
Moderate	47	38	60	39	42	56	+4
Liberal	20	11	87	20	8	90	-3

Source: Pew Research Center Publications, November 2012.

ports, "the proportion of self identified conservatives increased nearly by 1/3" which represented the highest level of conservative identifiers in two decades.[4] Another critical change was the shift that occurred among Independents. In 2006, while the overall totals of Independents were about the same, the GOP got the support of just 39 percent of the Independents while the Democrats received 57 percent of that vote. As highlighted in table 9.2, in 2010 almost the exact reverse was true. In that election, the Independents broke for the Republicans by a margin of 55 to 39 percent which represented a 16 point gain among Independents for the GOP. This represents a critical shift among a key demographic and the partisan choices of these voters, especially in close elections, often decide the outcome of midterm and general elections.[5]

Regional and State Results

The most significant aspect of the GOP victory was the gains in House that gave them majority control and ushered in divided government in 2010. Looking beyond the broad national outlines of this win, election results in individual states obviously reflect myriad local political factors as well as traditional candidate variables associated with these races. It would be difficult to produce precise correlations by state for gains in the U.S. House for the Republicans and Democrats. Looking at presidential approval ratings, levels of unemployment, and the changes in House seats gives us a picture of the shape of the economy and the mood of the voters toward the administration in individual states and regions[6] at the time of the election. At that time, Obama's national job approval was at 46 percent and the national unemployment figures hovered around 10 percent. Within this framework, state and regional variations are instructive and the extent of gains made by the GOP in US House seats is impressive.[7]

Within the regions of the country (as defined by the Bureau of Labor Statistics) the New England states remained highly supportive of the Democrats. In that region, unemployment was generally below the national average and in most states the president ran strong. Rhode Island was an outlier with high levels of unemployment but approval for the president was also high and the Democratic delegation remained intact. Indeed, approval for the president was solid in all states except New Hampshire, where the two congressional seats flipped to the GOP.

In the Mid Atlantic states, however, despite relatively low unemployment levels and fairly robust presidential approval ratings (except in West Virginia) the GOP picked up significant support. In Maryland, New Jersey, and West Virginia they took one seat, and won big in New York, gaining six seats. In Pennsylvania they took five seats and in Virginia they gained three. Only in Delaware did the Democrats pick up a seat.

Table 9.2. Party Gains in House Seats, 2010

Region/State	November 2010 Unemployment Rate*	Presidential Approval Ratings**	Congressional Results
National	9.8%	46.0%	
New England			
Connecticut	9.0	54.0	
Maine	7.3	46.4	
Massachusetts	8.2	55.2	
New Hampshire	5.4	41.3	+2R
Vermont	5.7	52.6	
Rhode Island	11.6	55.1	
Mid-Atlantic			
Delaware	8.4	56.3	+1D
District of Columbia	9.8	84.4	
Maryland	7.4	57.6	+1R
New Jersey	9.2	51.3	+1R
New York	8.3	56.6	+6R
Pennsylvania	8.6	46.3	+5R
Virginia	6.8	46.6	+3R
West Virginia	9.3	33.4	+1R
Mountain-Plains			
Colorado	8.6	45.2	+2R
Kansas	6.8	39.3	+1R
Missouri	9.4	41.4	+1R
Montana	7.2	39.1	
Utah	7.5	33.8	
Wyoming	6.6	27.6	
Mid-West			
Illinois	9.6	53.4	+4R
Indiana	9.8	43.9	+2R
Iowa	6.6	47.5	
Michigan	12.4	48.9	+2R
Minnesota	7.1	48.2	+1R
Nebraska	4.2	44.7	
North Dakota	3.8	41.4	+1R
Ohio	9.8	47.4	+5R
South Dakota	4.5	43.0	+1R
Wisconsin	7.6	47.8	+2R
South East			
Alabama	9.0	41.0	
Florida	12.0	45.8	+4R
Georgia	10.1	45.5	+1R
Kentucky	10.2	38.6	
Mississippi	9.9	47.1	+2R
North Carolina	9.7	46.9	+1R
South Carolina	10.6	43.9	+1R
Tennessee	9.4	40.9	+3R

Table 9.2. continued:

Region/State	November 2010 Unemployment Rate*	Presidential Approval Ratings**	Congressional Results
South West			
Arkansas	7.9	39.2	+2R
Louisiana	8.2	42.6	+1R+1D
New Mexico	8.5	48.6	+1R
Oklahoma	6.8	36.6	
Texas	8.2	44.8	+3R
West			
Alaska	8.0	38.5	+1R
Arizona	9.4	40.2	+2R
California	12.4	54.5	
Hawaii	6.4	65.9	+1D
Idaho	9.4	31.6	
Nevada	14.2	47.0	+1R
Oregon	10.6	47.8	
Washington	9.2	50.2	+1R

*Source: U.S. Bureau of Labor Statistics, October 2010
**Source: Gallup Polling, www.gallup.com/poll/146294/Hawaii-Approving-Obama-States-Decline.aspx

In the Mountain Plains, while all these states had unemployment rates below the national average, Obama did not run well in the region. Most approval rankings were well below the national average (except in Colorado) and the Republicans picked up additional seats in Colorado, Kansas, and Missouri.

States in the Midwest also provided big wins for the GOP. They added two seats in Michigan, where unemployment was the highest in the country. In other states, unemployment was at or well below national averages and approval ratings were mixed. Yet the Republicans scored victories in Illinois (four), Indiana (two), and made gains in Minnesota and North and South Dakota. The big victory in the Midwest was Ohio where the Republicans picked up five seats.

In the Southeast, unemployment ran high in most states and presidential approval was generally tepid. Republicans claimed four more seats in Florida, three in Tennessee, two in Mississippi, and one each in North and South Carolina. In the Southwest, although again unemployment levels were well below the national average, Obama's approval rankings were, for the most part, quite low and the GOP gained seats in Arkansas (two) and Texas (three), picked up a seat in New Mexico, and traded even in Louisiana.

In the West, not surprisingly, the Democrats picked up a seat in Hawaii. Low approval rankings in Alaska and Arizona probably contributed to losses in those states, yet remarkably high unemployment but strong approval levels in California and Oregon allowed the Democrats to hold their own in those states. High unemployment in Nevada probably contributed to a Republican win there but in spite of lower unemployment and high approval, the Democrats still lost a seat in Washington.

Allowing that each state had particular factors that contributed to the individual election, the overall picture is one that suggests the economy and levels of approval of the president influenced the ability of the Republicans to take over the U.S. House.

The results in state elections, as we noted, had Republicans picking up seven gubernatorial seats and controlling twenty-nine state legislatures. This has significant implications for the redistricting of congressional and state legislative seats which will occur over the next two years and be in effect for the 2012 election. Here the GOP has a decided advantage. While some states have opted for nonpartisan commissions, even in those states, partisanship comes into play on the margins—especially given the party of the governor. But after 2010, the Republicans will control the redistricting process in seventeen states redrawing the districts for a total of 195 House seats. The Democrats will only control the process in forty-nine House districts. Allowing that there are limits to the extent one can gerrymander districts, the expectation is that the GOP could pick up over ten seats and make many more significant gains at the state legislative level (Sabato, 2011, 29).

Venting and Moving On

The results of the midterm losses stunned the elected Democratic establishment and created a frenzy of media speculation about the president's relevance and prospects for a second term. But given the volatile nature of contemporary national politics, the debate soon changed to questions related to budget battles and a pending government shutdown as well as tumultuous events in the Middle East and North Africa.

As Alan Abromowitz notes, midterm elections represent a discrete event, a kind of correction course that can, in fact, set the stage for presidential comebacks. He notes that "what happens in the midterm election stays in the midterm election" (2010, 58). Indeed, in 2010 the loss of the House actually set up a dynamic whereby the strategy of parliamentary opposition that proved so effective before the election could no longer operate for the GOP. As the majority party in the House, they were forced to begin a difficult game of offering an alternative budget proposal and resolving the potential shutdown debate. Just saying "no" was no longer an option. This was made more difficult by the fact that within the ranks of the Republicans, newly elected representatives, many backed by the Tea Party, and other Republican officials made extreme and vocal demands for spending cuts, and were more willing than mainstream Republicans to risk the fallout from a government shutdown.[8]

This put the newly elected speaker, John Boehner, in an awkward position. It undermined his image and leverage as the opposition leader. This provided the president with an opportunity to cast himself as the singular, consensus builder and the face of measured opposition in response to diffuse bickering from partisan factions of the opposition. His calling the congressional leaders to a series of last minute late night meetings at the White House to avoid a government shutdown enhanced this perception. The president brokered a compromise that included no new taxes, and although it disappointed many liberals in his own party, he avoided a potentially contentious standoff. He would save this for another day.

The outlines of the Republicans' budget proposals, pushed by a young, forceful conservative contingent, provided more political opportunity for the president. In addition to resisting the idea of any new taxes and proposing drastic government spending cuts, the GOP plan, among other things, included holding the line on taxes but eliminating many popular deductions. It also proposed to transform Medicaid into a block grant to the states and recast Medicare to a voucher like program linked to private insurance. These GOP proposals were serious and responsible positions that attempted to grapple with the escalating national debt and social welfare costs. But the recasting of Medicare, among other proposals, represented a considerable political risk. Most Republicans knew they were treading in dangerous political territory by giving the Democrats the opportunity to turn Obamascare into Mediscare—a ploy the congressional Democrats had used quite successfully during the Clinton administration. But it was an honest attempt to come to terms with an unsustainable social welfare program.

In the midst of these confrontations, Obama's standing with the general public improved considerably while GOP fortunes declined. As table 9.3 illustrates, by March 2011, 47 percent of the general public—as opposed to midterm voters—indicated they were in favor of the president's reelection.[9] He enjoyed a 51 percent job approval rating and a favorability score of 58 percent. In addition, the Democrat party had a favorability rating of 48 percent to the GOP's 42 percent and a majority of respondents (51 percent) had an unfavorable view of Republicans, although 45 percent of the public viewed the Democrats unfavorably. Democrats recaptured the lead in party affiliation with 32 percent of the public identifying with them, in comparison with only 25 percent that identified as Republicans. But the biggest factor in these assessments was the spike in Independents to 37 percent of the respondents. These potential voters could provide the "swing voters" that will likely influence the outcome of the election. As of March 2011 they preferred Obama (47 percent) to a generic Republican (34 percent). In another sobering statistic, 73 percent of the nation was dissatisfied with the state of the nation, creating an unsettling cast to this early political overview.

The role of the Independents remains a key dynamic in the next election. We know, for example, that a critical segment of the president's electoral victory in 2008 was the Independents, who broke for Obama roughly at about 60-40.

In the 2010 midterm, the reverse was true, in that Independents supported the GOP over Democrats, 60-40. This kind of variability is likely to continue

Table 9.3. Obama Presidential Reelection Scorecard, March 2011

Generic Ballot	%
Like to see president reelected	47
Prefer other party's candidate	37
Prefer Independent	NA
Other/Don't Know	16
President's job rating	
Approve	51
Disapprove	39
Favorable Ratings:	
President	
Favorable	58
Unfavorable	39
Republican Party	
Favorable	42
Unfavorable	51
Democratic Party	
Favorable	48
Unfavorable	45
State of Nation	
Satisfied	22
Unsatisfied	73
Party Affiliation	
Republican	25
Democrat	32
Independent	37

Source: Pew Research Center, March 2011

among this important segment of the electorate.[10]

Obama should enjoy another incumbent advantage in that he will likely avoid a primary challenge and thus be able to position himself more to the center of the political spectrum in the reelection debates. The Republicans on the other hand will be forced by the dynamics of a GOP primary to initially position themselves far to the right. This has the potential to weaken their position in the general election. In juxtaposition to the polarization that tends to characterize the debate among elites, Morris Fiorina makes a compelling argument that most voters tend to be moderate and more in the middle of the ideological spectrum. He notes that the "culture war" promoted by elected officials and extreme partisans belies a more moderate disposition among a majority of voters especially in general elections (Fiorina, 2006).

Thus the impact of "swing" voters is likely to play a key role. Whites, moderates and women tend to be key demographic groups that can "swing" and influence the outcome of presidential contests.[11] Fiorina notes that in the election of 2004, a shift of women voters toward the Republican Bush, especially in three states closely affected by 9/11, appears to have had a critical effect on the outcome of the race and the victory for Bush. Furthermore, the shape of the general electorate is likely to reflect more support from more ethnically diverse, younger, less affluent voters—constituencies that should be more favorable to Obama. Here, the challenge will be turnout, always a critical factor in these demographic groups. The falloff among these voters in the 2010 election was significant and the challenge for Obama is to motivate them to get to the polls.

Another institutional advantage of an incumbent president is early media coverage of the upcoming presidential primaries. Pushed by the demand for 24/7 coverage of politics by the diffuse media outlets, the early polls and speculation about the likely GOP presidential contenders provide innumerable distractions. Celebrity types like Michelle Bachmann, Sarah Palin, and Donald Trump dominated the early news cycles taking attention away from more serious contenders. Mitt Romney, with little fanfare and recognition, did announce his exploratory committee via a web video while others continued to dominate blogs and cable with claims and positions far to the right of mainstream Republicans and the general public. At the time, the budget issues had yet to be resolved, massive cuts and pending taxes loomed on the horizon and the United States was involved in three foreign interventions. One would have thought it an ideal time for the potential Republican opponents to begin to stake out their positions on a range of legitimate issues. Yet, a halting bevy of potential Republican candidates seemed reluctant to enter the fray. The traditional jockeying of possible opposition candidates took on a particularly off-putting turn as celebrity hounds like Donald Trump took advantage of the 24/7 demand for attention drawing the oxygen out of the emerging contests of more serious and capable candidates.

During this same period Obama announced, with a confident flourish, his reelection bid. Using new social media and capitalizing on his incumbent position, the announcement hinted at a repeat of the disciplined and savvy campaign effort that characterized his first run. Shortly thereafter, he plunged into the budget debate setting out his budget priorities for 2011 and essentially outlining his domestic campaign position. Obama seized the initiative with a plan that essentially rejected the GOP plan for Medicare. He proposed extensive long term spending cuts in most sectors and also included a plan to rescind the Bush tax cuts for upper income taxpayers. This was not a surprise. During his first election campaign, he promoted a proposal for a national health insurance program and indicated, however obliquely, that he would ultimately pay for the program by rescinding the Bush tax cuts for the wealthy. A central struggle of his first term was to pass the insurance initiative without linking it to taxes. The tax proposal, as a deficit reduction measure, would be part of his reelection campaign strategy.

Initially, the tax increase proposal for the wealthy played fairly well. During this period, continued revelations of the machinations of the financial sector and the damage they caused to millions of American were starkly laid out. A Senate committee released a report that underscored the "shoddy, risky and deceptive practices" that were "aided and abetted by deferential regulators and credit rating agencies that had conflicts of interest."[12] And while the Senate committee issued recommendations for reform, no prosecutions of individuals who profited from these excesses were forthcoming. At the same time, huge profits from corporate entities, many of which were the beneficiaries of government bailouts were in the news. In addition, revelations of profits and bonuses to members of the financial sector drew the attention of the public, many of whom were still experiencing severe financial dislocation. In this soured environment, taxes on the rich were a lot more palatable than they otherwise might have been.

Conclusion

In terms of foreign policy, events on the international scene played to the advantage of the incumbent president. The dawning of the "Arab Spring" began and popular protests erupted in Tunisia and Egypt toppling existing regimes. The protests then spread to Yemen, Lybia, Syria, and Bahrain. While the United States offered peripheral assistance to the democracy movement and provided strong covert diplomatic leadership, Obama resisted calls from many at home and abroad to become actively engaged, particularly in Libya. Instead, the administration took a measured approach to assistance, and let European leaders and NATO play a more visible, leading role. While some critics at home were dismayed that Prime Minister David Cameron and other European leaders became a voice of the allied opposition, it hinted at a recalibration of the role of the United States in foreign affairs.

While this new direction began to generate some criticism as to the superpower status and role of the United States, a series of fortunate events allowed the president to order a daring commando raid into Pakistan that resulted in the death of Osama bin Laden. This displaced, at least in the short term, any impressions that Obama did not have the experience or the fortitude to be an effective commander in chief. Our continued engagement in Iraq and Afghanistan, however, remains a potential problem for the Administration, and as gas prices soar, the president is likely to take criticism for our continued entanglement in the Middle East.

As the financial markets calm and employment begins to pick up, the common focus of the post midterm environment is likely to be issues related to the economy. Debates about the budget, taxes, deficits, and the restructuring of social welfare programs and health care insurance will be in the forefront. It is worth noting that during George H. W. Bush's administration, he enjoyed soaring approval levels of over 80 percent after the successful war in Kuwait but lost his reelection bid in 1992 as a result of perceptions about the slow pace of the economic recovery.

In counter distinction to Bush, President Obama should have a reasonable media platform on which to promote his agenda and launch his reelection campaign. We know that the cumulative coverage of the mainstream media can tilt in the favor of particular candidates. Research documents that during the George H. W. Bush and Clinton campaign of 1992, Clinton was the beneficiary of more positive campaign coverage. Likewise, selected research findings tend to confirm the impression that the mainstream media coverage of Obama's presidency and agenda thus far appears to be at least fair, if not supportive. Early studies of his 2008 campaign indicate that he received more positive coverage during his campaign, particularly in contrast to John McCain. Other studies show that during the period of his early presidency, Obama received much more favorable coverage than either George H. W. Bush or Bill Clinton over the same time period.[13]

Clearly the foreign press has been good to Obama and the coverage of his foreign policy by the national media appears to be even handed, especially in light of the administration's forays in the Middle East and North Africa. Scathing criticisms on both sides by partisan cable networks notwithstanding, if the present trends continue, mainstream coverage of the Obama presidency should provide the administration with a supportive opportunity to correct the communication failures of his early term and more clearly articulate his domestic and foreign policy agenda.

The prospects for the Democrats in the Congress, however, are more daunting. Unless Obama can extend strong coattails, the Democrats are in a precarious position particularly in the U.S. Senate in that two-thirds of the seats up for election are held by Democrats. On the House side, while the exposure of newly elected Republicans and an incumbent president on the top of the ticket may provide some opportunity for the Democrats, gaining twenty-five seats to secure control would be a reach, especially given the potential gains that the Republicans should realize as a result of their redistricting advantage. Moreover, in the upcoming political battles, particularly over the budget, we probably will see the kind of partisan gridlock that is not likely to endear members of Congress from either party to the American voters.

Allowing for the volatile nature of contemporary politics, Obama appears to be in a good position to be reelected for a second term. If he succeeds, he has the opportunity to institutionalize his landmark achievement, national health insurance, mobilize and inspire a younger and more diverse electorate, reframe our global position, and oversee a long term economic recovery based on a more transparent and accountable financial system. A very tall order.

Notes

1. Florida went from a former Republican tuned Independent to a Republican Rick Scott and in Rhode Island, former Republican now Independent Lincoln Chafee was elected.

2. Calculations of some of these results were drawn from Larry Sabato's chapter, *Pendulum Swing* from his book, Pendulum Swing.

3. Estimates of this National sample are drawn from the National Election Exit Polls conducted by Edison Research.

4. Pew Research Center Publications, "*A Clear Rejection of the Status Quo, No Consensus about Future Policies.*

5. See table 9.1 Primary Voters 2006 and 2010.

6. Election day exit poll data only surveyed those states with a U.S. Senate race. We use Gallup data and note that national averages and individual state results give a consistent picture of where the voters were around election day, allowing for the fact that the Gallup responses were from a general population sample.

7. See table 9.2 Party Gains in House Seats, 2010.

8. "Budget Details Stir Republican dissent ahead of House vote" New York Times, April 14, 2011.

9. Table 9.3 percentages drawn from an article released by the Pew Research Center, "Obama Tests Well at Start of the Re-election Run," March 2011.

10. Statistics are drawn from a Pew Research Center article, "Obama Tests Well at Start of the Re-election Run," March 2011.

11. Mayer, William, "The Swing Voter in American Presidential elections," American Politics Research 35 (May 2007):358-88.

12. "Naming Culprits in the Financial Crisis," *New York Times*, April 13, 2011.

13. "Obama's First Hundred Days, April 29, 2009. Pew Project for Excellence in Journalism; "Winning the Media Campaign," October 22, 2008. Pew Project for Excellence in Journalism.

References

Abramowitz, Alan I. 2010. "Right Turn: The 2010 Midterm Elections." In *Pendulum Swing*, ed. Larry J. Sabato. Boston: Longman.

Busch, Andrew E. 2010. "The 2010 Midterm Elections: An Overview," *The Forum* 8 (4): Article 2: 1-15. http://www.bepress.com/forum/vol8/iss4/art2

Butler, Lawrence R. "Legislative Gridlock and the Unfinished Obama Agenda."

Campbell, James E. 2010. "The Midterm Landslide of 2010: A Triple Wave Election," *The Forum* 8 (4): Article 3:1-17. http://www.bepress.com/forum/vol8/iss4/art3

Cook, Rhodes. 2010. "The Battle for the Senate: The Republicans Fall Short." In *Pendulum Swing*, ed. Larry J. Sabato. Boston: Longman.

Edison Research. 2010. *National Exit Polls*. Retrieved from www.electiontonight.com/EAS/XTabPrintWindow.htm

Gallup Poll. 2011. "D.C., Hawaii Still Most Approving of Obama; All States Decline."

Gallup Poll. 2011. "D.C., Hawaii Still Most Approving of Obama; All States Decline."

Hulse, Carl. 2011. "Budget Details Stir Republican Dissent Ahead of House Vote." *New York Times*, April 14. www.nytimes.com/2011/04/14/us/politics/14congress.html?_r=1

Mayer, William. 2007. "The Swing Voter in American Presidential Elections," *American Politics Research* 5 (May 2007): 358-88.

Morgenson, Gretchen, and Louise Story. 2011. "Naming Culprits in the Financial Crisis." *New York Times*, April 14. www.nytimes.com/2011/04/14/business/14crisis.html February 23. www.gallup.com/poll/146294/Hawaii-Approving-Obama-States-Decli ne.aspx

Pew Research Center Publications. 2010. "A Clear Rejection of the Status Quo, No Consensus about Future Policies." Nov. 3. pewresearch.org/pubs/1789/2010-midterm-elections-exit-poll-analysis

Pew Research Center Publications. 2011. "Obama Tests Well at Start of Reelection Run." March 23. pewresearch.org/pubs/1937/poll-2012-campaign-obama-reelection-republican-primary-romney-huckabee-palin

Pew Research Center for Excellence in Journalism. 2009. "Obama's First 100 Days." April 28. www.journalism.org/analysis_report/obamas_first_100_days

Pew Research Center for Excellence in Journalism. 2008. "Winning the Media Campaign: How the Press Reported the 2008 Election." October 22. www.journalism.org/node/13307 (accessed May 14, 2011)

Sabato, Larry J. 2010. "Pendulum Swing." In *Pendulum Swing*, ed. Larry J. Sabato. Boston: Longman.

U.S. Bureau of Labor Statistics. 2011. "Regional and State Employment and Unemployment Summary." April 19. www.bls.gov/news.release/laus.nr0.htm

Wood, Isaac T. 2010. "Bringing Down the House: Reliving the GOP's Historic House Gains." In *Pendulum Swing*, ed. Larry J. Sabato. Boston: Longman.

Chapter 10

Principles and Pragmatism in the Obama Presidency

William Crotty

Introduction

In his first budget message to the Congress, the recently-elected Barack Obama delivered a strong condemnation of the economic and governing philosophy dominant during the post-Reagan Conservative Ascendancy. He attacked the burden placed on ordinary Americans, the misplaced priorities of previous administrations and their policies that promoted the interests of corporations and the wealthiest at the expense of the rest of the society. It was he said the programmatic agenda that brought on the nation's economic collapse and one he committed to changing. The message was clear and unsparing and in line with his campaign for the presidency.

In his budget message preceding the reelection campaign, President Obama emphasized financial retrenchment, deficit reduction and called for the nation to live within its means. He went on in this and related messages to call for a restructuring of entitlement programs including Medicare, Medicaid and in time Social Security, a new tax code, a review of environmental, and economic regulations affecting corporate America in addition to a reevaluation of the costs of doing business in the United States, all intended to strengthen an economic recovery.

Debt reduction had become the new watchword of the Obama presidency. A residue of objections to the greater extremes of the Tea Party/Republican move to eliminate social programs and to legislate a fundamentalist Christian

Right agenda through budgetary provisions remained. Beyond that, whatever the progressive tendencies that had motivated the campaign for office and underlay the initial budget message to Congress would seem to be long past.

The president had chosen to take the lead at what he presented as establishing a mature and responsible program emphasizing fiscal restraint and an economic recovery. He put himself in position to claim the leadership of the cut-the-budget debate sweeping Washington and the media. It was in effect a return to the economic free market orthodoxy that had dominated previous presidencies and in reality despite the financial industry's collapse and its consequences had never been really threatened.

The change in orientation and in the prioritization of interests was fundamental for the administration. It had taken hold over the course of a few brief years. What explained it? This is the question to be addressed in and the point of this chapter. It draws on those chapters that preceded it and links back to the introduction and the issues raised there. Additionally it calls on assessments from a variety of perspectives, center, right and left, most often in their own words, expressing their view of the Obama presidency and its course of action. The intent is to provide a necessarily brief cross-section of evaluations, many negative to be sure, and to offer possible explanations for the restructuring of objectives experienced. It should provide a framework for judging the Obama presidency in the context of mainline contemporary politics.

As indicated, a competition had developed to get out in front of the economic recovery debate, increasingly seen in terms of budgetary cuts and used as the framework for overall policy and political decision-making. The debate was not designed to initiate a broad public exchange of competing visions for the society or to present options as to who should benefit or sacrifice the most to recharge the economy (these issues had been quietly agreed upon). It did not raise questions on how to reign in a financial sector returned to pre-collapse profitability and old habits (large bonuses, high salaries and subprime lending were back in vogue). It was not to reconsider America's military role worldwide (and its costs to the nation) or conceptually the nation's post-cold war approach to international affairs or to identify and resolve the structural inequalities built into the economy that provided the basis for the financial and political power polarization at the root of the nation's problems.

What it did involve was a short-term if intense contest for political positioning to advantage one side or the other in the election to come. The targeted audience for the president was the moderate centrists, poorly informed about national affairs and depending on impressions as to what conditions were in the nation and which party best met their needs in making voting decisions. The Republicans committed to enacting policies (almost exclusively tax cuts), the demand for which had fueled their off-year election gains. For them, there was the issue of accountability to the electorate that had favored them. Their hope was that such a budget-dominated assault would satisfy their supporters and insure their loyalty in the next electoral go-around (Hacker and Pierson, 2006).

Not incidentally, efforts to rewrite the midterm operating budget had afforded lobbyists and partisans of different issue positions the opportunity to reopen financial and other areas of interest, reversing decisions made earlier. Much of this involved economic advantages for those involved.[1] Beyond that were the efforts to promote a social/religious/fundamentalist Christian agenda championed by the Far Right in line with their views, ones not likely to survive any normal policy-making process.

All of this was familiar. In the short-term, crisis-driven atmosphere that shapes decision-making in Washington, it was an exercise in politics as usual. It was a far cry from the political vision Candidate Obama had inspired in running for office or seen in his first budgetary message. The obvious questions as indicated were: Why the change? What accounted for it?

Definitive answers are few. Still the nature of the actions taken are clear while the motivations as to why they were taken may be speculative. The decisions made have real-world consequences and these can provide the basis for different evaluations as to the changing tenor and the success of the Obama presidency.

This chapter then establishes some benchmarks for evaluating the programmatic side of the Obama presidency. It begins with a return to the most compelling of them all, his campaign for office, the extraordinary nature of his success and, most pointedly, the promise contained in the victory. In the process it touches on the severity of the problems confronting Obama on taking office, a legacy of the Bush administration. The chapter then proceeds to consider interpretations from a variety of perspectives of his actions in office and it makes reference to continuing structural issues of concern that plague the economy and the society. It concludes with an overview of the promise and performance of the Obama presidency.

The Legacy (Largely Forgotten) of the Bush Years

George W. Bush left office with an economy in crisis: home foreclosures soaring; two continuing wars; a record of legal and constitutional abuse; an unprecedented aggrandizement of executive power; the endorsement of a policy of torture, secret detentions, and a denial of rights to anyone caught in or accused of terrorism; and record budgetary deficits. Bush also ended as one of the least popular presidents in modern history. The abuses of office and the excesses of power have been well covered elsewhere.[2] Summary judgments as to the Bush legacy provided by prominent historians and political scientists provide an idea of how the Bush presidency has come to be been assessed: Bush is "headed for a colossal historical disgrace" (historian Sean Wilentz); the constitutional and legal violations of the Bush presidency and its disregard for human rights "endangered democracy itself" (political scientist James P. Pfiffner); "there is no alternative but to rank [Bush] as the worst president in history" (political scien-

tist Eric Foner); and the Bush abuses of power reinforced and expanded the ex-
tra-legal prerogatives of the imperial presidency. Even former president Jimmy
Carter was to pass judgment that the Bush "administration has been the worst in
history" (quoted in White, 2009a, pp. 224-225).

The judgments were strong but for most observers deserved.

Reviewing the Election

Barack Obama began the campaign as the longest of long shots, modestly hop-
ing according to his top advisor not to be embarrassed. He was relatively unknown as a national figure with but one electrifying speech to draw attention to
his potential (to the 2004 Democratic National Convention). He had limited legislative experience. He had served three terms in the Illinois Senate from 1997 to
2004. Following an unsuccessful bid against the Democratic incumbent for a
seat in the United States House of Representatives in 2000, he ran for the United
States Senate in 2004.

Several events brought him to national attention during the campaign,
including his victory in the March 2004 Democratic primary and his keynote
address at the Democratic National Convention in July of 2004. He won election
to the U.S. Senate in November 2004 and his presidential campaign began in
February 2007. After a tight race in the 2008 Democratic Party's presidential
primaries against Hillary Rodham Clinton, he won the party's nomination. He
was an African-American candidate in a society still dealing with the fallout
from its racial issues. He had begun his presidential campaign with no funding
to speak of; his organization was non-existent and it would be created and managed by aides new, as he was, to national politics. He was challenging Hillary
Clinton, the candidate with the greatest name recognition and the strongest base
in the Democratic Party's electorate, the most experience on the national scene
and one with access it seemed to unlimited funding and to a pool of talented and
proven consultants. Clinton was the first serious female candidate to seek the
presidency and given her advantages had been conceded the Democratic nomination by most observers before the race began. Despite it all, Obama entered
the race early and went on to win the nomination and then the general election.
The story of his campaign has been well told and will not be repeated in detail
here.[3]

Basically he ran an insurgent effort that focused on the smaller state primaries and the caucuses neglected by Clinton who in turn won convincingly in the
big states. His campaign depended on a highly motivated, exceptionally well
organized grassroots effort by predominately young people new to partisan politics. After a lengthy and at times bitter campaign he won by a relatively narrow
margin (although the timing was such that he could claim a majority early in the
process).

In the general election, the Republican nominee ran an erratic campaign, one severely under-funded and punctuated by crises, strategic mistakes and poor decision-making. Most notably in this regard was the selection of Sarah Palin, an unknown Alaska governor and a temperamental addition to a failing effort, as its vice presidential nominee. McCain chose to champion the economic and war policies of the outgoing administration, in itself a curious decision given his reputation as a party maverick, the state of the economy and the unpopularity of the incumbent. Just prior to the financial collapse in echoing the president, McCain claimed the economy to be strong. In turn, Obama would be shown to gain consistently in support as the stock market fell, by itself enough to account for his decisive victory by more than an eight million vote margin over McCain (Crotty, 2009a, 2009b, 2009d).

His election attracted an enormous amount of positive attention as to its meaning and its potential for opening a new chapter in America's political history. Katrina vanden Heuvel in *The Nation* was not alone in her views:

> [T]he election was a referendum on an extremist conservatism that has guided (and deformed) American politics and society since the 1980s. . . . [It] presented a mandate for bold action and a historic opportunity for a progressive governing agenda.

> [Barack Obama] is clearly a reform president committed to the improvement of people's lives and to the renewal and reconstruction of America. (Vanden Heuvel, 2009, p. 1).

This is an assessment not unlike many others. At times it seemed to be bordering on euphoria, to be recalled down the road in light of Obama's actions in office.

There was another aspect to the Obama campaign. Many supporters also believed it to be both the repudiation of conservative politics and the rebirth of a progressive era. Such a belief was based on the candidate's rhetoric (Crotty, 2011) and the nature of the electoral shifts in the vote and its projected consequences.

> [T]he political demography that gave Nixon, Reagan, and both Bushes the presidency . . . near-lockstep southern support and backing among suburban whites who . . . has changed dramatically. With each passing year, the Republican share of the presidential vote has declined to the point where old rules are again about to be broken (White, 2009a, p. 202).

And White again:

> [T]he 2008 election represented . . . a moment when a new demography caught up to a new politics. That fact, combined with an actively engaged public, has given Barack Obama and his fellow Democratic officeholders an enormous opportunity to make the policy changes they seek and consolidate their political gains. . . . We are entering a period of consequence (White, 2009b, p. 204; Judis and Teixeira, 2002).

It would seem that a new era was coming. It was a vision encouraged by Obama's definition of what he stood for and what could be expected with his election.

A realignment of political programs and patterns of electoral support for the party coalitions along the lines projected with the Obama election is rare in American politics. It is difficult to orchestrate, requiring demographic shifts in the population; crises conditions, most frequently in relation to economic concerns that affect most every sector of the nation; a charismatic candidate with a broad and mobilizing appeal who can deliver a message of hope and renewal with conviction; and an election victory that allows a party and a candidate to follow through with a program of national renaissance once in power. Each element on its own is not enough and the balance among them, while of different potential importance, nonetheless has to be woven together under a committed leader into programs that change a nation's direction.[4]

The most dramatic realignment by consensus was Franklin D. Roosevelt's New Deal which dominated American politics for generations and to this day provides the target of conservative efforts to eliminate its programmatic legacy. Less universally agreed upon but also seen as more modern efforts at realignments were the 1968 victory of Richard M. Nixon, the Reagan successes that initiated the Conservative Ascendancy and, more in line with both extending the Reagan policy approaches and transforming the nature and powers of the national government, and George W. Bush's post-9/11 presidency.

Obama's victory was cast in this context. The demographic changes in population shifts and voting patterns were clear and provided the building blocks for such a transformation. Obama was a gifted orator and campaigner and held out the promise of a fundamental redirection of national priorities that would unite leader, party, voters and policy agenda in directing the nation into a new era.

The pressure was then on Obama to follow through, to provide the inspirational leadership and policy directions that would make realignment, and the rejection of the conservative neo-liberal politics and its failures of the past, a living reality. As was to be seen, it was asking a lot of the new president, more than he could (or chose to) deliver and likely more than he ever intended whatever the electorate's perceptions and expectations of him. As a consequence, the realignment projected to mark the new progressive dominance of politics was not to be.

The Promise

Most directly, Barack Obama's words best convey his message and the power of its appeal. These give an idea as to what Obamaism was all about and how the campaign managed to move a broad segment of the voting public, often resembling a mass social movement rather than a more traditional political campaign.

The speeches also convey why the level of expectation for an Obama presidency was set so ambitiously high (Crotty, 2011).

The speeches could be stirring and the problem areas precisely drawn. The call to action, the vision of decisive change, the commitment to stand and fight for working Americans, for what was right and what was needed and the emphasis on the fortitude and the promise of America and its people, all would come across forcefully in his speeches. These would come to establish the expectations as to what the Obama presidency would be all about.

The diagnosis of the problems facing the country was stark and clear. However the promise of a new direction turned out to be ephemeral, too much for an Obama presidency to achieve or even to show a willingness to propose. It was on balance a far cry from later positions taken and the appeals for budgetary restraints, program cuts, relaxed corporate regulations, a tax policy review, restructured entitlement programs with reduced benefits and the other features of a neoliberal governing framework. To observers it might appear to be a program often little removed from that of the administration that had preceded it. The creation of an aggressive globalized economy became the major objective. "Win the Future" (vague as it may seem) had become the new war cry and slogan of the Obama administration.

Perspectives on the Obama Presidency

The views on and reactions to the accomplishments, motivations and approaches of the Obama administration varied. It could be said there were almost as many of these as those willing to offer them. The conservative/Republican response was consistently negative, differing only in the intensity of a rejection of compromise and the willingness to push to extremes (most obviously but not restricted to the Tea Party insurgents elected to the Congress). The opinions of more centrist commentators varied primarily in relation to the issue under discussion and most frequently the moderation of the initiatives and the willingness to attempt to work with the opposition. Liberals and many Democrats on the other hand found much to object to. The views expressed serve to convey the divisiveness and lack of consensus of the period.

Following the midterm elections the complaints brought to the President about the operations of the White House by a number of outside advisors were extensive and frank. These included the following:

- The White House was provincial in outlook and lacked an understanding of Washington politics.
- The staff and the White House were "insular," supporters and advisors could not get through to senior aides.
- The president needed to "reach out" to more of the public and to members of the Congress.

- Obama did not pay enough attention to business or its representatives.
- The president needed to create a "narrative" or "story line" to help people understand his overall purpose and intent.
- He neglected his liberal base in the Congress and in the Democratic Party.
- He had in journalist Elizabeth Drew's words "a worrisome tendency to seem eager to appease those who bring open sustained pressure on him."
- He needed a redefinition of goals.
- He had to reshuffle his administration, replace some people and bring in new blood.
- The White House needed more order and discipline.
- He should be more "business-friendly."
- He should cut spending and the budget to better appeal to Republicans.
- He had to find a way to end the cycle of constant attacks on and charges and counter-charges with the Congress and with his opponents.
- He had to avoid big ticket items and laundry lists of programs being sent to the Congress (Drew, 2011).

Obama listened and acted. Regarding his advisors, some of his senior staff were returned to Chicago to begin preparations for the reelection campaign. He brought in William Daley of JP Morgan as his new chief of staff and appointed Jeffrey Immelt, chairman of GE, to lead a newly created President's Commission on Jobs and Competitiveness. He placed an increased emphasis on "competitiveness" in a globalized economy, the basic theme in his 2011 State of the Union Address and in his policy thereafter.

The "business-friendly" agenda to be enacted would include a review and simplification of tax policy, including a cut in corporate tax rates; a reduction in business regulations; a willingness to make a greater effort to reach out to Republicans; a delay in enforcing EPA standards; an emphasis on stimulating international trade; and overall a sensitivity to business interests and a commitment to making the nation's economy more productive.

Drew, an experienced Washington insider, a veteran author and a former correspondent for two U.S. magazines, *The Atlantic* (1967-1973) and *The New Yorker* (1973-1992) commented in her review of the Obama presidency:

> Obama has ceded the Republicans considerable territory and is arguing on their terms. He has accepted the long-held Republican premises that the government is too big and unwieldy, that regulations can get in the way of jobs, that the huge deficit can be handled by spending reductions without tax increases (Drew, 2011, p. 1).

It represents a fair assessment of the views and policy positioning that manifested itself in the post-2012 years.

To assess Barack Obama as president it is necessary to understand what got him elected, so says Marshall Ganz, a long-time labor organizer with experience mobilizing mass movements of African-Americans, feminists, California farm workers and Middle East activists while teaching at Harvard's Kennedy School of Government. Ganz, "the brains behind the movement-building," played a pivotal role in the Obama election effort. It was Ganz's job to employ his expertise in bringing the campaign message home to the voters. As he related it in an interview with *The Nation*, Ganz "realized Obama's ability to connect with his audiences through his powerful voice, his ability to weave a personal narrative into a larger political morality tale" and "he felt Obama had a rare opportunity to transform America's culture" (Abramsky, 2011, p. 26).

A main concern was to provide a rationale and motivational context for the young workers who did the grass-roots, door-to-door campaigning. The idea was to tie Obama's moving life experience and his oratory into a more comprehensive ideological framework as to its assumptions and objectives, one that would serve as the motivating rationale for the campaign and its nuts-and-bolts ground troops.

The article continues: "He understood how to unlock the 'prophetic imagination' of youth; the willingness to take the world from where it is to where you want it to be. 'The blending of grassroots organizing capacity with Obama really worked.'"

Where then was the problem? It may be enough to say that Ganz is back teaching at the Kennedy School. According to Ganz, Obama as President "lost his voice." He did not want his policy choices and the debate over the direction of his presidency "pushed from below." He seemed to be "afraid of people getting out of control." He effectively dismantled his volunteer base from the campaign, placing it under the control of the Democratic National Committee.

Obama in turn in Ganz's estimation moved from transformational candidate in the campaign symbolizing the promise of a new political order once in office to "a transactional leader, a maker of deals, a compromiser in chief." A "historic opening" had been lost. Ganz's basic point is that Obama did not understand or appreciate the dimensions or the dynamics of the movement that elected him and the nature of the opportunity presented.

This account could provide a key part of the puzzle: Candidate Obama's morphing into President Obama. The mass social movement was dismantled, although there would be an effort to rebuild it for the reelection drive. The president's advisers at one early meeting with supporters made it clear that he as president did not want to hear their views on policy issues and from them the directions his administration should take. He would decide (exercising control has always been important to Obama). Their job was to carry the message to the voters. That is not quite what many felt they had signed on for and as a consequence a mass organizing tool disintegrated into the more familiar surroundings of Washington politics.

There have been other efforts to explain the disconnection between what seemed to be and what came to be. Some are more sympathetic to Obama's positioning politically given the urgency of the problems inherited and the implacable opposition from the Republicans in the Congress. Conservatives were unrelenting in their criticism and others, particularly the liberal critiques of the President's in-office performance, were less forgiving. The intensity of the reactions could be unsettling, adding to the divisions in the political culture already in evidence (Crotty, 2011).

Whatever the administration did, or more frequently did not do, or the paths it chose to follow, was subject to debate and criticism. There were supporters but they were less vocal and in the minority. The critics in contrast, conservative, liberal or centrist were plentiful. However Obama's performance in office is approached it is worth remembering that there were major structural problems facing the society and however successful the Obama presidency might have been, or might turn out to be, the most basic of these were left unaddressed.

Structural Issues: A Society in Trouble

Speaker of the House Tip O'Neill once reminded the first Democratic president of the post-New Deal era, Jimmy Carter, that the Democrats were the party of the poor and the less fortunate. It had little impact on Carter whose priorities were elsewhere. Barack Obama lays claim to that mantle and calls on his experience as a community organizer on the South Side of Chicago to make the point. It has been contended by Democrats and liberals in particular, confused and put-off by his actions as president, that his priorities and legislative record speak to other concerns. He may be, as is often contended, a prisoner of historical circumstances. His preference is for short-run solutions dictated it would seem mainly by his Republican opposition and/or his projections of what it would take for him to be re-elected. The agenda is far from the needs of what was his electoral constituency. Whatever the explanation, his rhetoric in seeking office and his unwillingness to fight for issues close to the heart of his Democratic constituents for some of his former supporters speaks otherwise.

Economic and Social Inequality in America

The Republican Party has unequivocally identified itself with the best-off in the society and consistently and successfully advanced their interests. This can be seen clearly in the tax code and its redesign in recent decades, especially noticeable in the Conservative Ascendancy. As evidence: from the end of World War II up through the sixties the top income categories had a 90 percent tax rate (although it is unlikely many actually paid that). In the contemporary period it is in contrast set at 35 percent and it is claimed that few pay anything close to that. The nation's tax burden has been shifted primarily to the middle class and the working poor (Wolfe, 2011, p. 1, 3; see also Wolffe, 2010). "The top one-hundredth of one percent . . . made an average of $27 million per household [as against] . . . the bottom 90 percent [with] . . . $31,244." (Gibson and Perot, 2011, p. 2; see also Hacker and Pierson, 2010, 2005; Page and Jacobs, 2008; Page and

Simmons, 2000; and Verba and Orren, 1985). Nonetheless a major argument of the Republican Party is that taxes remain too high and need to be reduced further.

The disparity in impact from the Great Recession reemphasizes the differences in wealth in America. Minorities were especially hit. In assessing the consequences, The Pew Research Center reported that the recession

> from late 2007 to mid-2009 took a far greater toll on the wealth of minorities than whites. From 2005 to 2009, inflation adjusted median wealth fell by 66% among Hispanic households and 53% among black households, compared with just 16% among white households.

These lopsided wealth ratios are the largest since the government began publishing such data a quarter century ago and roughly twice the size of the ratios that had prevailed between these groups for the two decades prior to the Great Recession that ended in 2009 (Pew Research Center, 2011, p. 1).

Among the report's findings are the following:

- The typical black household had $5,677 in wealth in 2009; the typical Hispanic household had $6,325; and the typical white household $113,149 (calculated as assets less debts).
- The percentage change in median net worth of households, 2005 to 2009 was: whites, -16 percent; Hispanics, -66 percent; and blacks, -53 percent.
- The median wealth ratios, 1984 to 2009: white-to-black, 12 to 1 increased to 19 to 1; and white-to-Hispanics, 8 to 1 increased to 15 to 1.
- The median net worth of households, for 2005 and 2009: whites, $134,992 and $113,149; Hispanics, $18,359 and $6,325; and blacks, $12,124 and $5,667 (Pew Research Center, 2011, pp. 2, 3, 13).

In addition, the wealth rankings of the top 10 percent within each racial and ethnic group also increased disproportionately for the years 2005-2009 along with the increasing disparity in wealth.

There is a direct correspondence between money and political power. One leads inexorably to the other. The trend from the 1980s and the early twenty-first century has been to increase to record levels the imbalance in income and in addition political power and the policies that accompany both between a very small percentage of the wealthiest and the vast majority (as indicated 90 percent or better) of Americans. The trends in wealth and political polarization have been achieved through the increasing reliance on and dominance of money in elective politics. The institutions of government have been active participants in the process: the presidency from Reagan and Bush II to Obama; the Congress in its reliance on campaign financing and its embrace (along with the other branches of government) of free enterprise economics; and the Supreme Court through its case decisions (*United Citizens v. Federal Election Commission*, 2010, as an example). There is little prospect much will change and in fact the severe imbalance in power, economics and political, give every indication of

being permanent. It has been a curious but unusually successful and self con-
scious effort to reverse what in the not very distant past was one of, if not the
most, equalized distributions of wealth within its citizenry among advanced democratic nations (and arguably all countries worldwide). The Great Recession
and the reactions to it in the private sector and by the administrations and others
in power have served to reemphasize the trend.

Income taxes and payroll taxes have increased over recent decades to each
account for over 40 percent of tax revenues; corporate taxes have decreased
from the 1950s when they accounted for 40 percent or more of the federal government's income to less than 10 percent by 2007. An explanation of the financial gains and losses for the period 2007-2009 shows Wall Street profits up 720
percent; the unemployment rate up 102 percent; and Americans' home equity
down 35 percent (Gilson and Perot, 2011).

There is no confusion as to the reasons for such a severe redistribution of
wealth. The increasing inequality is directly related to the political dominance of
the Republican Party from the late 1960s on and was particularly pronounced
during the period of the Conservative Ascendancy and the shift from a Keynesian economic framework to a neo-liberal one (Pollin, 2010, p. 23).

Larry M. Bartels in a well-documented analysis (*Unequal Democracy*,
2008) examines the continuing surge of economic inequality and with it life
opportunities in America. Bartels quotes Jacob S. Hacker and Paul Pierson's
(2008) argument that the contemporary Republican Party is directly responsible
for "tilting the balance of benefits and protections away from ordinary Americans and toward the well-off, the well-connected, and the Republican base."
(Bartels, 2008, p. 291). The problem may be worse than assumed. Bartels concludes "my analyses suggest that the specific policy views of citizens, whether
rich or poor, have less impact on policy-making than the ideological convictions
of elected officials" (Bartels, 2008, pp. 289, 287).

Tax policy is a mystery to most voters. Consequently and despite its importance in establishing a society's economic opportunity structure, they have little
information on or interest in it. The results can be unfortunate:

> [A]ffluent people have considerable clout, while the preferences of people in
> the bottom third of the income distribution have *no* apparent impact on the be-
> havior of their elected officials. . . . The statistical results are remarkably con-
> sistent in suggesting an utter lack of responsiveness to the views of millions of
> people whose only distinguishing characteristic is their low incomes. Observers
> of contemporary American politics may be unsurprised to hear that elected of-
> ficials attached more weight to the preferences of affluent and middle-class
> constituents than of low-income constituents. However, only the most cynical
> critic of American democracy could be unsurprised to learn that low-income
> constituents seem to have been entirely ignored in the policy-making process
> (Bartels, 2008, pp. 285-286).

And:

These disparities in representation are especially troubling because they suggest the potential for a debilitating feedback cycle linking the economic and political realms: increasing economic inequality may produce increasing inequality in political responsiveness, which in turn produces public policies that are increasingly detrimental to the interest of poor citizens, which in turn produces even greater economic inequality, and so on. . . . Shifts in the income distribution triggered by technological change, demographic shifts, or global economic development may in time become augmented, entrenched, and immutable (Bartels, 2008, p. 286).

Martin Gilens in an analysis similar to Bartels and called on by him draws the obvious if painful conclusion: "representational biases of this magnitude call into question the very democratic character of our society" (quoted in Bartels, 2008, p. 286).

The United States in International Context

The United States faces some fundamental decisions. Beyond the Great Recession and long in the making, the country is also not doing as impressively in an international comparison of a variety of key economic and social indicators as Americans might choose to believe. To illustrate: ranked among thirty-three countries, from Germany and France to Taiwan and Slovenia, the United States did poorly. On inequality indices, the United States scored better only than Hong Kong and Singapore; on prison population it ranked last; and on employment and measures of life expectancy near the bottom. Overall it is not an especially impressive or encouraging statistical portrait nor is it one that receives much public or media attention or one that is a subject of political concern. Charles M. Blow concludes in presenting these data that the United States has "become the laggards of the industrialized world. Not only are we not No. 1 . . . we are among the worst of the worst" (Blow, 2011). This is a far cry from how Americans picture themselves and their country. The differences are sobering and seemingly should demand attention from those with the power and responsibility to do something to change the picture.

In this perspective much was expected (possibly much too much in retrospect) from Barack Obama's election. In office he has talked of making America more competitive and in the campaign (see excerpts from his speeches in Crotty, 2011). Obama had committed to "spreading the wealth." That would have been a beginning, but it did not happen. Additionally the problems faced go beyond this and would require broadly-based, informed and serious attention, little of which is in evidence.

Third, while it received a good deal of attention in the campaign it has received little attention once Obama took office. There is a serious imbalance in powers and authority among America's governing institutions. The presidency has continued to gain power, often in the process reframing the Constitution to suit its own ends, at the direct expense of the Congress, expected to be the public's most representative branch, and to a lesser degree in the judicial system (although the direction of change is clear). The accumulation of executive powers has been long underway and it received added impetus during the Bush years and the institutionalization of the 9/11 presidency. As was mentioned earlier in its fundamental redirection of American governing institutions and its redefinition of citizen rights and legal protections, the Bush administration could be considered transformative, leaving a permanent impact on American democratic governance (Crenson and Ginsberg, 2007; Schwartz, Jr. and Huq, 2007; and Savage, 2007). Many believed the Obama presidency would offer a corrective (as had been promised). It did not. A consequence is that the changes instituted have been quietly accepted as defining a new, and by implication, acceptable conception of the role of the American presidency and its increased dominance in the political order.

The transformations may well be enduring. There is little in the present political debates to indicate that either it or the social inequities in the system will be addressed in any meaningful capacity.

Discussion

A combination of forces came together to create what many believed would be a "perfect storm" for reshaping the American political landscape: a strong repudiation of the incumbent, his administration and his conception of government; the moving, at times edging towards the messianic, tenor of the pre-election campaign; and a candidate who brilliantly articulated a call for change, an "audacity of hope."

During the campaign and early into his administration, Obama had been compared at various times (as noted) to the most successful presidents in American history, including the transformative presidencies of Abraham Lincoln (on race); Franklin D. Roosevelt (the New Deal and the creation of the welfare state); and Ronald Reagan ("Morning in America," a reassertion of national pride and optimism). There were parallels drawn to John F. Kennedy, Bill Clinton and, as a negative point of reference, contrasts with George W. Bush. The projections as to the future and the level of anticipation went well beyond the reality of the moment: a candidate with superior oratorical skills and the power to communicate with and to move to action large segments of the population; the architect of a stunningly successful election campaign under unusually adverse conditions; the first African-American president in history; and a man of enormous intelligence and even greater self-confidence with a picture-perfect family and private life and a personal story that fit nicely with the American belief in opportunity realized. These were all significant pluses and they received a great deal of positive attention.

On the other hand, there was the reality of a highly ambitious politician, one who had stopped only briefly along the way in the offices he had been elected to; one who had a limited knowledge of or experience in national politics, had no administrative experience and depended on a small number of equally inexperienced but trusted and personally-committed advisors; and previously a man little known or politically-tested in ways relevant to taking on the duties of the most demanding office in the nation. Additionally for those who chose to listen closely the soaring rhetoric more often than not built on promise and trust in the candidate, his integrity, his ability and his willingness to fight for the commitments made; few specifics or in-depth policy development of issues were made (in comparison with his principal opponent for the Democratic Party's nomination Hillary Clinton); and as it turned out later broad as they may have been most of these proved to be non-binding, subject to the politics and pressures of the time.

President Obama as against Candidate Obama proved to be something of a study in opposites. Calls for change gave way to an emphasis on continuity, especially in the most significant of areas, the economy, defense and (less recognized) anti-terrorism policies. He was seen as a politician not willing to stand and fight for concerns he had championed and continued to say were close to his heart. As president he appeared satisfied to get from the Congress whatever legislation in whatever form he could ("putting points on the board" as Rahm Emmanuel, his chief legislative advisor, put it). He neglected his base in the electorate, moving away from it to cultivate a different voting sector (moderates) for his reelection drive; and he was often disdainful of his party in the Congress and its concerns (calling it "sanctimonious" and out for its own ends rather than the public good, charges made in the fallout from the vote to continue the Bush tax cuts). Yet he expected the party's full and unqualified support in pursuit of his legislative program (he tolerated its advice poorly and kept it out of most of the significant decision-making) and in his re-election campaign. He proved to be over-sensitive to the opposition and its demands and constantly emphasized, even with the Democratic majorities in both the House and Senate in his first two years, the critical nature of consensus-building and Republican support for key initiatives (neither came to pass). The mass organization that provided the base for his election was effectively retired or neutered.

The Barack Obama who took office proved to be far more of a centrist or moderate establishment conservative (a breed that no longer existed) and an advocate for the status quo than supporters or opponents would have expected. His skill in governing, his ability to negotiate and compromise, his failure to present a coherent political strategy or to communicate clearly and unambiguously with the public and the Congress, his lack of tolerance for dissent in his own party's ranks, his hesitancy and tentativeness in taking or holding positions and his weak response to unexpected and unplanned-for crises (the BP disaster in the Gulf, the earthquake in Haiti, the uprisings in the Middle East) and, most surprisingly of all, his inability or refusal to effectively communicate his objectives to the American public, his most compelling and attractive weapon in the campaign, all came to be seen as hallmarks of his presidency. Consensus-building (difficult if not impossible to achieve), qualified and modest objectives and the movement, at first gradual and then more clearly embraced, towards a corporate-sensitive agenda surfaced as the major themes as the trajectory of his presidency continued to define itself. It was one well removed from the forces and groups that got it to where it was. As a marking point in his 2011 State of the Union address to the Congress and the nation, the president did not once mention poverty or the crisis of the working class, extraordinary omissions for any president and especially for a Democratic one.

Barack Obama was far more of a transactional president and a centrist than the progressive he had appeared to be earlier. He insisted repeatedly he was not an ideologue, which was true enough, and he was far from a party man as his actions demonstrated. The point would likely be contested but the Obama elected president was not the Obama who ran for office.

One advantage (if there is any) of a highly-charged, politically volatile polarization in national politics is that at least the clarity of the opposing conceptions of government and its role in the society in advancing the nation's interest are obvious enough. For the Republicans, as it had been for decades, it was the intention to dismantle the safety net and the remains of the New Deal and to follow a free-market dynamic in allocating resources within the society. The social contract was to be rewritten. The problem was that the assumptions underlying the ideology were faulty and proven to be so by the financial collapse of 2008. Nonetheless with little regard for what the nation had experienced, they were embraced with continued fervor by the party. They appeared to be of little concern to the public, the victims of operating a government on the basis of beliefs in a system that had failed.

There is another vision for government, one that emphasizes its role in protecting the public interest and equitably dividing the resources of the society among its citizens, ensuring their wellbeing and a reasonably comfortable and productive life. This seemed to be what Candidate Obama offered the voters. Whatever the underlying reasons, it was not the one Barack Obama chose to put forward as president.

The reactions in assessing the adequacy and impact of the administration's policy initiatives varied widely (as shown). Some were intense in nature, others more balanced. To a large extent, these were the product of a number of forces. First, Barack Obama may have misread the situation he inherited, the acuteness of the problems to be faced, their intransigence and resistance to quick solutions and the inability of elites on the contemporary political scene to come together and agree on a reasonable middle ground in seeking answers.

A second is the discrete and individualized nature of the presidential decision-making process. There was little evidence of any controlling value structure or broader ideological conceptions in what was to be proposed. Consequently any judgments as to the relative merits or outcomes in a given policy area was approached on an issue-by-issue basis and reflected the criteria that the observer chose to apply as to what was best or most achievable in the culture of the times and politically supportable or acceptable. Such a decision-making matrix invites a variety of responses. Abstracting the broader message from the mix of decisions also becomes more contentious and subject to debate.

Third, there is a distinction between a process-oriented and substantive-oriented approach to policy-making. Obama comes down on the process-oriented side. This most often seem to be his major concern; the way in which things are to be done more so than the substantive content that defines what should be done.

Fourth, the amount of emotion invested in assessing the Obama presidency and its actions reflects the high level of expectation that accompanied the Obama candidacy and entrance to office. The level of concern for those impacted by the policy directions taken and the personal investment in Obama's election are factors of consequence in how one chooses to judge his presidency. If the actions taken appear significantly at odds with the promise to attack and attempt to resolve fundamental social problems (in particular) within the progressive framework evidenced in the campaign then the reaction can be, and as indicated frequently have been, intense, angry and at times unforgiving.

This chapter and others in this volume have drawn attention to the promise of the Obama presidency, open-ended and ambitious as it appeared, and the performance, difference in direction and more limited in operation. The question to be answered may well be what accounts for the difference. More than likely it is best explained by a combination of forces, some obvious, others less so and still others yet to be known. Among the explanations that have been offered at one point in time or another are the following:

- Barack Obama is not and never intended to be a transformative force in American politics bent on redesigning the country's economic structure or its politics, a view at odds with his message to voters in the election.
- Campaigns are little more than pathways to office, a marketing of a candidate and the positions most likely to win support. They should be seen in this light and not taken too seriously.
- The hope ("promise") of the campaign was illusory; the commitments made were general and vague, allowing the incumbent great latitude in how he chose to act. This has been a characteristic of Obama's campaign since he first decided to run for public office,
- Candidate Obama did not fully grasp the meaning of his own campaign or the opportunities the election provided for new policy ventures and a rebuilt coalitional base in the electorate.
- There is a fundamental difference between governing and campaigning and whatever the original intentions, the actuality of exercising power is considerably more difficult and subject to severe limits than many who enter the presidency realize.
- Governing responds to the conditions prevalent at the time and it seldom can move beyond them. The question to be asked in reality is how effectively does a president deal with these? In this context Obama and

the standards by which he is to be judged differ little from previous administrations.

- The Republican party's strategy of total opposition to the president's agenda was too strong, too unyielding, too effectively communicated to the public at large and too electorally successful as shown in the mid-term elections to allow for any other course of action. The use of structural barriers (such as the threat of a filibuster in the Senate) was simply too much to overcome.

- Continuity and stability are more important objectives to Obama than any others and these are the ones he emphasized in the presidency.

- Obama's embrace of a centrist governing strategy was more a measure of the man, his personality, his temperament and his values than anyone might have realized.

- Obama does not like confrontation and divisiveness as his emphasis on civility in political discourse attests; at heart he is a consensus-builder, an objective he has made a priority in office.

- His one real domestic policy passion was a national health insurance plan however framed which he realized.

- President Obama's principal concern from the beginning has been ree-lection, not forging a new strategy for governing or promoting his party and its electoral chances. What he chose to do can best be understood in the context of appealing to the center and repositioning himself for the election to come.

- Barack Obama is an exceptionally intelligent and personally, intellec-tually and emotionally disciplined and forward-looking individual. It is an unusual combination of qualities for any politician and ones that give him an insight and a capacity to frame governing in a context few can readily appreciate. The future will be the judge and is likely to look more kindly on his accomplishments than his contemporaries, as hap-pened with several presidents after leaving office. It is quite possible that Obama would see himself in this more positive light.

Barack Obama has written in *The Audacity of Hope*: "I am new enough on the national political scene that I serve as a blank screen on which people of vastly different political stripes project their own views. As such, I am bound to disap-point some, if not all, of them."

Obama went on: "Which . . . perhaps indicates a second, more intimate theme . . . namely, how I, or anybody in public office, can avoid the pitfalls of fame, the hunger to please, the fear of loss, and thereby retain that kernel of truth, that singular voice within each of us that reminds us of our deepest com-mitments" (Obama, 2006, p. 15).

All of this may ring true. But there is enough of a record from the campaign and from Barack Obama's time in office to make reasonable judgments as to his approach to politics and to governing and the strengths and vulnerabilities of his presidency.

Notes

1. See Government Accountability Office, 2008.

2. Among the accounts of the Bush presidency and its actions, are: Ball, 2007; Cole and Dempsey, 2006; Cole and Loebel, 2007; Crotty, ed., 2004, 2009a and 2009b; Danner, 2004; Goldsmith, 2007; Greenberg and Dratel, eds., 2005; Lichtblau, 2008; Mayer, 2008; the 9/11 Commission, 2004; Sands, 2008; Savage, 2007; and Strasser, 2004.

3. Among a number of accounts, see: Kenski, et. al., 2010; Jamieson, ed., 2009; Balz and Johnson, 2009; Plouffe, 2010; Heilman and Halperin, 2010; Crotty, ed., 2009a, 2009b, 2009c and 2009d.

4. See Burnham, 1970; Key, 1955; Sundquist, 1983; Paulson, 2000, 2007; Reiter and Stonecash, 2010; and Crotty, 2006.

References

Abramsky, Sasha. 2011. "A Conversation with Marshall Ganz." *The Nation*, February 21, p. 23GG.

Ball, Howard. 2007. *Bush, the Detainees, and the Constitution: The Battle Over Presidential Power in the War on Terror.* Lawrence: University Press of Kansas.

Balz, Dan and Haynes Johnson. 2009. *The Battle for America 2008: The Story of an Extraordinary Election.* New York: Viking.

Bartels, Larry M. 2008. *Unequal Democracy: The Political Economy of the New Gilded Age.* Princeton, NJ: Princeton University Press.

Blinder, Alan S. and Mark Zandi. 2010. "How the Great Recession Was Brought to an End." July 27. http://www.economy.com/mark-zandi/documents/End-of-Great-Recession.pdf (accessed May 13, 2011).

Blow, Charles M. 2011. "Empire at the End of Decadence." *New York Times*, February 18. http://www.nytimes.com/2011/02/19/opinion/19blow.html (accessed February 19, 2011.

Burnham, Walter Dean. 1970. *Critical Elections and the Mainsprings of American Democracy.* New York: W.W. Norton & Company.

Canellos, Peter S. 2011. "Obama's Speech Problem: The President, It Turns Out, Is Not A Great Communicator." *Boston Sunday Globe*, January 23, p. K1.

Cole, David and James X. Dempsey. 2006. *Terrorism and the Constitution.* New York: The New Press.

Cole, David and Jules Lobel. 2007. *Less Safe, Less Free: Only America is Losing the War on Terror.* New York: The New Press.

Crenson, Matthew and Benjamin Ginsberg. 2007. *Presidential Power: Unchecked and Unbalanced.* New York: W.W. Norton and Company.

Crotty, William, ed. 2004. *The Politics of Terror: The U.S. Response to 9/11.* Boston: Northeastern University Press.

———. 2006. "Party Transformations: the United States and Western Europe." In *Handbook of Party Politics*, eds. Richard S. Katz and William Crotty. London: Sage Publications. Pp. 499-514.

———. 2009a. "The Bush Presidency and the 2008 Presidential Election: Context and Imprint." In William Crotty, ed., *Winning the Presidency 2008.* Boulder, CO: Paradigm Publishers. Pp. 1-19.

———. 2009b. "The 2008 Election: Introduction." In William Crotty, "Special Issue: The 2008 Election." *Polity*, July, pp. 279-311.

———, ed. 2009c. "Special Issue: The 2008 Elections." *Polity*, July. New York: Palgrave.

———, ed. 2009d. *Winning the Presidency 2008.* Boulder, CO: Paradigm Publishers.

———, ed. 2011. *Barack Obama and the Politics of Survival.* Boston: Center for the Study of Democracy/Northeastern University.

Danner, Mark. 2004. *Torture and Truth: America, Abu Ghraib, and the War on Terror.* New York: New York Review of Books.

Democratic Underground. 2010. November 8, p. 1.

Drew, Elizabeth. 2011 "Obama and the Republicans." *The New Yorker*, March 10. http://www.nybooks.com/articles/archives/2011/mar/10/obama-republicans/   (accessed May 12, 2011)

Gilson, Dave and Carolyn Perot. "It's the Inequality, Stupid." *Mother Jones*, March/April 2011. http://motherjones.com/print/99036 (accessed February 24, 2011)

Goldsmith, Jack. 2007. *The Terror Presidency: Law and Judgment Inside the Bush Administration.* New York: W.W. Norton and Company.

Government Accountability Office. July, 2008. "Tax Administration: Comparison of the Reported Tax Liabilities of Foreign- and U.S.-Controlled Corporations, 1998-2005." Washington, DC: Government Accountability Office. http://www.gao.gov/new.item s/d08957.pdf (accessed May 12, 2011).

Greenberg, Karen J. and Joshua L. Dratel, eds. 2005. *The Torture Papers: The Road to Abu Ghraib.* Cambridge: Cambridge University Press.

Hacker, Jacob S. and Paul Pierson. 2010. *Winner-Take-All Politics: How Washington Made the Rich Richer—and Turned Its Back on the Middle Class.* New York: Simon and Schuster.

Hacker, Jacob S. and Paul Pierson. 2006. *Off Center: The Republican Revolution and the Erosion of American Democracy.* New Haven, CT: Yale University Press.

Heilemann, John and Mark Halperin. 2010. *Game Change: Obama and the Clintons, McCain, and Palin, and the Race of a Lifetime.* New York: Harper.

Jamieson, Kathleen Hall, ed. 2009. *Electing the President 2008: The Insider's View.* Philadelphia: University of Pennsylvania Press.

Judis, John B. and Ruy Teixeira. 2002. *The Emerging Democratic Majority.* New York: Scribner.

Kenski, Kate, Bruce W. Hardy and Kathleen Hall Jamieson. 2010. *The Obama Victory: How Media, Money, and Message Shaped the 2008 Election.* Cambridge: Oxford University Press.

Key, Jr., V.O. 1955. "A Theory of Critical Elections." *Journal of Politics* 17: 3-18.

Lichtblau, Eric. 2008. *Bush's Law: The Remaking of American Justice.* New York: Pantheon Books.

Mayer, Jane. 2008. *The Dark Side: The Inside Story of How the War on Terror Turned into a War on American Ideals.* New York: Doubleday.

National Commission on Terrorists Attacks Upon the United States (The 9/11 Commission). 2004. *The 9/11 Commission Report.* New York: W.W. Norton and Company.

Obama, Barack. 2006. *The Audacity of Hope.* New York: Vintage.

———. 2009. "Inheriting a Legacy of Misplaced Priorities." http://www.gpoaccess.gov/ usbudget/fy10/pdf/fy10-newera.pdf (accessed May 12, 2011).

Page, Benjamin I. and Lawrence R. Jacobs. 2009. *Class War: What Americans Really Think About Economic Inequality.* Chicago: The University of Chicago Press.

Page, Benjamin I. and James T. Simmons. 2000. *What Government Can Do: Dealing With Poverty and Inequality.* Chicago: The University of Chicago Press.

Paulson, Arthur C. 2000. *Realignment and Party Revival: Understanding American Electoral Politics at the Turn of the Twenty-First Century.* Westport, CT: Praeger.

Paulson, Arthur C. 2007. *Electoral Realignment and the Outlook for American Democracy.* Boston: Northeastern University Press.

Phillips, Kevin. 2002. *Wealth and Democracy: A Political History of the American Rich.* New York: Broadway Books.

Plouffe, David. 2009. *The Audacity to Win: The Inside Story and Lessons of Barack Obama's Historic Victory.* New York: Viking.

Pollin, Robert. 2010. "It's Not the Party—It's the Policies." *The Nation,* September 27, p. 23.

Sands, Philippe. 2008. *Torture Team: Rumsfeld's Memo and the Betrayal of American Values.* New York: Palgrave Macmillan.

Saslow, Eli. 2010. "Despite His Roots, Obama Struggles to Show He's Connected to Middle Class." *Washington Post,* February 3, p. A11.

Savage, Charlie. 2007. *Takeover: The Return of the Imperial Presidency and the Subversion of American Democracy.* New York: Little Brown and Company.

Schwarz, Jr. Frederick A. O. and Aziz Z. Huq. 2007. *Unchecked and Unbalanced: Presidential Power in a Time of Terror.* New York: W.W. Norton and Company.

Stiglitz, Joseph E. 2010. *Freefall: America, Free Markets, and the Sinking of the World Economy.* New York: W.W. Norton and Company.

Strasser, Steven. 2004. *The Abu Ghraib Investigations: The Official Independent Panel and Pentagon Reports on the Shocking Prisoner Abuse in Iraq.* New York: PublicAffairs.

Subcommittee on Investigations, U.S. Senate. April 13, 2011. *Wall Street and the Financial Collapse: Anatomy of a Financial Collapse.* Washington, DC: Permanent Subcommittee on Investigations.

Sundquist, James L. 1983. *Dynamics of the Party System: Alignment and Realignment of Political Parties in the United States.* Washington, DC: Brookings Institution.

Taylor, Paul, Rakesh Kochhar, Richard Fry, Gabriel Velasco and Seth Motel. 2011. "Wealth Gaps Rise to Record Highs Between Whites, Blacks and Hispanics." Washington, DC: Pew Research Center/Social and Demographic Trends.

Vanden Heuvel, Katrina. 2009. "Obama, Year One." *The Nation,* November 23, p. 1.

Verba, Sidney and Gary R. Orren. 1985. *Equality in America: The View From the Top.* Cambridge, MA: Harvard University Press.

White, John Kenneth. 2009a. *Barack Obama's America: How New Conceptions of Race, Family, and Religion Ended the Reagan Era.* Ann Arbor: The University of Michigan Press.

White, John Kenneth. 2009b. "Transforming Election: How Barack Obama Changed American Politics." In W. Crotty, ed., *Winning the Presidency 2008.* Boulder, CO: Paradigm Publishers. Pp. 185-208.

Wolffe, Richard D. 2011. "How the Rich Soaked the Rest of Us." *Truthout.* March 2. http://www.truth-out.org (accessed March 2, 2011).

Wolffe, Richard. 2010. *Revival: The Struggle for Survival Inside the Obama White House.* New York: Crown Publishers.

About the Contributors

John C. Berg is professor of government at Suffolk University. His research and teaching interests include legislative politics, environmental politics, interest groups and lobbying, Massachusetts state and local politics, minority parties in the United States, ethical issues in politics, and American political development. His publications include *Teamsters and Turtles? Progressive U.S. Political Movements in the 21st Century* (Rowman & Littlefield, 2003) and *Unequal Struggle: Class, Gender, Race and Power in the U.S. Congress* (Westview, 1994).

R. Lawrence Butler is associate professor of political science at Rowan University. His research investigates the role of political parties and party leaders in the institutional structure and legislative activity of the U.S. Congress. He has been featured on several cable television programs discussing issues of presidential politics. He is currently working on a book manuscript titled *Party Governance in the U.S. House*. He is also the author of *Claiming the Mantle: How Presidential Nominations Are Won and Lost Before the Votes Are Cast*, published by Westview Press.

Bruce E. Caswell is associate professor of political science at Rowan University. His research interests include forecasting presidential and congressional elections, campaign finance, local political party activists, radical American political thought, and the portrayal of American politics in popular culture. He is past president of the New Jersey and the Northeastern Political Science Associations and currently a member of the council of the Political Science Education Section of the APSA. He is author of "The Presidency, The Vote, and the Formation of New Coalitions," *Policy*, Volume 41, Number 3, July 2009.

William Crotty is the Thomas P. O'Neill Chair in Public Life and professor of political science at Northeastern University. His interests include political parties (American and comparative); democratization procedures and developments; electoral behavior, political behavior, and representation; American politics; presidential nominating systems and procedures; electoral change and voting behavior; comparative public policy; political representation; and democratization processes and development. He has been a recipient of the Samuel J. Eldersveld Lifetime Achievement Award of the American Political Science Association's Political Organization and Parties Section and has served as president of the Midwest Political Science Association and the Policy Studies Organization. Among his publications are *Winning the Presidency 2008* (Paradigm Publishers, 2009) and *Handbook of Party Politics* (Sage Publications, 2006), with Richard S. Katz.

Maureen F. Moakley is professor of political science at the University of Rhode Island. She specializes in state politics, political parties, and women in politics and teaches American government, state politics, and media and politics. Her publications include *The Political Life of the American States, Party Alignment and State Politics, Rhode Island Politics and Government* (Nebraska University Press, 2001), with Elmer Cornwell, and *The Rhode Island Senate Race* in *The Sixth Year Itch*, edited by Larry Sabato (CQ Press, 2007). In addition to academic work, she is a regular political commentator on state politics on Rhode Island PBS and Rhode Island NPR.

James A. Morone is professor and chair of political science at Brown University. He has published eight books. His *Democratic Wish* (Yale University Press, 1998) won the APSA Gladys M. Kammerer prize for the best book on American politics and was named a notable book by the *New York Times*. His most recent book *The Heart of Power: Health and Politics in the Oval Office*, coauthored with David Blumenthal, was also named a *New York Times* "Editors' Choice" book and received a front page review in the *Book Review*. Morone has published over 150 articles, essays, and reviews. He has testified before Congress numerous times and has served as president of the New England Political Science Association and the Politics and History section of the American Political Science Association.

Shayla C. Nunnally is professor of political science at the University of Connecticut. Her teaching and research interests include African American politics, African American public opinion and political behavior, and race and politics. Her research focuses on black Americans' trust in social and political contexts, intraracial and interracial attitudes, racial and political socializations, and political development. She has a forthcoming book, *Trust in Black America: Race, Discrimination, and Politics*, which will be published with New York University Press (2011).

Arthur C. Paulson is professor of political science and pre-law adviser at Southern Connecticut State University, where he serves as chairman of the political science department. He is a life-long student of parties and elections and his teaching and research interests include American politics, presidential elections, and constitutional law. Among his publications are *Electoral Realignment and the Outlook for American Democracy* (University of New England Press, 2006) and *Realignment and Party Revival: Understanding Electoral Politics at the Turn of the Twentieth Century* (Praeger Publishers, 2000).

Lawrence C. Reardon holds the Hood House Professorship and is an associate professor of political science at the University of New Hampshire. He also is a research associate at Harvard University's Fairbank Center for Chinese Studies. A China specialist, he is author of several publications including *The Reluctant Dragon: Crisis Cycles in Chinese Foreign Economic Policy* (University of Washington Press, 2002) and coedited *The Catholic Church and the Nation-State* (Georgetown University Press, 2006). He currently has a publication in progress, *Learning to Globalize China: Development Paradigm Change and the Opening of China's Economy*. Reardon has been involved with the prestigious Fulbright Program on many levels, including as a participating scholar, as a campus committee member with the U.S. student program, and as a consultant and national screening committee member for China.

CPSIA information can be obtained at www.ICGtesting.com
Printed in the USA
BVOW082114220812

298490BV00001B/2/P